Movin' East

Also by Harry Bruce

Each Moment As It Flies
The Gulf of St. Lawrence
The Man and the Empire: Frank Sobey
A Basket of Apples: Recollections of Historic Nova Scotia
R.A.—The Story of R.A. Jodrey, Entrepreneur
Lifeline
Nova Scotia
The Short Happy Walks of Max MacPherson

Movin' East

Further Writings by

HARRY BRUCE

METHUEN

Toronto   New York
London   Sydney   Auckland

CANADIAN CATALOGUING IN PUBLICATION DATA

Bruce, Harry, 1934–
    Movin' east

ISBN 0-458-99670-X (bound). – ISBN 0-458-99680-7 (pbk.)

I. Title

PS8553.R83M68 1985   C814'.54   C85-099079-3
PR9199.3.B78M68 1985

Printed and bound in Canada

1 2 3 4   85   89 88 87 86

Contents

Fare Thee Well. Down Here, It's a Sad, Old Story

Good-bye, good luck, God bless...Take care...Keep in touch, eh?...Yeah, you too...Be sure to write...Think you'll be down home for a while next summer?...I'll sure as heck try...Well, looks like it's time to climb aboard...No tears now, none of that...Here blow your nose...

The words are old in our family, and so is the sorrow. Times were tough in Guysborough County near the turn of the century and my grandfather, William Henry Bruce, went all the way down to Boston to find work. He came home, bought the family farm from his father in 1904, and died in 1934. By then Charles had gone down the road to work for Canadian Press in Toronto, where I was born.

But William Harry Bruce—that's me—came back *up* the road some four decades later, settled in Nova Scotia, wrote books and magazine articles in Halifax, and took over the old homestead in Guysborough County. With him, he brought his Toronto-born family, which included a 10-year-old kid named Alexander Bruce. In the fullness of time (actually only nine years), Alec married Vivien Cunningham of Halifax, begat Melinda and Jessica Bruce, and at the ripe age of 23 moved his family back *down* the road to Toronto.

He didn't want to leave Nova Scotia any more than his great-grandfather or his grandfather had wanted to leave, but he is a journalist (a third-generation journalist, as it happens), and the *Globe and Mail* offered him a better job than he could find anywhere in the Maritimes.

May I summarize? Charles was born and raised in Nova Scotia but ended up in Toronto. Harry was born and raised in Toronto but he's ending up in Nova Scotia. Alec was born in Toronto and raised in Nova Scotia, but he's now settled in Toronto. Vivien, Melinda and Jessica Bruce were all born in

Nova Scotia, but now they're Torontonians. If history repeats itself, repeats itself, and repeats itself, I'll see my granddaughters' bylines in newspapers and magazines around the year AD 2004, when I'll be a mere 70. I'll also see the girls themselves in Nova Scotia. For we Bruces are obviously doomed to sail back and forth between Toronto and Nova Scotia for centuries, like a phantom ship in the grip of a Force 10 curse.

Homesickness runs in the family. It's our oldest tradition. James Bruce, my great-great-great-grandfather, arrived in Guysborough County when the French Revolution was picking up steam; and, like other Scottish emigrants, he doubtless remembered faces on the shore, the hills of home. The heartbreak of wandering Scots inspired a plaintive branch of literature, a poetry of homesickness that so mourned a lost land of gloom that it struck those from sunnier cultures as perverse, like the love of haggis.

But as British essayist Robert Lynd once put it, "In the absence of homesickness, man is but a prodigal, glad to be allowed to live on the husks, without memory of his father's home." My father certainly had memories of *his* father's home. Construction tycoon Robert McAlpine was at Mount Allison University in 1923 when Charles Bruce, 17, fresh off the farm, arrived on the campus. My father was so homesick, McAlpine recently told me, that he could scarcely talk or move. It was as though his homesickness was a crushing physical ailment. He seemed partially paralysed.

A decade later, he was Toronto-bound. He'd scarcely arrived in Hog Town, however, when he started to angle for jobs on newspapers in the Maritimes. If his Toronto colleagues in the depths of the Depression had known that he'd actually offered to work for a down-home newspaper for a lower salary than he was earning up there, they'd surely have misidentified his homesickness as insanity. But children and promotions kept coming, and eventually he resigned himself to a life in Toronto. In his fiction and poetry, however, he never stopped returning to the old homestead.

"The late-August easterlies and the line storms have blown themselves out," he wrote in *The Channel Shore*

(1954). "Slowly the slopes begin to blaze with reds and yellows, wild splashes of cold dramatic fire along the sombre hills of spruce. The days are crisp and clear, or windless under a mild and clouded sky. The nights are those a man remembers, looking upward through the murk of cities, his instinct looking back. There are nights in the full moon of October when darkness is a kind of silver daylight, when the sea is a sheet of twinkling light, the shadows of barn and fence and apple tree black and incredible, the air vibrant and alive but still as a dreamless sleep."

He was in Toronto when he wrote that. He'd been there two decades when, in 1952, his *The Mulgrave Road* won the Governor General's Award for Poetry; but that's a book in which nearly all the important things occur in Nova Scotia. "I haven't seen Queensport Light over the loom of Ragged Head in years," he wrote in one poem. "And never a smell of rollers coming up the bay from Canso." He also referred to "A few homesick men, walking an alien street;/A few women remembering misty stars/And the long grumbling sigh of the bay at night."

No critic I've ever read, no professor I've ever heard, has grasped that the creative juice in my father's writing flowed from something so elementary as homesickness. For decade after decade, he endured Toronto while remembering Nova Scotia, and the effort of his writing was itself a return of the native. I dare to wonder: If he'd never left Nova Scotia could he ever have written about it as superbly as he did in Toronto?

As late as June 1971, only six months before he died in Toronto, he wrote a brief, loving description of the farmhouse where he was born and reared. The piece appeared in the *Globe and Mail*, and its ending was so prescient it strikes me now as eerie: "Four generations have lived in the house. Various members of a fifth (MacMillans, Schulzes, Bruces) have occupied it in summer and overflowed to the fields and the beach that edges water a quarter-mile away. A sixth will be along. The heart of a home is use."

The sixth *has* come along. It's my wife and I. We've bought the old place from my aunt Bess, and some day we'll

3

settle in there, not just for weekends but year-round for the rest of our lives. Meanwhile, only two weeks after our son Alec, his wife Vivien and their baby girls moved into an apartment in the west end of Toronto, we got a call from him.

"What's up?" I asked.

"Oh, it's nothing. We're just feeling a bit homesick."

Walking an alien street. Remembering the long grumbling sigh of the bay at night.

So what else is new, Alec?

Atlantic Insight, January 1985

The Comeback of Hugh MacLennan

Half a lifetime had passed since I'd first heard Hugh MacLennan's name and now, at last, I was going to meet him—not in Toronto where, long ago, my mother had warned, "If you don't read Hugh MacLennan's *Two Solitudes*, Harry, you'll never understand Canada," but in Halifax where MacLennan, as a bare-legged boy, barely escaped having his face torn off by the Halifax Explosion. It was here too that, as a youngster hooked on the terrible drama of the First World War, he haunted the waterfront and saved cigarette cards that featured all the deadly warships of the time. He has an astounding memory. More than 60 years later, some of what little Hugh learned about those same ships pops up in his seventh and, some say, his finest novel. It's called *Voices in Time*, it should be out any day now, and when I phoned him at his summer place in North Hatley, Que., to arrange our meeting in Halifax, he spoke about it with a voice that was weary and British. "It's not like anything I've ever written

4

before," he said. "It may not be like anything anyone has ever written before. I am very tired." He is also 73.

Voices in Time is heroically ambitious. "It's been with me for 10 years," MacLennan told me in Halifax. Reading an advance copy, I was sure it was the work of a man who'd decided he'd damn well write a masterpiece that, once and for all, would settle his critics' hash. No one can tag *Voices in Time* with the old put-down that it's "too Canadian." No one can sneer that *Voices in Time* is the Canadian version of Jacqueline Susann's potboiler, *Valley of the Dolls*. That's what a TV interviewer called MacLennan's last novel, *Return of the Sphinx* (1967), and he remembers, he remembers. Especially the Toronto critics. "I agree with Robertson Davies about Toronto," he says. "Rob said a Toronto audience won't laugh at a joke unless they've got a written guarantee that it's already been laughed at in New York. They're a terribly narrow, provincial people. Nova Scotians aren't like that."

Critics crucified *Return of the Sphinx* with such sadistic relish that it would have been understandable if he'd quit writing fiction forever; but here he is, 13 years later, in the eighth decade of his life, and he's roaring back with a book that CanLit authority Elspeth Cameron calls the greatest novel he's ever written. Such a man, I thought, is worth meeting.

But I also had older reasons for wanting to see him. I grew up in Toronto knowing that Hugh MacLennan—along with such lesser lights as Louis St. Laurent, hockey player Bill Ezinicki and skater Barbara Ann Scott—was a celebrity. For he was a *writer*, like my father. Books were so important to my parents that they switched on the radio only one night a week (for Jack Benny), and for years after television had arrived in virtually every other house on our street, they continued to dismiss it as a contemptible toy. Reading was all. And when Elspeth Cameron says that *Barometer Rising* (1941)—the novel MacLennan set in Halifax at the time of the explosion he witnessed in his boyhood—was the book that *launched* Canadian fiction, I'm happy to agree. After all, it was the first adult book I ever read, and right into the

Sixties, my father insisted it was "still Hugh's best."

My father was Charles Bruce. He was pretty good at tennis and he once told me, "Hugh was a terrific tennis player, you know." Back in '28, when Hugh was a 21-year-old Halifax scholar and Charles was a 22-year-old Halifax newspaper reporter, Hugh won the Maritimes singles tennis championship. He also won a Rhodes Scholarship, went off to Oxford, bounced around Europe, got his Ph.D. at Princeton and, by the mid-Thirties, had settled down in Montreal as a schoolteacher who tried to write novels on the side. He'd once wanted to be a poet. And Charles? Well, he was already a poet. He stayed in Halifax a while, went to New York, came home and, by the mid-Thirties, had settled down in Toronto as a newspaperman who tried to write novels on the side. They were both bluenosers who found that you really can't go home again—except on summer visits, and on winter vessels of the mind that run before gusts of memory and sail right onto a printed page.

MacLennan's novels punctuated my entire childhood and youth. *Barometer Rising*'s explosion on Canada's literary scene occurred when I was seven. *Two Solitudes*—the work one critic said was "at the very core of Canada's future" and another simply called "the Great Canadian novel"—came out when I was 11. *The Precipice* appeared when I was 15, *Each Man's Son* when I was 17, *The Watch That Ends the Night* when I was 25. My parents read them all, talked about them, compared them. The man's very name triggers memories of my mother and father, stretched out on chesterfields, silently reading away the nights of 25, 30, 35 years ago. I grew up thinking that the emergence of a MacLennan book was as important as a national election (and a lot more interesting), and I was far from unique. Among readers all across the country, Hugh MacLennan was the undisputed heavyweight champ of Canadian fiction and, indeed, even its inventor.

For all these reasons, I awaited his visit to Halifax with the eagerness of a baseball fanatic who's been invited to dinner by Hank Aaron. After all, I thought, what other

Canadian author has earned no less than 10 honorary degrees, the Molson Award, the Lorne Pierce Medal for Literature, the Quebec Prize for Literature, and *five* Governor General's Awards?

MacLennan's work has appeared in 12 languages. *The Watch That Ends the Night* sold a quarter-million copies in Germany alone. His work is the subject of seven books, 68 sections of books and 13 university theses, and when critics analyse his fiction they toss around the names of the great: Tolstoy, Turgenev, Balzac, Wordsworth, Proust, Spinoza.... Mind you, some have also faintly damned him with "decent" and "workmanlike," and others have not-so-faintly damned him with "banal," "melodramatic" and "artistic duds." Elspeth Cameron asks, "How can so much praise walk hand-in-hand with such condescension?" She believes that now, four decades after *Barometer Rising*, "the full blooming" of MacLennan criticism "can and will take place." It may already be here. Among CanLit profs, assessing Hugh MacLennan is a minor industry.

All of which explains why it was that, in Halifax, a hulking Cape Breton school principal named Al Thomson introduced MacLennan to an international gathering of high-school English teachers with such charming brevity. Thomson said, "Lord tunderin' Jesus, boy, if dose fellows don't know who Hugh MacLennan is, den what are dey doin' at dat meetin?" And with that, MacLennan shambled over to the microphone and, for 45 minutes, captivated 300-odd reverent men and women with an erudite, funny, sometimes outrageous and highly personal disquisition on the evolution of English prose. (My father, who died in '71, would have liked that speech, or most of it anyway. He would *not* have liked MacLennan's opinion that "it is much more difficult to write good fictional prose than to write poetry. All you need for poetry is genius, but fiction is truly a combination of nearly all the writing techniques there are," including poetry.)

After the speech, women closed in on him, their eyes shining, paperback MacLennans clutched to their breasts. He gently chatted with them and signed their books with his odd cramped writing. "Though it was obviously the writing of a scholar," his first wife, Dorothy Duncan, wrote in 1942, "its characters might have been formed by the same fellow who carved the Rosetta Stone, for all the sense they made." She was an American, and her book, *Bluenose: Portrait of a Province*, was also a loving portrait of the young Hugh MacLennan. She first caught sight of him on a dock in Southampton: "Untidy grey slacks, a brown tweed jacket, a scarf knotted about his throat, and no hat. . . . A head of wavy, tousled brown hair and a mobile face that broke into laughter as easily as it receded into a frown . . . the movements of his hands were quick in outlining the body of a phrase, with a tensed nervousness that comes through breeding rather than worry." When they met, she tried to guess his nationality. Danish? German? English? "I am a Nova Scotian," he said. About 45 years ago.

He was smaller than I expected. His hair was still brown but now it was neither wavy nor tousled. It was lank. His face was still mobile and his hands quick but now, as ex-tennis champs go, he was frail. He no longer plays tennis; he has "distant vision" and cannot judge the ball's approach. Moreover, while his wife Dorothy was in hospital with her third brain embolism, he was suffering from a spastic back, and landed in hospital himself for eight agonizing days. That was 23 years ago, and every day since then he has done special exercises to keep his spine from disintegrating. It's still risky for him to sneeze while standing up, and as he addressed the English teachers he looked so frail I thought that if he didn't hang onto the podium with both hands their gusts of applause might blow him away.

He wore a yellow shirt, striped woollen tie, a brown suit. His pants were too long. He had some books in a plastic bag from the Halifax public library. ("I see you've got a Cape Breton attaché case," Al Thomson said.) In profile, his face was lean, aristocratic, perfectly suited to the Oxford accent he picked up half a century ago. But later we were alone together, and when he took off his suitcoat, loosened his tie, puffed Matinees and faced me across a table, he appeared

8

neither fragile nor uppercrust. He looked like a wiry, ruddy, opinionated Cape Breton miner, a bloke who'd be at ease in any beer hall in the country.

He talked about death.

Oh, he talked about other things, to be sure: his home town, Glace Bay, which he pronounced the old way, "Gloss Bay"; the weird fact that, during an argument in Germany in 1932, he recalled his boyhood cigarette-card statistics about German naval armaments with such accuracy that police arrested him as a spy; the fact that his father, a colliery doctor in Glace Bay and an ear, nose and throat specialist in Halifax, was "a casualty of the Presbyterians"; and the fact that another Presbyterian doctor, a Scot, used to put both the fear of God and the fear of sex into Dalhousie students with "perfectly brutal talks" about syphilis that "made kids faint all over the place."

He talked, too, about his writing. "I have a very vivid memory, ever since 1915," he said. "Until you have a perspective of time, you can't write novels, not if you're a man anyway. It's different with women. Women can write about a woman's world, about themselves. I don't mean that in any condescending way, but they're comfortable doing that. Men writers aren't." Somewhere, D.H. Lawrence had said, "The novel begins at the point where the soul encounters history," and MacLennan liked that.

But nudged by my own curiosity, this fascinating, meandering soliloquy kept swinging back, like a compass needle, to the dark fact. Death, visions of death. On the day the *Titanic* sank, April 15, 1912, MacLennan's mother saw her going down in a dream and awoke in terror. A year later, the family took a passenger ship to Europe, and one day far out at sea little Hugh noticed that the engines had stopped. Flowers from an upper deck plopped into the ocean. Deep, sad voices sang, "Nearer my God to Thee." It was the first anniversary of the tragedy, and they were above the *Titanic*'s hulk. An eerie moment for a boy who'd just turned six (not to mention his mother). MacLennan has remembered it ever since.

His father lit a match in the basement of their Halifax

9

home in 1916, and ignited gas fumes. "I was sitting in a chair, eating bread and molasses," MacLennan recalls, "and I was blown right up to the ceiling. For a while after that, my parents were living in one room at the Waverley Hotel with their faces half burned off." But that mishap was only a tiny preview of the following year's hideous Halifax Explosion. MacLennan was 13. He was about to go to school and had just washed his knees. The fact that he was in an alcove in an upstairs hall may be the only reason he survived to help define 20th-century Canadian fiction. Moments after the blast, he saw a truck hurtling down South Park Street. It carried a man. His face was in his hands. Blood squirted between his fingers. The truck hit a tree, the man was dead. "I went out," MacLennan says, "and I saw another man. Window glass must have cut his throat and, with some curious instinct for neatness, he'd crawled over to a catchbasin." He, too, was dead.

"My father said he could usually tell whether or not a patient was going to die," MacLennan continued, and as it had turned out, Dr. MacLennan had known even when his own time was up. One February night in 1939 he went by sleigh to Rawdon, 35 miles north of Halifax, to perform an operation on a dying girl, and the next morning he told his wife, "Bring me a chequebook. Now cash this. I shall be unconscious by 5 p.m. You can call the children." Hugh arrived half an hour before the old man expired. MacLennan was still an unknown schoolteacher in those days.

If his deathwatch over his father lasted 30 minutes, his deathwatch over Dorothy lasted 10 years. She suffered brain embolism after brain embolism, and it was she who inspired his creation of Catherine, the dying heroine of *The Watch That Ends the Night*. Of Catherine's last months, he wrote, "Her face had never seemed to me as beautiful as it was then....It had become so transparent one almost felt one looked at a spirit. Light was in it. Light came out of it. Light came from her constantly into me....She was alive and yet she was not; she was half-translated and yet she was still here....Enter thou into the joy of the Lord. So, in the end,

10

did Catherine, and her face showed what I can only describe as the joy of the Lord."

"As a boy," I asked him, "were you very religious?"

"Yes. *Very*."

"And though you may have lost your...let's say your orthodox religion...did you ever lose *religion*?"

"Not really."

Dorothy died on Easter, 1957, and the following morning, before dawn, MacLennan awoke, "and I knew she was with me. I saw her hand. I knew she was saying, 'I don't want to be here [on earth] anymore.' That *happened*. It was no hallucination. She was saying, 'Don't bother about me anymore. I won't bother about you.'"

So he was alone while writing *The Watch* (he married Frances Walker in '59, the year it came out), and found inspiration not in any writer who'd ever lived but in Bach and Beethoven. Their work had conquered death. Beethoven, too, had struggled alone "to find grace in a terribly harsh environment." His mass, *Benedictus*, was "a miracle.... What a man! I felt so near to him all those years." It wasn't only that immortal music helped MacLennan write, it was also that "a novel itself has got to have symphonic form. *Voices in Time*, you know, it's a symphonic exercise."

But it's far more than that. *Voices in Time* is an epic that sweeps its tormented characters through the First World War, and into the delusions of the Twenties, the sickening rise of the Nazis in the Thirties, the horrors of Hitler's Germany in the Forties, the triumph of greed and materialism in the Fifties and Sixties, briefly backward all the way to the collapse of the Roman Empire, further forward to the threats of our own time, then horribly forward again to the 21st century.

The plot spins round a ghastly build-up of uncontrollable events: Millions of impoverished run amok in riots such as no one has ever seen before. Unknown fiends take advantage of the chaos by announcing that, unless the Smiling Bureaucracy pays them fabulous amounts of gold and diamonds, they'll nuke whole cities. The bureaucrats pay up five times but when they finally refuse, a bomb kills half a million

11

people. The Great Fear grips the Western world, hate-filled rednecks support a nightmarish international dictatorship by committee; and, one fine day, the computer networks of rival bureaucracies suffer "a collective breakdown." The bombs start flying, but at least they're "clean" bombs, and outside "the metros" pockets of people survive.

Voices in Time ends with a straw of hope that reminds me of novelist Dave Godfrey's opinion that what MacLennan really writes about is "the idea of the holy city and how people become part of it." But as Wayne Grady says in *Saturday Night*, the hope in *Voices* is "subdued... a thin hedge against total despair."

"I know *Return of the Sphinx* foresaw the kidnappings and violence of the October Crisis in Quebec," I said to MacLennan. "I certainly hope *Voices in Time* is not that prophetic."

"What do you mean?"

"I mean the slaughter of hundreds of millions of people."

"Do you really think they've got a chance?" he said. "People no longer run the world. It's computers.... And when you have a prognosis that, by the year 2000, there'll be 50 million people in Mexico City alone, well that's a prescription for disaster. They'll all die of hunger, disease, pollution or whatever.... No one can even count them in Calcutta.... There are just too many people.... God is *not* democratic."

He said this with such utter conviction that I remembered a sentence by Dorothy Duncan: "From the day a Nova Scotian is born until the day he dies, he knows he is right." I hoped he was wrong, and then, out of the blue, he said an odd thing: "You know, Harry, men can get stronger imaginations when they're older. That's what's dangerous. Imagination can kill them."

I drove him back to his sister's house. It's near Dalhousie University, where a hot young tennis player studied classics a full quarter-century before atomic bombs hit two cities on the far side of the world. An ocean breeze washed the summer air, sunlight filled the trees, and it was one of those afternoons when the Halifax "metro" shimmers with a strangely vulnera-

12

ble beauty. Hugh MacLennan, author of *Voices in Time*, said he was glad to be back, and in a way, I was glad, too. I had finally met this remarkable voice in this remarkable time, and the chance might not come round again.

Atlantic Insight, November 1980

Harvey's Daughter

"We've had a cat for 14 years," Penny announced, "and you've always wanted a dog. We aren't getting any younger." I went to the Halifax library and borrowed five books, all jammed with photos of impossibly cute dogs, tips on canine care, and warnings never to buy a puppy on a whim. I ignored such spoilsport advice. A yellow Labrador Retriever would suit me fine. Labs were friendly, intelligent, patient, loyal, lovable, and a cinch to train.

The very next morning an ad in the Halifax *Chronicle-Herald* announced that a woman in Riverport was selling puppies for $100 each and, wonder of wonders, they were yellow Labs. We phoned the woman, who had a pleasant English accent. She had brought the father dog, Harvey, from Britain, and had papers to prove he was pure Lab. The mother dog was a young Nova Scotian, and would we like to inspect the parents and the litter? Would a seagull like a smelt?

We headed for Riverport, and I remember the day: November 28, a freak gift from a hotter season. The sun glittered on the moving waters of the fishing coves, lit up the haze among the last, tough, golden leaves of the hardwoods, brightened the walls of wooden houses that had once belonged to rum-runners and master mariners. We'd never been on the road to Riverport, and plunging into unknown country lent enchantment to our mission.

Harvey and his mate were in a corral, and they were fine, amiable, tawny beasts. Indeed, they were so gorgeous we never paused to consider what a massive presence such a dog would be in our second-floor apartment in downtown Halifax. The pups were just inside the back door, eleven of them, a squirming, adorable mess. Two little children played in the rangy, country kitchen. The wood stove crackled. Harvey's bed was a stuffed armchair. A dog-wise neighbor woman sipped coffee at the table, smoked cigarettes, and swore by Labs.

"This one is specially responsive," said the English woman, plucking a female from the litter. "She's weaned, of course, and paper-trained." She held the pup up. If Scrooge had seen a dog with a mug like this, he'd never have needed ghosts to melt his heart. With less than a month till Christmas, the puppy's amazingly beseeching eyes said, "Take me, I am yours." We took her. She was ours. The English woman had been a fine person to do dog business with.

During the two-hour drive back to Halifax, the pup slept in Penny's arms. She was more than a foot long. She seemed a trifle large for a dog not yet seven weeks old but, what the heck, I had my Lab at last. Her scrunched-up face and silky ears were sweet in slumber. She moved only when a doggy dream stirred her. We named her Sophie, and we would never again love her as much as we did while driving her docile body home to the city.

But we could not destroy an old cat just to make room for a young dog. Sophie got the kitchen, the landing beyond the kitchen door, and the stairway down to the door to the backyard. The cat got the rest of the apartment, including the bathroom, where we fed him. He was no longer the killer he'd once been, and on the rare times he saw Sophie he merely uttered feeble spitting sounds. The cat was no problem. Sophie was a monumental problem.

Her crimes included yelping, nipping, chewing, leaping, sleeping too little, eating too much, growing too quickly,

14

learning too slowly, and leaving puddles and mounds on the kitchen floor. Penny is a fastidious housekeeper. Reasoning that we'd never house-train Sophie unless we expunged all odors of everything the pup eliminated, she spent much of the Yuletide season on her hands and knees with sponges and disinfectant. The stink of Javex mingled with the aroma of plum pudding and sizzling turkey.

Sophie's bed was a drawer on the landing outside the kitchen. This site enabled her to run downstairs to leave deposits just inside the back door. We therefore erected a wooden barricade to imprison her on the landing. But within days, she could curl her fat paws over the top of the barrier and hoist her whole rubbery, wriggling body up and over to freedom. Then she flopped downstairs to what she regarded as an indoor outhouse—or she charged at our latched kitchen door with the force of an NHL hockey player slamming an opponent against the boards.

Experienced dog-owners might argue that we weren't taking her outdoors often enough, but we were giving up much of our lives to take Sophie out. She got a dozen outings a day, six during daylight, six after dark. I often took the 11:30 p.m. shift, but Penny would be outside with Sophie three times between then and dawn. She'd say to herself, "Here I am, a grandmother of 48, and I am standing out here—under the stars, in the snow, in sub-zero weather, at 4 a.m.—and I am shivering, and waiting for a dog to decide when and where to let go. Why am I doing this?"

Why was I letting her do it? Penny's side of our bed is closer to the kitchen than mine. I'm a heavier sleeper than she is. I am less noble. I am a master of the fake snore. When Sophie yelped, Penny jumped to her feet, and I said, "No, no, it's my turn." "Never mind," she replied, "I've already got my boots on." That brave statement became a family joke. I'd return from work at noon, and find her flat on her back, out cold with her boots still on, like an exhausted soldier who may be called back into battle any second.

Sophie destroyed the quality of our conversation. Suppose I have just returned from dragging her twice around the

15

quarter-mile track at Dalhousie University during a blizzard. I am banging the snow out of my hat on the back stairs, and she has already exploded into the kitchen to gnaw on curtains, chair legs, Penny's jeans, even the radiator. "How'd she do?" the wife asks. "She went," the husband replies. The wife probes further. "Number One or Number Two?" Husband: "It was dark, but I think just Number One." Wife: "But she had her feeding 45 minutes ago. I'll have to take her out again." During Sophie's brief domination of our lives, we had a lot of discussions of that order.

The kitchen had always been our favorite hangout for joking, listening to radio, talking about our children, reviewing the day. Now, we discussed nothing in there except The Sophie Problem, and only in whispers. She was just beyond the door, stirring, whimpering, getting ready to yelp, demand entry, impose upon us once again her dynamic, muscular, waggling and hyperactive self. If she were silent, one guffaw would arouse her. When I wanted a drink, I carefully tilted the tumbler and let the icecubes soundlessly slide to the bottom. After Sophie was gone, I'd occasionally still find myself actually tiptoeing on my way to the refrigerator, with an ear tuned to the little ghost beyond the kitchen door.

Sophie's chewing was merely a nuisance. We weren't wild about the curtains she wrecked anyway. But if we couldn't control her yelping she'd disturb our downstairs tenants, and might later become one of those dogs whose ceaseless barking makes life miserable for every neighbor within earshot. Her love of leaping in the air to nip at your fingers was also ominous. Did it mean she might one day draw blood from a stranger? We didn't know.

We only knew we had to correct these habits. One book suggested we could make Sophie behave by reprimanding her loudly right after she'd done something bad. This advice was ludicrous. Her attitude was, "I yelp, you shout. What fun!" From another book, I learned that the way to discipline her was to lift her by the scruff of the neck till her front paws were off the ground and then chuck her firmly under the chin.

Penny could never bring herself to try this technique,

16

while I found its ineffectiveness so frustrating that my chucking soon became stiff little uppercuts. All this did was make Sophie yelp—which was exactly what I did not want her to do—and make me uncomfortable about the possibility I had a cruel streak I'd never known about. Moreover, Sophie could smell my mood so unerringly she knew exactly when to flip over on her back, spread her hind legs, dangle her front paws, tuck in her chin, and look at me as if to say, "I'm just a tiny helpless girl, and I'll love you forever, but please, sir, don't grab my neck and smash my jaw."

Once, while Penny and I were hiding in the living room at the front of the apartment, Sophie body-checked the kitchen door so fiercely she sprung the latch. She tore into the bathroom, and gobbled up a full bowl of the cat's food so fast it was all gone by the time we got down the hall to find out what was going on. One dog-food package advised that at each feeding we should give her enough food to keep her munching comfortably for 20 minutes, and I cannot remember ever having received so ridiculous a tip. We gave Sophie almost four cups of food a day, the right amount for a Lab her age, and she took them in like a street-cleaning vehicle that sucks leaves out of urban gutters in the late fall.

Instructions on a dog-food package indicated that before Sophie reached the age of one year, she'd require more than 12 cups a day. She'd be eating 90 cups a week! By her fifth week in our house, when she was just shy of three months old, she'd already outgrown her puppy's collar but not her puppy's habits. Standing on her hind legs she could sweep stuff off the kitchen table with her front paws. Mature Labs weigh more than 50 pounds. If her body matured before her behavior we'd have a monster on our hands. *Dear Sophie*, I thought, *you have to go, and you have to go before we learn to love you.*

For she was lovable, make no mistake. We will never forget her playing with a leaf in the wind, proudly carrying her own stick along a beach while the ocean roared beside her, or charging over a field, ears flopping, to answer my, "Here, Sophie. Come on girl." Until I knew Sophie, I did not believe

17

any animal could be attractive while excreting; but she had a way of looking over her shoulder to ask "Is it okay if I go here?"

Our daughter, 22, betrayed the cat by declaring Sophie the most beautiful creature she had ever seen, and an elderly Russian woman almost swooned when she first saw the pup in our kitchen. She picked Sophie up, cradled her in her arms, and squealed, "Ooo, she iss lickink me all over, and I am lovink it." Sophie was worming her way into all of our souls, but she was just too huge a presence in the routine of our lives.

We could not turn her in for destruction. We could not advertise her in the newspaper because a stranger might not guarantee she'd live happily ever after in the countryside. She deserved nothing less than that, and now, on the third day of the New Year, Penny phones the woman in Riverport. "No, we don't want any money back," she says. "It was our mistake. We thought it would be like raising a cat, but it isn't like that at all. She doesn't belong in the city, and we'd like you to take her back. You will? We'll be there in two hours."

On the drive to Riverport, Penny reveals the woman's sad story. She had sold the entire litter, and then delivered Sophie's mother to a veterinarian for spaying. The bitch died during the operation, only last week. Sophie's father Harvey, without mate or offspring, is the last dog in the household. He's in mourning. The English woman doesn't sound all that chipper either.

Harvey greets us uproariously. He reaches my shoulders with his front paws, and his long-lost daughter makes him giddy as a pup. The tail wags the dog. He hugely fusses over Sophie. His bulk cows her for a moment, but then she is up and at him, chasing him, nipping his thrashing tail. I wish our Russian friend could see them together. They are lovink each other.

"Thanks for renting your dog to us," I say to the English woman, "and thanks for taking her back."

"Well, I guess it was meant to be."

The cat's in the kitchen when we get home. He is king of

18

the castle. He is too polite to remind us of our recent foolishness, but I glance out the window and down at the yard, and I see hundreds upon hundreds of Penny's and my own bootprints in the snow. Winding among them are trails of pawprints. Soon, fresh snow will bury the prints, and then all the snow will melt. We never took even one photograph of Harvey's daughter. Good-bye, Sophie. Have a good life.

Harrowsmith, May 1985

Stepping Out On England's Green and Pleasant Hiking Trails

Walking is the noblest and most contemplative of sports, but its noncompetitive nature is probably why sports reference books give it short shrift. They recognize dog shows, canoeing, checkers, jumping out of airplanes, and *kabaddi*—an Asian game that requires players to hold their breath for a long time—but refuse to give walking its due as a sport in its own right.

When the *Toronto Star* paid me to describe my weekly rambles, I was a professional walker. That was 16 years ago. But the old rhythm never really leaves a once-superb athlete, and now, on a magnificently English spring day, I find joy and personal competence while trekking the walker's equivalent to Yankee Stadium, Wembley, or Wimbledon. I am striding along England's 500-mile Southwest Peninsula Coast Path. My guide calls himself "Backpack Man," and though his garb is a shade pretentious for so gentle an outing, you could scarcely find a better bloke to introduce the path.

19

It is two centuries old. Its original purpose was to enable "sarchers," or government agents, to snoop on every cove, cave, creek and beach during the stupendous heyday of smuggling in Somerset, Dorset, Devon and Cornwall. Thanks to this ancient contest between the hated revenue spies and the ubiquitous community of churchgoing smugglers, England now boasts the world's finest hiking trail for lovers of the sea.

It carries you along the tops of huge, dark cliffs, through juicy pastures, under singing pines, out to breezy seaside meadows, and then inland to medieval churches that reek history, to sun-dappled hardwood forests, to perfect pubs and perfect pub lunches beside perfect babbling brooks and, always, back again to the sweep of the great Atlantic. "Here where the cliff rises so high," wrote poet Andrew Young in "Cornish Flower-Farm," "The sea below fills half the sky,/ And ships hang in mid-air. . . ." Far below your feet, seagulls wheel above white explosions of surf, and their squawks rise in the smelling-salts air to mingle with the aroma of wild garlic, fresh manure and blossoms whose names I'll never know.

Backpack Man chats ceaselessly, cheerfully, knowledgeably. Flourishing his walking stick, he points out the straw-lined lair of a badger, a feather-lined foxhole, scenes of ghastly shipwrecks and a 14th century Norman church with a gnarled tree growing out of one wall. In the coal cellar of this church, he says, villagers once imprisoned Captain William Bligh, later the hated skipper of the *Bounty*, in the mistaken belief that he was a French spy. The words on one gravestone are so legible they look as though they'd been carved last week rather than 179 years ago. They mourn John Williams, dead at 24:

> *His strength much resembled the*
> *Firmness of Oak*
> *And his Health the gay verdure of May*
> *But Death cut him down in full Bloom*
> *at a Stroke*
> *To admonish the Healthy and Gay*

20

Chastened, we plunge on through the gay verdure of May. Leading us through a sea of mud, Backpack Man chimes, "Don't worry about it. Just walk right through it. It's a mixture of good, clean English water and good, clean English soil to make good, clean English paste. If you feel yourself slipping on the wet grass as we go down the slope, don't worry about it. Just slide and sit down.... There are more than 100,000 miles of public footpaths in Britain. By law, anyone is free to use them, and they have to be wide enough to enable two men with burdens to pass in opposite directions. It's really the only way to see the country. You can't understand anything when you're all boxed-up and tense in an automobile." Backpack Man says the Age of the Automobile has dreadful things to answer for.

I am with seven other Canadians, and diverting though Backpack Man's patter may be, we are decidedly peckish by 1 p.m. But he has booked a fisherman to meet us at Helford Passage, ferry us upriver to Frenchman's Creek (scene of Daphne du Maurier's *Frenchman's Creek*), then dump us at the Shipwright's Arms. There I down a thick crabmeat sandwich with a succulent salad, a cream-filled cake under an extra gob of Cornwall clotted cream and a pint and a half of local bitter. I also satisfy my curiosity about Backpack Man.

He is Ken Ward, 56, an ad executive not from southwest England but from the Midlands. As a beloved sideline, he and his wife, Margaret, conduct what they are pleased to call "Civilized Walking Tours" in assorted lovely corners of England. Today, for instance, we are enjoying a segment of "A Walk in Poldark Country," a two-week, 100-mile, coastal jaunt from St. Ives around Land's End to St. Mawes. Margaret, a quiet woman with dark eyes and short, dark hair, is not all that wild about walking herself. She prefers to oil the machinery of the business, set up pub lunches and hotel accommodations and take luggage on ahead in a "trek-support vehicle." The detestable automobile, it seems, has certain uses after all. The Wards take the worry out of walking. When you put yourself in their hands, you need worry only about how you're going to hit it off with a bunch

21

of strangers for a couple of weeks. You can even get by without a backpack.

Backpack Man, of course, will have his. After all, in addition to having walked extensively in three continents, he is president of the British Backpackers Club. Engaged by the Thomas Cook travel empire, he once took trekkers to Swedish Lapland and the Mount Everest base camp; and indeed, here at this riverside pub on a mild May morning in gentle Cornwall, he looks as though he's ready for an assault on the Himalayas. His face is nut brown and shines as though it were polished. Strings of curly grey hair bounce around his bald dome, and there is something in his benign countenance that reminds me of an immensely healthy Alastair Sim. His outfit suggests he likes backpacking gear almost as much as he likes backpacking.

He's wearing rock-climbing boots with tough crusts of tread, a professional-looking olive-green jacket and knee-high gaiters to keep the lower legs of his tweedy trousers clean. When leading scruffy trekkers into a respectable pub, he removes the dirty gaiters so that he at least doesn't look like a bum who's been wading in good, clean English paste. Mobs of boisterous, thirsty, muddy trekkers apparently do not always bring joy to the hearts of English pubkeepers.

"Okay, Backpack Man, I get the gaiters, but what's in your backpack?" I demand. Before he can answer, a comely, pregnant Vancouverite complains about a blister on her heel. Backpack Man triumphantly produces an adhesive pad so she can trek on in comfort. "You saw that, didn't you?" he says to me. "Well, I have a complete first-aid kit, plenty of warm, dry clothing, confections, water, brandy and rum. I also have a bivvy."

"A bivvy?"

"Yes, it's a large, warm bag. If someone sprains an ankle or otherwise injures himself so he cannot carry on, I put him in the bivvy, fetch help and come back later to get him."

"Backpack Man, I've got to hand it to you. You think of everything." He is pleased, and so am I. I am a 48-year-old grandfather, I smoke a pack a day and my fitness program consists of a daily stroll to a nearby bar, but I have no difficulty walking stride-for-stride with Backpack Man for 10 miles along this fabulous coast. Some walks are like a shot of adrenalin.

But as the bumper sticker says, "I'd rather be sailing." I've loved sailing ever since I was a schoolboy and knocked around Toronto Harbor in a 14-foot dinghy. Three years ago, however, I sold the last of the five sailboats I've owned, and for a man who thinks he's learned to live without sailing, southwest England is a bad place to be. This morning, an onshore breeze is as steady as the earth's turning, and it seems to declare that for century after century after century the men of this treacherous coast have been fishing, smuggling, looting wrecks and setting out in sailing vessels to find strange lands. You cannot amble down the dark alleys of these little white ports, with their curiously Mediterranean flavor, without remembering that no corner of the world has sent better sailors to sea.

On the grassy heights of Rosemullion Head, I look seaward. Big sloops bravely bash through heavy seas on the English Channel. I look inland. Two miles up, on Helford Passage, hundreds of sailboats dance at their moorings in the morning sun; and later, when the fisherman ferries us through these same boats on our way to lunch, I hear again the old, sweet sound of halyards slapping masts. Several boats are Drascombe Luggers. A Drascombe Lugger is a British-built 18-footer with two masts and three small, brown, loose-footed sails. She is pretty and exceptionally seaworthy. In rough weather, she sails as an antelope runs. I know. I owned one 10 years ago, and now, in anchorage after anchorage on the Cornish coast, Drascombe Luggers remind me of the fine times I abandoned and reproach me for my faithlessness. I am like a man who turns from a cocktail-party conversation and, for the first time in years, finds himself gazing into the eyes of an old flame. Seeing her again leaves him unexpectedly desolate.

Then I meet Billy Trebilcock, who has something Backpack Man will never pluck from his backpack: a little wooden

23

racing sloop with sky-blue sails. Billy is 18 and built like a pocket weight-lifter. He's shy but he has the confidence of a man who knows he's good at doing what he most likes to do. He's been sailing since he was seven and now is a member of a national sailing team. Along with his father, Ted, and brother, Mark, he accepts money to take strangers sailing. The Trebilcocks—all of whom, incidentally, are madly competitive table-tennis players—run their modest sailing business from Mylor Bridge on the western shore of Cornwall's biggest estuary. The Fal River feeds the estuary and Falmouth sits at its mouth.

It was 315 years ago that the swift and lightly armed Falmouth packets began their mail service to America, and more than a century before that, in the reign of Henry VIII, Pendennis and St. Mawes castles rose on opposite sides of the harbor. Between them lies Carrick Roads, the main channel of the estuary. Three hundred sailing vessels used to tug at their anchors there, and now, just upriver, while a mighty breeze howls off the ocean and past the castles and through the roads, little Billy takes me and the pregnant Vancouverite for a furious, shocking, punishing, drenching sail.

We tear across the estuary with the wind abeam—the fastest point of sail—and as we shift our weight aft, the bow suddenly lifts. Now, the craft skims along on a plane like a speedboat. To keep her flat, we hook our toes under the hiking straps and lean our bodies out over the racing sea. I'm working the foresail so I have a line to hold, and since Billy is working both the tiller and mainsail, his hands are busy. But the brave Vancouver mom, sandwiched between us, has nothing to grab but the back of my pants. She thus turns them into a scoop for seawater, giving me the wettest 48-year-old bum in all Cornwall. Spray pours aft in an icy, relentless shower, slapping our faces, spattering my glasses until I can't see, wrenching strange shouts from us. Billy says, "Ready about," slams the tiller over and heads back on another beam reach. This promptly soaks the few parts of our bodies that remained dry during the outbound charge. I scarcely notice

24

because Billy now pays me the supreme compliment. He lets me take the tiller.

In the calmer lee of the shore, I sail to a white pub with a thatched roof. "It's the loveliest thing, to arrive at the Pandora Inn by water," a hotel proprietor has told me, and he's right. That's something you can't do in Canada: sail right up to an historic pub with a beer garden, change into dry clothes and, with two pints of St. Austell bitter ale, wash down a Cornish pasty the size of a first-baseman's glove.

The romp on the estuary has conquered Billy's shyness. This is Methodist country, he volunteers, but that doesn't mean the locals don't booze a lot. The Pandora is "the tenth- or twelfth-oldest pub in England." Billy offers some hearsay history, but I'm not really listening. My thighs still shudder and my stomach is already getting sore from the effort of hiking the boat flat. I haven't done that for a long time, but if there's anything that beats walking by the sea, it's sailing on the sea.

I raise my St. Austell to my lips. If I can get $5,000 for the family car, I can buy a sweet little sailboat. After all, she'll only be the sixth one I've owned.

Quest, September 1983

We Found a New Place for
Our Third Child to Break
His Collarbone

We lived in the house on MacPherson Ave. in Toronto for five years, less thirteen days, and this is supposed to be an age of such residential rootlessness that I suppose that qualifies as quite a long time. Things had been pretty good in that steep old place, and maybe we should have been sad to leave, but the other day, as we all drove off together—and forever away from the house on MacPherson—my wife said, "Did you feel any pang?" and all I could answer was, "No, not really, hardly at all."

"I know," she said. "Funny, neither did I."

There are no seats in the back of our minivan, so one kid was sitting on the engine box between my wife and me; another kid was leaning on the back of my wife's seat; she was holding the baby in her lap; and we were all five of us looking out the front window. The rear of the van was full of household gear that suddenly looked older than it had before; and it rattled and clanked so that, for a while, I thought of the Okies in *The Grapes of Wrath*.

There were pots and pans back there; mountains of shiny, green, garbage bags, full of clothes; wrenches, hammers, nuts, bolts, garden tools, curtain rods; a television set, a radio-record player; lamps all over the place; beer steins, pretty bottles, a fantastic collection of treasured toys; a yachting compass, a microscope, an artist's easel, a soapstone polar bear from Frobisher Bay; books, records, cutlery, dishes, can-openers; and God only knows what other junk that, an hour before, had all belonged in the skinny house on MacPherson Ave.

A big wicker basket with handles made ominous noises

whenever railroad tracks crossed the highway because it held nothing but loose tumblers—the glasses that had served a hundred drinking parties, a thousand drinks of milk after school, a thousand shots of orange juice in the morning.

Our older son was three when we moved into that house, and he had never negotiated a staircase. Our daughter was two. Both of them broke collarbones on the stairs that led down from their bedrooms to the living room, and they both made those miserable Sunday-evening journeys by taxi to the emergency ward of the Hospital for Sick Children. They are eight and seven now, fat and happy. Their brother is only seven months, so he won't remember the old house at all. He'll get his chance to break a collarbone in an old, rosy-brick farmhouse out in Newcastle, Ontario, east of Oshawa.

Our reasons for forsaking MacPherson Ave. are obscure even to ourselves. They probably have something to do with the huge lot in Newcastle. The house on MacPherson was only about 15 feet wide, and the western and eastern walls were forever dark. Our reasons may also be related to the fresher air out there, and the closeness to Lake Ontario, and the peonies, rose bushes, asparagus, strawberries, crab apple trees, 15 big evergreens, and daffodils and tulips and petunias that all grow on the big plain of grass at the house in Newcastle.

Or perhaps those are merely what we think are the reasons. Maybe the real ones lie deeper. Except for the homes of our childhood, we have never lived in any house or apartment for as long as five years, and maybe there are millions of parents in their thirties who feel that every few years, whether there's any logical reason or not, it is just time to move. *This has been just fine, hasn't it, just fine for quite a while, but you're ready now, aren't you? Yes. Well, let's go.*

We had our own van packed by the time the movers came to take the heavier stuff—the day, appropriately, was grey—so there wasn't much to do but sit around and keep out of the way while all the rooms became empty. We had watched the neighborhood grow, in only five years, from what was not far from a slum to a renovator's heaven.

27

We had watched a few friends move on and off the street, but when the time came to lock the doors for the last time, we realized that the nice old lady on the west was in hospital, the house on the east had been under renovation and unoccupied for almost two years, and there really was hardly anyone left on all of MacPherson Ave. to whom we wanted to entrust our house keys. There was only Lou's variety store at the corner of Avenue Rd., but it was a few hundred yards down the street and we were in a hurry. Somehow, we would deliver the keys to the new owners of the house on MacPherson Ave. on our own.

We had never installed the sundeck outside the third-floor bedroom on the south. We had never turned the basement into a clean hangout for the children. We had never ripped off the stale wooden shed behind the kitchen and built a sunroom. We went over to a cottage on Toronto Island for months each summer so we rarely even cut the lawn on MacPherson, and we never used the great stone patio that I built in a burst of sweaty, house-proud effort in the first hot months of the first year we ever lived in the house. But it's a good place, and maybe the new people will do more.

At the moment, most of what we own and need in order to get through the days of our lives is all out at the house in Newcastle. Thanks to the small-town kindness of the former owners there, we were allowed to install our junk on the day we left MacPherson.

But when we got to Newcastle, we discovered that for one incredibly complex legal reason or another, we could not move into our new house. We arrived back in Toronto at midnight, and now the five of us are staying in a big, sleazy suite with yellow walls and red curtains on the fifth floor of a hotel on Jarvis St. near Carlton. Hooker territory. Oddly enough—and perhaps because we're members of The Transient Generation—we are fond of this place, too.

The Toronto Star, March 1969

Alden Nowlan
(January 25, 1933–
June 27, 1983)

Alden Nowlan wrote 30 pieces for *Atlantic Insight* before he died last June 27 and in one of them, he asked, "Where else [but in Fredericton] could you meet the premier, the mayor, a poet and Stompin' Tom Connors walking arm-in-arm together at 4 a.m., or drive past a wild black bear on the way to work and attend a reception for the Dalai Lama that same afternoon?" He called Fredericton "a city of almost surrealist surprises," and he was a man of almost surrealistic surprises. I suspect the poet who deigned to honor the mayor, the premier and the country singer by walking with them at a black and raucous hour was Alden himself, and I wish I'd been there. I wish I'd known him better. I thought we'd have a quarter century to let our acquaintanceship ripen into something deeper. He's gone, at 50.

Fraser Sutherland, who did know him, wrote in the *Globe and Mail*, "Born to a family that was Irish, rural and hardscrabble poor, he quit school early to work on farms and sawmills in Nova Scotia's Annapolis Valley. Nowlan's roots were the kind you had to split with a wedge and a sledge-hammer, and he never forgot them throughout his career as a prolific journalist, poet, short story writer, novelist and play-wright."

I was glad Sutherland mentioned "journalist." Scholars, creative writers, readers of creative writing are already aware—and will remain aware for God only knows how many generations to come—that Alden was a blunt and magical, terrifying and comforting, harsh and humane wizard of words. But I knew him mostly as a fellow journalist, a master of the transitory in print, and simply as "a gentleman of the press." Some theorize that slugging it out in journalism drowns the imaginative spark that's vital to creative writing. Others theorize that Alden, in his poetry and fiction, owed a bit of his flat, biting, economical style to his long slavery at daily newspapers. Alden's theory was simpler: Good writing was good writing. Whether you were writing a poem, a novel, or a magazine article on "the King of New Brunswick swing," your job was to make it sing.

I once made a self-deprecating remark in a letter to him. I said something about my craft, magazine-writing, being on a lower order than his art. His reply was vehement and scolding. Did I, of all people, not know that one superior magazine article was worth more than a dozen inferior novels? Why did I rank categories of writing so foolishly? "I write for the same reason I'm six feet three inches tall," he once said. "I can't do anything about it." Maybe that's why it was that, out of the blue one summer day in '81, there arrived on my desk a gift from him. It goes like this:

> If the day comes when an editor
> realizes it's a crime
> that the Devil down in Hell
> is never given equal time;
> then he'll look for a writer
> to give us Satan's side,
> and it oughtn't to be difficult
> to guess what he'll decide.
> No, it oughtn't to be difficult
> to guess that he will pick
> Harry Bruce or Alden Nowlan
> to interview Old Nick.
>
> "Satan's a gruff old devil,"
> Harry Bruce will write,
> "but his skill with the pitchfork
> is an absolute delight."
> "It's true he's a little smelly,"
> Alden Nowlan will add,

"but nobody who wags his tail like that
can be all bad."
And whichever of them does it,
the nation will be told
that no citizen of Hell
need ever suffer from the cold.

Now, I'll have to get that framed.

For *Atlantic Insight*, he wrote tough opinion pieces ("Canadian Doctors Should Pay for Their Mistakes"); funny arguments that some didn't think were so funny ("It's Time to Get Tough with Teetotallers"); travel articles ("Cuba Is a Great Place to Visit," which won a national gold medal for travel writing); political analysis ("Can Daigle Beat Hatfield? Maybe. Place Your Bets"); small-town articles on Minto, Gagetown and Hartland, N.B.; stories on medicine, theatre, writers, artists, Orange lodges, musicians, virtually anything that an editor asked him to try. He even wrote a cooking piece ("Battle of the Blueberries: It's Grunt Against Cobbler"), complete with recipes.

He always delivered on time, never complained of "writer's block," never submitted messy manuscripts. They were flawlessly typed, with the typos whited out and corrected. His stuff read so smoothly we almost never asked him if we could change a phrase or shuffle paragraphs, but when we did, he said, "Yes. I think you're right. That'll be better." You may not know what such skills, habits and attitudes mean to editors. As a freelance magazine writer, Alden was the Complete Pro.

But he was more than that. He was a friend to the magazine. When it ran into financial horrors that threatened to destroy it as a market for writers, when it no longer had a nickel to pay the writers (including Alden) to whom it had owed money for months, he did not write outraged letters, he did not hire lawyers to threaten it, he did not drag it into court. Moreover, when *Atlantic Insight* offered to pay him for the right to reprint his prize-winning article on Cuba, he said that, in view of the magazine's plight, he didn't want the money. (*Atlantic Insight* paid him anyway.) Alden was not rich, nor even "comfortably off." You can be a major literary figure in this country, and still be hardup.

I mean none of this as a rebuke to writers who get tough with a magazine that owes them money. I've done that myself, and anyway that's their business. I only want to say that, in the experience of *Atlantic Insight*, Alden was not only a fine magazine writer but also a man of immense generosity. I remember his throaty, roaring, cancer-throttled voice, and the hair that didn't matter sprouting all over his face and head, and his eyes that seemed to hide so much. I remember the few rums we had together. When I was handing him an award on a stage he leaned his large, soft, bear-like body toward me and then, before hundreds of people, threw his arms around my neck. He made me feel that I was a member of some glorious brotherhood of writers.

His poem, "Sharon, Sharon," goes like this:

> *Sharon, you are*
> *one of the reasons*
> *we needn't be*
> *afraid of computers.*
> *I touch the tip*
> *of your nose with*
> *the tip of my finger,*
> *in salute; you*
> *are singular,*
> *a woman whose*
> *loveliness no*
> *micrometer could ever*
> *appraise, it*
> *is so wholly human.*

So were you Alden. So are you.

Atlantic Insight, August 1983

Kathi Anne II Could Do No Wrong

In a lifetime of worshipping other men's yawls, ketches, cutters and sloops, I have never seen such beauties. They are wooden schooners. They swoop around each other in a light breeze just off the Lunenburg Yacht Club, and I think of two huge, mythical birds in a sky-high dance of flight.

The American boat, the challenger, is *Agamemnon*. She has an elegant clipper bow, a black hull, white trim, and a long, tapered bowsprit, like the sword on a fish. If you count the sword *Agamemnon* is 54 feet long, but on deck, she has only 38 feet. She's 11 years old, sailed out of Nassau, registered in Florida, and built in California along the lines of the classic New England coasters. As she slides through the mist towards shore, with the Stars and Stripes fluttering on high, you'd swear she was sailing up out of another century to loot the town. Her ambition, however, is more honorable.

She has already whipped the cream of American wooden schooners in the Great Schooner Race at Gloucester, Mass., and what she's after now is the championship of the annual International Schooner Races near Lunenburg. To get it, she has only to beat *Kathi Anne II*. *Kathi Anne II* is blue and sleek. Her deck is creamy, her trim varnished wood. Overall, she's 46 feet long. She is lighter, slipperier, more slender, less serious than *Agamemnon*. If boats could laugh, *Kathi Anne II* would laugh more than most. For a two-year-old, her reputation is already formidable. She was only 17 days old when she beat *Outward Bound* of Dedham, Mass., in these same races. In '73, she beat *Amberjack* of Needham, Mass., and, in competition against American boats, the margin of her victories has been huge enough to embarrass even her own crew.

Captain Mike Daniel, owner of *Agamemnon*, is a British-born architect who spends several months each year sailing her up and down the North American coast. He's a tall, lean, charming man with the air of someone who'd be quite at home at the better yacht clubs around the world. His cap is rakish and looks like authentic captain's gear.

Captain David Stevens is not like him at all. He wears a green, baseball-style cap. There are no crossed anchors on it, only the words "Tree Farmer." Stevens will never sail far. The schooners he builds may take other men to Caribbean shores but these familiar waters—this corner of this county in this province—are the only home he ever wants to know. He's an old-age pensioner, a stubby, agile man, a trifle shy with strangers. He's a non-smoker, a non-drinker, the beloved grandfather of nine, a master shipbuilder, and the most good-natured man at the helm of a racing sailboat that I've ever met.

For him, the international championship is an excuse for a family picnic on the sea, and his crew today includes sons, daughter, grandsons, a granddaughter (Kathi Anne herself) a son-in-law, old friends, and me. Thirteen in all, and most have nothing to do but eat, talk, and revel in the light breeze, the misty afternoon, and the exquisite silence of *Kathi Anne II*'s ghosting rush over the ocean's swell. They talk about cabbages. They talk about sauerkraut, turnips, and the pears one of the boys grows. That kid's pears, David insists, are so juicy you have to wear rubber boots and a slicker when you eat them. They talk about old salts they have known, the rum-running era, the hard days of dory fishing, and about whales.

Porpoises lope along beside us, and a power launch—built by David and full of younger Stevens'—cheers us on from our starboard beam. And all along the shore, there are parked cars and people at houses and cottages and boatsheds that belong to still more Stevens', and we keep on waving at their waving. Then, a beautiful thing happens. Stevens announces that *Kathi Anne II* has slipped into a groove in which she is so finely balanced she will sail herself. We go below as a joke. When the committee boat pulls near, race officials see a fully rigged schooner, with her sails perfectly set, flying over the Atlantic Ocean with no crew.

She heads straight for Tancook Island, where David was born, and by now, *Agamemnon* is a mile astern. In the evening, after more than 20 miles and just under five hours of sailing, the sun shoots down like a searchlight to light up the whole sea. A southwest breeze gives *Kathi Anne II* a burst of strength and she leaps across the finishing line.

    Agamemnon crosses 12 minutes later. She's flying every inch of sail she can hoist; and schooners, even in defeat, have a lyrical kind of dignity. "Beautiful," Captain Daniel shouts over to Captain Stevens. "Beautiful race." *Agamemnon* is a lady. Her skipper is a gentleman. He's also a challenger of stupendous odds.

The Toronto Star, August 1974

Win the Marathon?
Sure, Harry, Sure

I'll trounce Ralph Hollett. Yes, that's the idea. I'll whip his arse. At 47, I'll wipe the floor with the middleweight champeen of Canada. Or rather, I'll run him into the ground. A superkeen guy named Barry Walsh has phoned to say, "We're going to have this Terry Fox Marathon of Hope, Mr. Bruce. The lieutenant-governor's coming, and even Reid Dexter [beloved weatherman on CBC Halifax's *Information Morning*]. The CBC's going to film it. The Saint Mary's Huskies are running, and a whole bunch of politicians and real celebrities, and we'd sure like you to be with us at the starting line." *Did he really call me a celebrity?* I fight the hook, but not for long.

    "Oh, I don't think so, Mr. Walsh," I say, lighting another

35

Rothman's Special Mild. "I haven't jogged for weeks. I'm in terrible shape. I couldn't run my way out of a paper bag. I'd have to quit smoking.... Um, what's the course like?"

"Well, it's 10 kilometres. That's a bit better than six miles, but it's nice and level. No hills. You just trot around this pretty little duck pond. Ralph Hollett's running, too."

I have two weeks to train. I swear off the Special Milds, blow $100 on snowy socks, silky shorts, a snazzy T-shirt of the sort worn by winners of the Boston Marathon, and an elegant pair of Brooks runner's shoes, with blue and grey stripes. (Poor Hollett. He'll probably turn up in boxer's shoes, fine for the ring but pathetic against top marathon talent.) Then, day after day, I hurl myself round Point Pleasant Park. I do all the stretching exercises that *Runners' World* magazine recommends, and at last I can snap off 10 km in 54 minutes. That, my fat friends, is roughly six nine-minute miles. Watch out, Sebastian Coe. Here I come, Ralph Hollett.

An omen I should heed: Max Bruce, 13, bursts into the kitchen just before I drive out to the starting line, and he says he's been to an earlier Marathon of Hope. He has never before shown the slightest interest in running, and he's wearing an old pair of his mother's shoes. "Well, well, well," I say. "I guess you had to walk most of the way, eh?"

"Oh no, Dad, but my time wasn't too good. It took me 54 minutes. That's only about six nine-minute miles."

Another omen: In the Celebrity Zone at Tantallon Junior High School, I find none other than Marilyn MacDonald, editor of *Atlantic Insight*. "Hello Marilyn," I say coolly. "You a celebrity, too?" She wears a grey sweatshirt, white shorts that look fine on her but certainly aren't *runner's* shorts, a beat-up pair of blue-and-yellow Adidas with frayed shoelaces and—har, har—blue socks with no stripes. Real runners always wear white socks with stripes. Besides, Marilyn's just a slip of a girl.

"I'll run along with you for a while, Marilyn, just to keep you company. But I'm out to beat Ralph Hollett so don't be sore when I leave you in the dust."

"Sure, Harry," she says. "Sure."

Bang! Off we go. She flies up the first huge hill (curse Barry Walsh) like a startled gazelle. She is supremely comfortable. I am gasping, wheezing, desperate. I can't talk. She is actually making funny remarks about the running style of those we keep passing. She chatters away, steps up the pace. Rivers of sweat roll down my face. A cramp in my left side makes me face the horrifying possibility that this little female person, my *editor* yet, may not only beat me but may force me out of the race entirely. The cramp fades. A rush of adrenalin, or masculine fear, hurls me ahead in a fantastic sprint for the finish. Surely I've left her hundreds of yards behind. I stagger up to the finish line, proudly announce, "Harry Bruce." Beside me, a small, firm voice says, "And Marilyn MacDonald." Migod, it's a tie. We both get certificates to prove our time is 50 minutes.

More than 700 runners and walkers started the race, and we're among the first 100 to finish. That plodding prizefighter must be a mile back in the pack and, sure enough, a full 20 minutes pass before I find him in the men's can. He has a luxuriant black mustache, dark and surprisingly gentle eyes, short legs, a massive hairy chest, a torso like the proverbial brick backhouse. I, of course, have a stringy body, a *runner's* body, and I challenge him on the spot.

"All right, champ, what was your time?"

"I don't know," he mildly replies. "I just run to keep in shape."

"Don't give me that, Hollett. You've got your certificate right there in your hand. That'll tell us your time."

I grab his certificate. It says, "Thank you for supporting Terry's Dream. Name: Ralph Hollett. Time: 39 minutes."

Oh.

The brick backhouse has merely run six miles at an average speed of better than six-and-a-half minutes per mile. Why doesn't the brute pick on someone his own age, anyway?

I find Marilyn. "Let's get the hell out of here," I tell her. "I need a Rothman's Special Mild."

"Sure, Harry," she says. "Sure."

Atlantic Insight, November 1981

In Toronto the Good,
Three Wrong Numbers

"This seat taken?" she asks. It isn't, so she sits beside me and
orders a club soda. Nice, sensible, abstemious lady. She is a
tall, lumpy woman in her early 40s, and wears a red pantsuit.
She carries a white purse with a shoulder strap. Her shoes are
white, too, like a nurse's. Her skin is the color of coffee, with
extra cream, and I take her to be a housewife from Buffalo or
Detroit who has come to Toronto to do a little shopping.

We are at Trader's. It's a ground-floor bar off the cavernous lobby of the Sheraton Centre. A single room in this hotel
can set you back $129. Near Trader's, glittering escalators
rise hundreds of feet, waterfalls tumble through a fake jungle,
and gangs of mildly raucous Oldsmobile dealers swarm
around. They're here for a convention, but it's nearly midnight now and they have other things on their minds.

"Where you from?" she asks amiably.

"I'm actually from Toronto, but I've lived in Nova Scotia
for 13 years."

"Now that's a beautiful, beautiful province," she says.
"Really, really beautiful. What brings you to Toronto?"

"I write for magazines, and there's a national convention
of magazine people here tomorrow night. I'm up for a prize. If
I win, I get $1,000."

"Well, isn't that fascinating? What magazines do you
write for?"

"Oh, I've written for pretty nearly all of them. *Atlantic
Insight*, *Maclean's*, *Saturday Night*, *Quest*, some that aren't
around anymore."

"No kidding? I read *Maclean's* all the time. That's a good
magazine."

Two Japanese men take seats at the bar, and now her talk
takes an odd twist.

38

"I think those two are Japanese," she says, "and not Koreans. I've lived in New York, and Vancouver, and I lived in San Francisco for four years. So I can always tell the difference. The Koreans have more moon-shaped heads. No really, I mean it. You know, in San Francisco there's this section of town where naked white women get up in glass cages and perform obscene gestures."

She stresses the first syllable of obscene. AWBseen.

"Yes," she continues, "and hundreds of Japanese men with cameras stand there and take photographs of these white women doing these obscene gestures."

"I never heard of that before."

"Well, you're a writer so I thought you'd be interested."

She studies me for a few seconds. Her chocolate eyes remind me of a Trinidadian woman I once knew.

"You a happily married man?"

"Yes," I reply, "As a matter of fact, I am."

"I guess that means I can't seduce you then."

"I'm afraid that's right."

But she doesn't leave. She chats for a while, as though it would be graceless to go abruptly just because she's failed to score. Then she gets up, leaving a $2.50 tip for the bartender.

"I sure hope you win the big prize," she says. How sincere she seems. How likable. "If you do, and you change your mind, I'll be right here tomorrow night at the same time."

"Well, thanks, but do you mind telling me one thing? Have you really seen Nova Scotia, or did you just say that?"

"Have I seen it?" she explodes. "Honey, I'm from Cape Breton."

"Go on! Why'd you ever leave?"

"I didn't want to marry some guy down there, and end up on welfare with 17 children."

"Do you ever go home?"

"I haven't been back for 17 years. I can't go back to that town. They all regard me down there as a fallen woman. And I *am* a fallen woman."

She says this as though she were truly a happy hooker

who's letting me in on a marvellous joke.

She walks a few feet, asks a plump man about his lapel badge. I can see them in the mirror over the bar, and from the rear she looks both animated and matronly. They leave together. She's won her prize.

A tall man with thin hair, wearing steel-rimmed glasses and a blue business suit, replaces her in the chair beside me. He seems to feel that since my tastes did not run to the lady from Cape Breton they might run to him. "May we have a little chat?" he pleads.

"Nope. The bar's closed, and I'm getting out of here."

He goes into deep mourning.

At 1:30 a.m., there's a soft, insistent rapping at my door on the 33rd floor. I am brushing my teeth, naked at the sink. I pull on my trenchcoat—which means I'm classically garbed for flashing—and yank open the door. A girl stands there, a small, young girl with dark, luminous eyes, gleaming lip gloss, and an overnight bag. She reminds me of *Flower Drum Song*, but she is not an actress.

"I'm sorry," I say, "but you've got the wrong room number."

"I see you got your house robe on," she replies mockingly. She traipses back along the corridor toward the elevator, leaving me to reflect that six whole hours have passed since I arrived back in my home town, Toronto the Good.

Atlantic Insight, August 1984

The Wonder That Was Expo

"What is that?" the African asks. He is squinting in the extravagant sunlight, looking north across the glittering action of the St. Lawrence to the grey towers and purple cliffs of downtown Montreal. A long, smooth wind is blowing into Expo like a train out of the Far West, and for a moment, the man's brilliant tribal robes fly around him, and rattle. He gets them back under control, and then his companion, a French Canadian, says, "That? Oh, that is only the city."

The Montreal skyline has a raw, spectacular beauty in this summer of triumph and romance, but here on the windy heights of the Canadian pavilion, here in the strange and Olympian atmosphere of Expo 67, the French Canadian's remark is not even surprising. It is simply right. For Montreal *is* only the city. It is merely life as it is; and Expo is life as it should be.

Expo 67 is a sprawling camp of buildings that look like huge jewels spilled from a bag. It is also a brave and boastful monument to our own genius. It is a happy land of sudden acts of kindness and unsolicited smiles; a garden of candy floss, of strange liquor, cars in the sky, sculpture, unearthly machines, and endless sensation. It is a place of international alliance, private liaison and weird community of spirit. It is the world's biggest party. The men there are forever shaking hands, and the girls are always laughing.

It is all, somehow, a taste of the world we are sure we could make, if only we could find the answers. And, for a little while anyway, it achieves a miracle: Each day, it makes hundreds of thousands of people feel that they have all stepped together into a better place than they've known, and that they have something in common because this is where people come when they want to be happy and good. That miracle is one of the great feelings of Expo.

Now, the electronic bells in the old tower on the hills of Île Sainte-Hélène have begun to send their Sunday-morning sounds out over the people, and some other feeling settles in the paths of Expo. The bells—by contrast with the beeps, the chirps, the mechanical clunks and clickety-clicks, and the other noises of tomorrow at Expo—have a deep, old-fashioned quality. They are an elderly man talking of his childhood, and they are sad.

They serenade the men in green suits who are down on the grass by the edge of the water raking up the dead fire-crackers of the night before. The bells argue that, tomorrow, everyone must go back to his job and that, by the time the snow falls, all the tents and most of the roofs of Expo must come down, and that the only permanent thing these millions of people will take away from the fair is the right to say, "Yes, I was there."

As the bells sound, a dark amphitheatre over in the French pavilion is showing a film about the modern history of Paris. The film gives you Mistinguett, the young Chevalier, girls kissing soldiers who are marching to the trenches, the alleys of Paris, the voice of Piaf, and the morning breaking after the blackness of the Second World War.

A beautiful woman sits by herself on a park bench, with the sunlight in her blonde hair, and the commentary tells us that, in Paris, love is brighter, and pain is deeper. The film starts with quaint scenes from the world's fair at Paris in 1901. That was more than two world wars ago; and now, the bells of Expo are saying that there are people, perhaps even here on the grounds, who can say about that fair, too, "Yes, I was there."

The bells speak of time, and they define the gap between the magnificent illusion of Expo and, across the water, the reality of the cities that are only cities. The bells, if you listen, give you the reverse side of Expo's joy, and that is another feeling of the fair.

The place where the African and the French Canadian are

standing is on the north side of the Katimavik. The Katimavik (from the Eskimo for "meeting place") is the crown of the Canadian pavilion. It's a blue-green glassy affair that opens like a strange, 1,000-ton flower to a height of nine storeys. The view from the Katimavik is dramatic in every direction. Moreover, the eerie electronic symphony up here in the wind, and the shadowy symbols that Canada has installed to represent "things universal to all men" combine to create an air of mystery and spiritual grandeur.

The Katimavik is more than striking architecture; it is a celebration. It celebrates the idea of Expo 67. It celebrates the gathering of nations to show their pride in human achievement and to demonstrate that, on remarkable occasions like this one, they can really manage to be nice to one another. The spirit of the Katimavik is the reason why there is a subtle quality to the good times at Expo—a quality that lifts *these* good times to something better, something more like fine wine, than the pleasures of ordinary world fairs.

On the level of the Canadian pavilion that lies just below the Katimavik, the idea of Expo is more explicit. Here, exposed to the winds of summer on all sides, there's a roughly circular network of triangular flags and white pennants that offer wise old sayings from many nations. Down in La Ronde, Expo's amusement area, there's a carnival game entitled "Knock Sputnik's Teeth Out," but up here, the pennants offer more hopeful reasons for coming to Expo:

"We cannot dwell in a house together without speaking to one another...help me to help you climb the ridge...do not protect yourself by a fence, but rather by friends...policy goes beyond strength...one is never a friend by force...not to injure is the first of virtues."

A lot of people are standing around reading this stuff, but even here in the heady air of Expo, you must expect the intrusions of the cities that are only cities. Two businessmen charge by the flags, and one is worriedly telling the other, "But I only hope I can write to him and say that we're making a lot of money." A young mother is trying to read a flag that says, "Without rules there can be no perfection," but her daughter is swinging on the mother's hand and wailing, "I want to go get some goodies."

Kids want goodies, men want a drink, old people want to sit down in the subway, hundreds upon thousands of people are wondering where in hell are the toilets, and why do we have to line up for a crummy hot dog? These, however, are the preoccupations of crowds at gatherings all over the world.

The thing that makes Expo remarkable, the thing that sometimes makes it seem superhuman, is the goodwill it manages to force on the people who go there. This atmosphere *opens* people to one another. It invests the smallest incident with significance and, somehow, makes idle conversation matter.

A puffy middle-aged Canadian businessman, who looks as though he has never spoken to a stranger in his life (much less a black stranger), finishes his Planter's Punch at the cool, outdoor bar of Trinidad, Tobago and Grenada. He turns and looks, more enviously than resentfully, at the skinny young guy on the stool beside him. The black has just arrived to work at Expo.

"You know," the businessman says, for no clear reason, "it ought to be a lot of fun, as time goes on, and you know where to go, people to meet." The youth unleashes a beautiful smile and, in his soft West Indian way, says, "Yeh, it's a swingin' place."

An eight-year-old boy stoops to pick up a key that an old woman in a blue and white polka-dot dress has dropped on one of the subway platforms. He hands it to her and, astonished, she says, "Why, thank you very much." He runs up the platform, blushing under the station's long, orange and white awning.

The Cuban pavilion sells the revolution hard. It offers ugly photographs of the Batista regime, movies of bloody battles, and references to "the shiverings of death and the singing summer joy of VICTORY." But the bar in the Cuban pavilion features rich, dark, polished wood, gleaming mirrors, suave bartenders and an atmosphere that speaks so clearly of the old days in Havana that the place is full of nostalgic Americans.

One of them—a jolly, round, tanned little man with a grey moustache—keeps asking the proprietor how old so-and-so is making out down there in Cuba these days. Then, he chats for a while with a lady who has brought her fur coat all the way from Labrador City and, after a while, the whole bunch of them move on. "Hasta la vista!" they shout. "Hasta la vista!" The waiters smile a lot and wave good-bye.

Outside the Ontario pavilion, two shockingly pretty French-Canadian girls wearing mini-mini-*mini* skirts, are teasing a sternly handsome member of the Ontario Provincial Police. They are asking for directions in French. He is blushing so hard he must be a rookie.

"Do you not speak *any* English?" he stammers. "Ah, non, monsieur," one of them says, pouting so very, very sadly. She reaches out, for a second, and touches the back of his hand. ("If it responds it lives," says a sign in the pavilion called Man The Explorer. "If it lives it responds.")

Thirty or forty teenagers of both sexes, wearing brown uniforms with orange scarfs, crowd aboard a subway car that's already so packed that the mob inside gives them furious looks. Then, as the subway moves out past the grey ships in the harbor and the astonishing structures of Expo, the kids all begin to sing French-Canadian folksongs. They are some sort of choir. They sing and sing and sing, and within a few minutes, they've got the whole carful of people laughing and grinning foolishly and singing along with them. They are still singing as they squeeze their way out of the car and head towards the Man And Life exhibit.

There, among the incredible representations of life cells, the human brain, and the processes of human thought, they will find a different kind of singing and, on one of the walls, a quote from Hamlet that indicates how well Shakespeare understood why men build things like Expo: "What a piece of work is a man! how noble in reason! how infinite in faculty! in form and moving, how express and admirable! in action, how like an angel! in apprehension, how like a god! the beauty of the world! the paragon of animals!"

One of Expo's pavilions tries to give us an idea of how small "the paragon of animals" really is. "If the world shrank until it was a ball just ten feet across, the highest mountains would be no thicker than a coat of paint," a sign tells us. "The deepest ocean trenches would become a faint scratch. Our biggest buildings would be smaller than specks of dust. And man would be invisible except under a powerful magnifying lens."

This, like so much at the fair, is fascinating stuff but it is a measure of Expo's joy that nothing there, no matter how deeply impressive, makes you feel that men are small. "Possibly," a sign in the French pavilion says, "one of the highest functions of Art is to make men conscious of the greatness which they ignore in themselves." Expo itself is a vast work of art; and it makes you feel your greatness. It makes you feel something the way Soviet cosmonaut Gherman Titov must have felt when, circling the earth, he spoke by radio to the cities that are only cities.

"I am eagle!" he said. "I am eagle! I am eagle!"

The Canadian, June 1967

Take to the Hills, Everybody. The City's Had It

I came down to the city recently after weeks away, and in the past when I had come back, there had always been a beautiful young surge of excitement but this time, for the first time, I did not feel it at all and it was painfully clear that, between me and the city, something had changed forever. Then, for four days, a blank, grey cover, an oppressive eiderdown of tarnished mist sat on the city, and intermittently it dribbled the sooty sort of rain that has turned clotheslines into an urban anachronism. The temperature was neutral. There was no season, no sunrise or sundown, or even a real noon.

I was born here. I had lived most of my life here, and it was here that I'd done most of my reading about air pollution. Pollution had always been something one only read about, but now, with every breath, it was here in my nostrils, surprising and unpleasant, and melodramatically, I thought, *Ah, my beloved city. My beloved city, you really do stink.*

Most of the people I know are lifelong lovers of the city. As children, some of us actually liked the smell of automobile-exhaust fumes, and we'd hang around gas stations to suck it in. The landscape of our memory is common. It consists of city softball, city hockey, city hopscotch and skipping, a peculiarly dusty and smelly kind of July heat, Saturday-afternoon movies, the learning of expertise in the use of streetcars, and roaming by bicycle for mile upon mile down corridors of houses in a hundred alien territories. It consists of street gangs, clubhouses made of stolen fence planks, a few concrete swimming pools (the chlorine was fierce), asphalt and, wherever we went, pavement. Pavement in the morning, pavement before coming in for bed, bloody noses and love on the schoolyard pavement. To people like us, you need only say the word "pavement" aloud, and the

47

images and urgings and colors and rivalries of childhood, they all begin to boil around in some obscure depth of the mind. At a downtown cocktail party, I have merely to name a particular dancehall where we teenaged "operators" used to go to see if we could "make out," and three or four strangers of my generation will all look up with a happy shock of recognition. We're city boys.

And later, did we change, did we settle in the square, healthy suburbs, or beyond? Not on your polluted life! We moved even farther downtown than our parents had lived. We were not exactly a Jet Set. We were the Taxi Generation. We put our kids in downtown schools. We traded our knowledge of the Saturday-movie matinées for a knowledge of "film." We moved out of the hot dancehalls and into the bars, coffeehouses, art galleries, delicatessens, laundromats, magazine stores, boutiques, hair-dressing salons, creative men's tailoring shops, bookshops, charity balls, theatres, and all the other places that a good city is supposed to provide to keep one's appearance interesting and one's mind moving. We made jokes about the rubes who were so unfortunate as to live more than two miles from City Hall and, if we were smug, it was only because we were rather pleased with the way we lived in our city and because, outside of being rich in Manhattan or London, we really could not imagine how anyone could have a better life than the ones we had arranged for ourselves.

But something has gone wrong, and I'm not sure what it is, or it is so many things that I can't get them all straight. Perhaps it's just that the longer you live in any one place the more oppressive and confining it becomes. Perhaps the bricks, and the pavement itself, in all their great familiarity, slowly cease to be a background to excitement and, instead, become reminders of the small defeats and private disillusionments that everyone must endure. Hardly any of the people I know are still living with the people they married in their twenties. A close friend suddenly died and, until then, I'd never had a close friend who did that, just died. She used to read rural real-estate ads, and she'd talk a lot about finding a place in the country and getting out of the crappy old city. And now, every other city boy I meet—and his wife, or his second wife, or his new girl friend—they are all scheming to find something "up north" that they have never found in their beloved city. They are buying Crown land, building log cabins, comparing prices per acre, forming little syndicates to buy bush and rock and pasture and brooks, and even before they've found these things, they are worrying about how they'll keep the hunters and the snowmobile nuts off their property. Even to my city-loving friends, the city is no longer the place where you choose to work to get a good life; it's becoming the place where you *have* to live to get good work.

Air pollution is nowhere near the whole reason for this change in feeling. Pollution is more symbol than cause, a pervasive reminder of our gentle despair over no longer caring much about the old city. For, if we loved the city enough, we who once enjoyed the smell of auto exhaust might even learn to stop worrying and love the smog. Your true city-lover, your Jimmy Breslin for instance, can celebrate even the more profound horrors of city life. Gangsterdom, ghetto life, power failures, transit strikes, bums, drought, crime waves, poverty, not to mention such minor unpleasantness as greed, rudeness and human callousness...they've all been endlessly deplored, but writers and politicians have also romanticized them, and sometimes even idealized them. *This is my town. You gotta know how to talk to the cab drivers. Don't let anyone give you any crap. I grew up on the pavement just across the river and, believe me, brother, that was murder. I can take care of myself in this town. This is my town, and I love every rotten, corrupt, rat-infested, disease-ridden, back-stabbing, throat-slitting, screwed-up inch of it. The dope addicts, too.*

I can understand that, I just don't like it much any more. A recent essay in *Time* said much the same sort of thing: "In countless different ways, [the great city] has almost always been an unpleasant, disagreeable, cheerless, uneasy and re-proachful place; in the end, it can only be described as magnificent." I can understand that, too. I just wonder if, in connection with cities, we shouldn't redefine such words as "great" and "magnificent." The dream of The Great City recently led Mayor Jean Drapeau to explain on television that, in a sense, the anarchy and murderous public violence that afflicted parts of Montreal in October were merely the price of Montreal's international greatness. "In England," Drapeau said, "it is London. In France, it is Paris, and in Canada it is Montreal." Praise be! Canada can hold her head up because Montreal, in addition to her big-league baseball, her big-league skyscrapers, her big-league gangland killings and her big-league slums, can now prove her greatness with big-league street violence as well. I thought I detected a note of pride in Drapeau's statement, as though he'd just talked the Metropolitan Opera Company into moving to Montreal, but no one seemed to think he'd said anything unusual, and I wondered, *Are we all quite sane?*

I'm moving back to the city myself soon. There's a job there, and I need the money. You see, I know a place on the coast of Nova Scotia where I can build a house that faces the ocean. There's a little bluff back from the beach, and though the water is very cold, it has always been clean and it marches up to the shore from somewhere I cannot see, and there are big evergreens. You can walk for miles, over a billion round beachstones, and hardly ever meet anyone.

Maclean's, February 1970

The Day Churchill Did Not Die

Back in the time of World War II—when not only the girls but even the boys in my class were knitting little woollen squares to make quilts for bombed-out British kids; when we were supposed to be saving our quarters for pink war-savings stamps; and when we all thought we'd beat the Germans if we could only collect enough metal paper from cigarette boxes— back in that time, there were big vacant lots on three of the four corners where our street met Yonge Street. The intersection is part of downtown Toronto now. It's many years since a couple of insurance firms and a soap company destroyed the vacant lots with squat, numb-looking office buildings.

The buildings are sorry monuments to the imaginary battles that occurred in those three fields. By 1945, the war had been on for half my life and I, along with some other battle-tough ten-year-olds whose fathers were overseas, had fought in most of its historic battles. Every Saturday we'd go to a neighborhood movie theatre that's gone now and pay 12 cents each to see Hollywood's version of the horrors of Bataan, say, or North Africa. Then, in the following week, we'd "go down to the lots to play guns" for all the waking moments we could escape home and school. We were expert in the use of every deadly weapon known to modern man. We knew the right way to take a bullet in the gut, scream, roll down hill, and then recover.

The vacant lots offered virtually every battle condition you could imagine: the dust of the Sahara, the mud of Italy, the mountains of Norway, the obscene growths of the Burmese jungle. Putrid smells, broken glass and cruel thistles lurked in their grass. (I still bear a small white scar on my left shin where a piece of concrete shrapnel got me.) You could climb up the intricate framework of any one of four huge billboards that flanked Yonge Street and bombard the slow,

51

wooden streetcars with whatever real or imaginary ammunition came to hand. Our mothers hated the vacant lots the way all mothers hate war.

I remember a spring day. Three or four of us were down in the dirt planning some bloody action when a boy named Dickie, who was not officer material, came running across the rubble. "Churchill's dead, Churchill's dead!" Dickie shouted. "My mother heard it on the radio." We all looked scared, and for a few minutes, we wondered if there weren't something we should do. I went home and told my mother that Dickie's mother had heard on the radio that Churchill was dead. *My* mother looked as though she were going to say, "Nonsense," and then she, too, began to look scared. Churchill, remember, was seventy. She phoned a newspaper, listened for a few seconds, and seemed to relax. "Well, I suppose that's bad enough," she said to the phone and then turning to me, "It's all right. It's only Roosevelt."

Saturday Night, March 1965

Highland Games, Florida Style: He Who Pays the Piper Calls the Tune

The palm trees sway in the sweet wind off the Gulf of Mexico, the fabulous white beach at Clearwater swarms with largely naked and largely beer-swilling college kids, and a few miles north, in the town of Dunedin, which officially defines itself as "delightfully different," the skirl of bagpipes floats on the semitropical air and men weighing more than an eighth of a ton each are gathering to throw telephone poles. Well, not exactly. What they toss is merely a tapered 20-foot log weighing anywhere up to 140 pounds. They call it the caber.

It is noon, I've checked out of my hotel, and my flight home from Tampa doesn't leave until 11:30 p.m. Should I join the nubility on the beach for hot hours of bikini watching? Or, as a sometime sportswriter, should I witness the softball game in Clearwater for guys over 65? After all, a 97-year-old centre fielder has told the press that that's where he hopes to croak, in centre field. Or should I take in the last day of the delightfully different Dunedin Scottish Games and Festival? The decision is easy. I'm a Bruce.

Kilt flaunting and caber tossing among the orange groves of the Florida "suncoast" are not really all that improbable. Surely the people of no other small nation have settled more corners of the earth than the Scots. This is why it was that before the gathering of the clans in Scotland in 1981, Scottish officials got inquiries from cities as exotic as Singapore and Beersheba; from Mrs. Dubinski in Yugoslavia, who said she was a Gordon; Mrs. Freitag in Australia, who insisted she was a Ferguson; and Maria Luisa Gallozi in Yonkers, N.Y., who knew in the marrow of her being that she was really a fighting Leslie. It is why there are Mexican MacGregors and

French Frasers, and it may also be why a man named Siegel once phoned from Milwaukee to Limekilns, Scotland, and at 4 a.m. awoke Lord Elgin, chief of the Bruces, to tell him that he, Siegel, was a direct descendant of King Robert the Bruce.

Just before the last big gathering in Scotland, a British magazine advised, "If, flying to Britain this summer, you find your aircraft carrying men with bare thighs and daggers in their socks, you need not panic. Those pale limbs are being exposed to the world because their owners—Auckland solicitors, Phoenix dentists, Vancouver estate agents, Brisbane Datsun dealers—have donned the kilt and, with their sporrans full of credit cards, are preparing to engage in a bit of ancestor worship." MacVanish, a Highland name, may have vanished, but the love of things Scottish still flourishes from Dunedin, New Zealand, to Dunedin, Florida.

Those who revel in their Scottish heritage but can't live in Scotland make up their own Scotlands, and that's what Dunedin's sixteenth annual games are all about. That, and tourist bucks. Dunedin is a sister city to Stirling, Scotland. It boasts Scottish street names and a sprawling high school with both a massive parking lot and a sports field, complete with spectator stands, that would put many Canadian universities to shame. It is here at the school—out under the southern sun, within a couple of miles of the palm-fringed beach, in the land of lizards and alligators—that I witness highland games, Florida style. Thanks to the *Clearwater Sun*, I already suspect that Scotland was never like this.

In a story by Shannon Brennan, who must be a mischievous Irish girl, the *Sun* reported that some of the 750 spectators at the opening-night ceilidh (pronounced "kay-lee")—a Scottish party with music—found the event culturally impure. The kilted band was so bold as to play "New York, New York," and this did not please Mary Armstrong, a Toronto Scot. "When we come for the ceilidh, we want the ceilidh," she complained. "It's a ceilidh. *All* Scotch." The star was Peter Glen, a fine Scottish tenor who lives in Toronto and had a spot in the film *The Black Stallion*; and, as Brennan reported, he not only "stole the show with his booming brogue and

Scottish favorites," but also mockingly confessed, "I love those Scottish songs: 'Kansas City' and 'New York, New York.'" Festival Committee President Frank Jennings— whose greetings in the printed program urged, "Lang may your lum reek, and your pat bile!"—defended the musical mélange on grounds that "the Scots are like everybody else. They like a little variety."

At the games on Saturday afternoon we get even more variety. Master of ceremonies Robert Barr, an Eastman Kodak regional sales manager and director of both the Burns Club and the St. Andrew's Society in Atlanta, genially urges us to try "southern-fried chicken in the fine Scottish tradition." Booths sell not only Cameron Meat Pies for $1.35, but also hot dogs, sausage dogs, popcorn, pizza, pretzels and T-shirts that define their wearers as "Dunedin Highlanders." (If Dunedin sits on high land, incidentally, so does Holland.) I settle for a hot dog. What the hell—it's a direct descendant of haggis, isn't it?

Under canopies hawkers preside over tables that bend under the weight of huge bolts of tartan, woollen sweaters, blankets, sporrans, dirks, shortbread from the auld sod, antique prints, records of Scottish music, clan front-door plaques, books, jewellery, trinkets, gewgaws and, all in all, more Scottish schlock than you'll find on Edinburgh's Royal Mile. If Arabs wore the kilt, the bazaars of Morocco might look like this, but the sales zone is in fact the cunning offspring of a perfect marriage of Scottish and American commercial instincts. Business is booming. A line of out-of-state Winnebagos nuzzles the sales booths like a herd of hungry bison.

A rack holding hundreds of men's tartan ties urges: "Support your clan, wear its color." The Bruce is not represented. The ties jump from Brodie to Buchanan. Oh well, maybe I'll buy a sign to remind the world that "God Made the Scots a Wee Bit Better." Or a bumper sticker that says, "Scots Make Better Lovers," or another that shows a Highland drummer and announces, "Drummers Do It on the Side." While I'm examining bumper stickers, an elderly saleswoman

55

with white hair and a mahogany tan suggests a particularly popular one. She smiles and points to it. It says, "Kiss My Thistle." I feel faint.

This is superb T-shirt country. I see a fat woman hand-in-hand with a fat boy, and they're both wearing Scottish tams and "Smokey and the Bandit" T-shirts. I see a wonderfully ample young woman in a tartan skirt. Her braless breasts celebrate "Famous Amos Chocolates" and her fine back insists that I "Have a Very Brown Day." Thanks, dear, that's just what I'm having. But my favorite character, the perfect symbol of the cultural smorgasbord of the day, is a young guy with straggling black hair and an unkempt beard. He wears a kilt, cowboy hat, dirty Adidas and a "Cock o' the North" T-shirt. That outfit is unbeatable, though after hearing his drawl I decide he's really a cock o' the South, possibly a member of the Dixieland branch of the MacGoon family.

Bands of the senior high school, wearing the dress Stewart kilt, and of the middle school, in royal Stewart, form up on the far side of the football field under flags of Canada, the United States, the Southern Confederacy and assorted tartans. Scotland's lion, of course, also flutters in the hot zephyr. The bands march up to the crowd and give us jazzy versions of Scottish tunes in which the pipes bravely but feebly compete with the brass. They haven't a chance. The middle-school band, for instance, includes more than 100 students, but only 13 of them are pipers. I do not think Mary Armstrong of Toronto would approve.

Still, bagpipes rule the gorgeous afternoon. Dunedin has invited pipe bands from Georgia, Texas, Burlington, Ontario, and from all over Florida, including the Space Coast Highlanders. The Burlington Teen Tour Band, a local official says, is "one of the international greats." There are so many pipers around that no matter what's happening on the field—whether it's superheavyweight athletes hurling the "stone of strength," or guys racing "the kilted mile," or a circuslike demonstration of primitive warfare, or honey blondes flashing tanned thighs while highland-flinging—you can hear, off in the sunny wings somewhere, the far wail of bagpipe rehearsals. That noise is one reason why Betty Carlyle of Toronto makes the touching statement that at the Dunedin festival, "We always feel we're a little bit nearer Scotland."

For me, to feel nearer Scotland, to amble around at what's more like a gigantic family picnic than a sports event, to watch the girls dancing and know that bikini watching at Clearwater is boring by comparison, and to get a tan, all at the same time—well, the day is all a man could ask for. Now, if I could only find a shot of single-malt whisky.

Dave Harrington completes my day. It is not often I get to see a Canadian athlete clean the clocks of half a dozen American bruisers, but even before the opening ceremonies, he grabs the 22-pound hammer by its handle, twirls around, lets out a karate scream and hurls the thing 101 feet $2^1/_2$ inches. This smashes the North American record, and the Florida Scots give the Canadian boy a mighty cheer. All in all, he wins four of the seven strange contests of strength that occur at Highland games the world over, and finishes second in the other three. The events include throwing a 20-pound stone, a 28-pound weight, a 56-pound weight, the caber and, with a pitchfork, tossing a 16-pound bag of hay up over a bar. Harrington, with ridiculous ease, cops the Professional Athlete of the Day trophy. He barely works up a sweat. He should change his name to MacJock.

The announcer repeatedly says Harrington is from "Ontario, Canada," but he lives on the Quebec side of the Ottawa River at Old Chelsea. He looks like a Mountie but in fact he is the branch manager of a photocopier firm. He's a genial giant with black eyes and moustache, and hairy forearms the size of footballs. He reminds me of Whipper Billy Watson, a good-guy wrestler of my childhood days in Toronto, but Watson was a shrimp by comparison. Harrington's chest and shoulders bulge under a red T-shirt, and his calves swell under red knee-socks. He wears black and yellow Puma running shoes and a Cameron Highlander kilt.

"How much do you weigh, Dave?"

"About 252 or 255," he says. "Unfortunately."

"You mean you'd like to lose weight?"

"Nope. I'm one of the lightest in the field. Some of these other fellows weigh in at about 280 to 330."

The difference, however, is that some of these other fellows have guts that suggest that if they can beat Harrington at anything it's probably beer-drinking. Harrington trains three hours a day, and looks as tough as India rubber. If I punched him on the arm or in the breadbasket, my fist would bounce off. I do not undertake this test. It's doubtful that anyone ever considers punching any of these guys, which may explain why they're such an affable elite. They rank with sumo wrestlers and football linemen as the world's biggest athletes, but unlike wrestlers and linemen, their sport never requires them to hurt anyone.

Harrington's rivals are not patsies. They include the cream of Highland-games competitors in the American South, fellows not only from Florida but also from Tennessee, Maryland, and both Carolinas. They travel a Highland-games circuit and, like Harrington, pick up enough money in expenses and prizes to get by. Harrington has competed in Australia and Nigeria, and right across Canada and the States. He has strutted his impressive stuff at the Highland games in Antigonish, N.S., almost every year since 1972; but now, downing a cold Budweiser in the Florida sun, he says, "My real ambition is to compete in Scotland." But of course. Almost everyone here would rather be in Scotland, for a little while anyway. For Scotland, too, is delightfully different and, as I know man-mountain Harrington will one day discover, delightfully familiar.

Quest, September 1982

That Was No Lady, That Was My Jeep

It was on the day we went to Prince Edward Island that I knew, at last, that I hated our Jeep Cherokee. How quickly love can turn to hate. Only three years ago, I spent whole Saturdays blissfully washing her, waxing her, stroking her ample curves, crooning sweet nothings into her pretty grille. But she repaid me with contempt and subtle cruelties. She milked me for everything she could get and never returned a favor. I blush to remember my devotion to this unworthy hag.

She has four-wheel drive and a vaguely hearselike appearance. If ever there's a funeral motorcade in the bush, she might actually be useful. She is scarlet and black and temperamental, and she reminds me of a fat flamenco dancer. My wife calls her Lola.

I bought her in March 1977, but since she was a '76 model, American Motors gave me "a good deal." You know the kind. All I had to fork over was $6,139 plus a Nova, which was in top shape. I got a $5,000 loan, and though my payments on that have now amounted to $4,961, I still owe $2,000 on it.

But the purchase price was merely the headache I invited. The surprise headaches came in the 40 months that have followed: no fewer than 29 bills, totaling nearly $1,500, some for such routine services as lube jobs and installing new filters and spark plugs, but most for replacing parts that wore out with baffling speed, for repairing the same mysterious flaws again and again, and in one case, for just getting the damn thing started on a *summer* morning. The car has travelled only 34,143 miles, but we've already had battery trouble, automatic choke trouble, carburetor trouble, heater trouble, fan belt trouble, muffler and tailpipe trouble, gas tank trouble, gas gauge trouble, driver's window trouble, doors-full-of-rainwater trouble, even glove compartment trouble (the lock kept sticking). Lola is a monument to either planned obsolescence or quality non-control.

We had to forgo a journey to our beloved cabin because Lola leaked transmission fluid all over the highway. On one trip, we couldn't even drive 20 miles to the Halifax airport without the whole jeezly car filling up with putrid smoke, and for a while last winter Lola had an even more terrifying habit: when she went over even a small bump, her engine cut out totally. This of course, suddenly killed the power in the power steering, which meant you really had to wrestle the bitch to get her safely to the side of the road. This habit mystified the mechanics over at the American Motors shop across the harbor in Dartmouth, Nova Scotia, who were already having enough trouble with the tailgate window. It often refused to close. Each time they admitted Lola to their emergency ward, incidentally, it cost us $10 in cab fares to get home, and later, to pick her up again. By the time we went to Prince Edward Island last July, they had fixed the window four times.

We'd been invited to the première of *Fauntleroy*, a musical comedy that the Charlottetown Summer Festival dreamed would be a smash hit like *Anne of Green Gables*, and I had high hopes not only for the production but also for the exclusive little cocktail party before the show and the cast bash after. So my wife, our 12-year-old boy and I piled into Lola and headed for the ferry dock at Cape Tormentine, New Brunswick. We left at 10 a.m., but one hour out of Halifax, Lola's water pump gave way, her rear window once again refused to close, and a leak developed in her gas line.

We left her at the American Motors shop in Truro, N.S., wandered Truro's streets and parks all through the afternoon as steaming hot as my funk was blue, paid the shop $130.49, reached Charlottetown after dark. *Fauntleroy* was over, and so was the last vestige of my once-passionate love for Lola. She's a filthy old bag, and if I knew how, I'd immolate her for the insurance.

Today, September 1980

Trivial Matters: The No-Errors Career of Harry "The Hat" Flemming, Baseball Trivia's Big Hitter

The undefeated and still heavyweight champion of sports trivia in Halifax, N.S., Canada, is a bald, bespectacled, cigar-puffing and frequently scowling 47-year-old boy named Harry Flemming. He is not, of course, a boy in every respect but when it comes to what really matters in life—such as every last statistic to define the batting career of Ted Williams—Harry's boyhood returns and, once again, he is the smartest kid on the block. Moreover, he *knows* he's the smartest kid on the block, and you have only to look at the thin set of his mouth to realize that in the field of baseball history he does not suffer fools gladly.

If some punk were to blow into town, aiming to build his reputation by knocking off the notorious Harry "The Hat" Flemming, and if this kid brashly fired a question that Harry had correctly answered over countless foaming beers during countless shoot-outs with countless trivia-wise worthies, Harry would respond as Lyndon Johnson once responded to a journalist: "You're asking me, the leader of the Western world, a chickenshit question like that?" Then, of course, he'd give the punk the answer and, for good measure, drown him in a gratuitous shower of related information about RBIS, ERAS, strikeouts, stolen bases, or whatever. I've seen it happen. I've seen these hopefuls grow more and more subdued as they witness the merciless flowering of Harry's encyclopedic memory. I've seen them slink out of assorted watering holes like whipped curs. They told their friends. The legend grew. Harry had respect.

61

Harry has never lost a public sports trivia competition—though Jimmy "The Spoiler" Miller, a Halifax accountant, once came thrillingly close to beating him—and therefore no one knows if he'd be a good loser. To competitors he respects, he is affable in victory, though a trifle condescending. My own guess is that as a loser, he'd show all the grace of tennis star John McEnroe after a woman umpire has declared a chalk-biting McEnroe serve to be out of bounds.

Though sports trivia is Harry's vocation, he has had a string of mere hobbies. He's a graduate of Dalhousie University Law School, but has never practised law. He has been a newspaperman, TV interviewer, radio commentator, magazine columnist, journalism teacher, federal bureaucrat, executive director of the Atlantic Provinces Economic Council and chief policy adviser to the premier of Nova Scotia, but he has stoutly refused to let such petty pursuits interfere with his true calling as master of sports trivia.

The public battles began when Paul Walsh, radio journalist, and "Buffalo" Moe Cody, a government information officer, designed a format for contests to increase the Saturday business of a Halifax bar two friends had just taken over. With Harry "The Hat" Flemming thumping challenger after challenger during tense, 100-question afternoons, and mobs of fans (95 percent men, the rest groupies) crowding in to witness the slaughter, the happy owners renamed the bar the Trivia Lounge, and rewarded Harry with $50 worth of free drinking after each contest.

"While competing," Harry says, "you're not very clever if you drink anything but a little beer." In victory, however, he was lordly. He bought rounds for friends and vanquished alike, and the $50 didn't go far. He'd arrive home out of pocket but feeling just fine, thank you, and always with another trophy to show his wife (whom he married in 1960, the year Bill Mazeroski of the Pittsburgh Pirates clouted his immortal bottom-of-the-ninth home run, and thereby demolished the Yankees in the seventh game of the World Series). Harry won so many dinky metal cups on pedestals that Mrs.

Flemming finally asked, "Why don't they ever give you something useful? Like an ashtray?"

The peak of Harry's career was his duel at the Halifax Press Club against a highly touted gunslinger from out of town. Brodie Snyder was not only the former sports editor of the Montreal *Gazette* but also the guy who made up the trivia questions for Montreal Expos TV broadcasts. He was charming in his tough, Montreal-Scottish way, but cocky, oh so cocky. On the big night you could scarcely squeeze a sardine into the club and—dare we admit it?—the crowd included even locals who, like those who once prayed for the downfall of Muhammad Ali, yearned to see the humbling of the unhumble Harry the Hat. Never big on Canadian nationalism, he wore a New York Yankees cap. Snyder sported Expo headgear. As the light of a CBC crew glared at them, sweat streamed down their faces. Especially Snyder's. After a dozen questions, he wore the bewildered, panicky look of a third-rate club fighter who realizes in the first round that he has somehow climbed into the ring with a title-bound pro who is about to give him a hideous pummelling.

The ensuing rounds were not a pretty sight. When the score reached 52–18 in Harry's favor, Snyder threw in his Expo hat. He had been bravely entertaining, but as Harry later confided to Jimmy "The Spoiler" Miller, "You could have taken him, Jimmy." A laconic fellow, Jimmy simply said, "I know." Since Harry's victory made the national news, it was his most satisfying achievement since the *Sporting News* had published a letter in which he'd firmly corrected an error in an article about Ted Williams by U.S. novelist John Updike.

When it comes to knowledge for knowledge's sake, Harry can also hold his own in the fields of country and western music (pre-1960), Italian tenors, movies, British history, U.S. presidential politics and German generals of World War II. In Toronto once, I saw him go head-to-head against ace magazine editor Alexander Ross in a spontaneous but titanic struggle to see who could name the most cabinet ministers of various modern African nations. Ross had gained his expertise while working for an international news service; Harry relied solely on what he'd picked up from routine reading of newspapers and magazines. The contest was a draw and later, when I introduced Harry to editor Robert Fulford (now of *Saturday Night*), Fulford narrowed his eyes, looked him up and down coldly, and said, "I hear you're a trivia expert, Flemming. This town isn't big enough for both of us."

He's in semiretirement now, a sort of grand middle-aged man of the Halifax trivia subculture. He rarely competes. What would be the point? He serves as emcee for general trivia contests at the Halifax Press Club, and at a north-end tavern, he put in a winter of Saturdays as the guy who asked the questions at sports trivia contests among younger men, softball players and their ilk. "It's the perfect tavern game," he says, "but the whole thing is beginning to smack of commercialism. It's just to get people into drinking joints on Saturdays."

He concedes that "some of the kids who're coming up are fantastic. They can answer questions on fourth-round draft choices, for Chrissakes." He lowers his voice, looks around, finally confides, "They could probably even take me, you know. But only on the past 15 years. They actually *study* for the goddamn contests, but they don't know from shit about the grand sweep of baseball history."

Quest, October 1981

On the Day the World
Runs Out of Air,
Where Will Your Kids Be?

It is as hard and pure and bright and cold a mid-winter morning as Ottawa could ever have experienced. There's a bit of snow falling but it's so clean it could be the world's first, and it's so slight that, down on the true ice at the rink around the corner, they've not even had to bring out the shovels, and though the time is only nine o'clock, some boys have gathered there already, and there's the good old sound again. The dull bang. The puck off the boards. The great old sound. The sun lights up the small snow in the air and turns it into a thin radiant mist, and since this happens to be a Sunday morning, the sulphite stink is not sweeping at us from the paper mills across the dying river (which I cannot see from where we live in Ottawa); and the stark and shapely maple on the lawn, and the grubby red box of apartments across the street, they exist this morning in the sort of air the town must have known every day in the time of, say, D'Arcy McGee's assassination.

We had an excessive party last night. Ten years ago, when I was only 25, hangovers had already ceased to be something I could bring myself to laugh about. Their ravages could tear down whatever protection good health puts up against spiritual terror, and during a bad hangover, a Presence would sometimes come to sit in my room, and I'd be so afraid of it that I could only lie there for a while, and not move even a finger. I would be wide awake, but the Presence had the same paralyzing effect as the amphibious creatures—both furry and slimy at once, fawning and carnivorous—that have sometimes slipped up on me during sleep. The Presence arrived only when I was in hotel rooms, never at home, and in the last couple of years our children have taken over some

65

corner of my mind, and they've expanded in there so that there's not much room for the Presence any more. Not for a while.

Still, the party has imposed its usual punishment (does experience teach nothing at all?), and the only influence that's strong enough to draw me out of bed—to pull the curtains and face the angelic brilliance of this particularly holy morning in Ottawa—is the noise of the two older ones chatting in the street below. The boy, nine. The girl, eight. There they go, way ahead of me...away, away down the white city avenue, and then they're gone. Joyous on their new skates. Now I remember. I bought the skates only yesterday. I was supposed to go skating with the children but I didn't, and hearing their voices from a moment ago, I know that that's not their loss, but mine.

I get under the bedclothes again. They get along, those two, better than any other brother and sister I've ever known. They looked good out there in the cold, *beautiful*. They swam together in the St. Lawrence once. Silly, brown, slippery, perfectly playful little animals. The water babies. We couldn't get them out for hours, not even to eat...

Can it really be true that population growth and industrial activity are destroying the earth's atmosphere so fast that there won't be enough food, or oxygen in the air, to keep us all alive? Some scientists argue that, the way we're going, we'll run out in 20 or 30 years, and that'll be it. For everybody. Some say it may already be too late to stop this thing happening. Can they really know what they're talking about? Do they *mean* it? If they do, why isn't the whole world yelling, and getting together to do something? Can it be that we just aren't able to worry about anything, even the Day of Judgment, when it's 20 or 30 years in the future? Maybe they don't really mean it. Maybe they just think the air's getting bad, and it would be a good idea to scare people into doing something. All right, so I'm scared. Why did I say "the Day of Judgment," anyway? I haven't been to church since they invented the H-Bomb. I haven't been to Sunday school since Hiroshima. I was about his age, nine or 10.

66

If The Bomb fell here but it failed to kill us all right away, how would you do it to them? Is that why the good man killed his young children in that Italian movie? We have no firearms. A hammer? A knife? God no. But there's nothing suicidal about me or my wife; why can't we have a family stock of those suicide pills anyway? And why is it that such questions have been just too horrible to ask in the open? Of course. Violence really is the one obscenity of our dwindling time, isn't it? Can we believe that the massacres at My Lai, the little dead boys and little dead girls, will not ultimately impose their equally terrible answer in our part of the world?

Maybe they won't. Maybe they'll just run out of oxygen first. If that takes 30 years, my wife will be 64, I'll be 65. Retirement age anyway. But the boy will be 39, the girl will be 38, the baby boy will be only 31. They may have children of their own. I wonder if people will just sort of fall down, maybe on their way home from the rink. Probably not. It would take a while...

But it doesn't do to lie in bed on a Sunday morning, feeling the way I feel. If I go further asleep, the wet mandibular things, the lizard creatures and their grotesque relations, may come for me, with their ghastly affection. If I lie here awake, I'm sure now that, for the first time, the Presence will enter my own home. I get up fast, go downstairs, pour some coffee, and my wife and I say things that we think are funny about the bad party of the night before. After a while, the two of them come in the kitchen door. They've still got their skates on, their faces are red, a gust of knifing Arctic air tears around the kitchen, we all start laughing and hollering and, sweet dying Jesus, they are beautiful children.

Maclean's, March 1970

Blessed Are the Cheeky

I've never been able to work up a public lather about Yuletide greed and commercialism for the simple reason that both were part of the most thrilling Christmas of my youth. I was 15, and from an older boy I inherited the best paper route in Canada: 131 customers in four posh apartment towers in central Toronto. While the hands of other paperboys turned stiff and sleet lashed their cheeks, I strolled through heated corridors, slapping papers on doormats.

What made this soft touch even softer was that many of my customers paid the newspaper directly by mail. Their cheques exactly covered the paper's share of my revenue and that meant I never had to go downtown to pay off the circulation department. I could keep all the cash I collected. Whenever I felt bored, I'd just make a few collections, go to a movie, top off the evening with a mucky banana split, and walk home burping and feeling independent.

Ah, but Christmas. Around December 15 I found in my bundle of newspapers enough Christmas cards for all my customers. All I had to do was sign them and slip them into the papers, but that would have been throwing away a silver opportunity. I decided to deliver each card in person—not only to those from whom I collected every week but also to the strangers who paid by mail and therefore never saw me (or tipped me). I mastered a facial expression that nicely combined shyness, respect for adults and a sense of responsibility that was rare in one so young, and then knocked on 131 doors. I handed the card to whomever answered, chirped, "Merry Christmas from your Globe and Mail carrier boy," and hovered there expectantly.

Even now I'm embarrassed to confess that this forelock-tugging, money-sucking campaign was a dazzling triumph: I came home with $102 in quarters and small bills. My father, who faced every Christmas with gloom and resignation, seemed disgusted by my loot gathering. To him, I think the money symbolized what he least liked about Christmas—the Urge to Get. And by what right did I deserve so much more than he could give my brothers? He made sure my dubiously gotten gains didn't net me a single banana split. The whole works went into my bank account.

I never told him, but even the style with which I'd scrawled my signature on the cards had been part of my strategy. I'd read in a book about handwriting that if you wrote your signature uphill you were optimistic. If you under-lined it you were self-reliant. Since optimistic, self-reliant people were bound to be successful in whatever they under-took, that's how I wrote my name. Uphill, underlined—131 times.

That signature had one queer result.

There was a door at which no one ever answered my knocking, and eventually I gave up on it. I just left a card and wrote off the customer as an unknown Scrooge. But when I got there the following dawn with a newspaper, a nurse greeted me. She ushered me into a bedroom where an old woman lay quivering under a quilt with my card in her left hand.

"Young man," she said. "I've been studying your signa-ture. You are optimistic. You are self-reliant. I think you will be successful in whatever you undertake, and I'd like to wish you a very merry Christmas." I knew we'd been reading the same book, but I just said, "Thank you, ma'am," and tried to look potentially successful. She pushed a beautiful blue $5 bill into my hand. It remains the biggest cash gift from a stranger of my entire life, and as a 31-year-old footnote to the Christ-mas of '49, I'd like to show you how I still write my signature. To the readers of *Today*, Merry Christmas from

Harry Bruce

Inflation and the Miscellaneous Hustler

A friend who remembers the Dirty Thirties says the finest achievement of his boyhood was harvesting a turnip from a highway. The turnip had fallen from a truck, and he'd proudly presented it to his mother. Now, 40 years later, he and I sometimes get together over a bottle and scare each other half-witless with hideous predictions about what the sticky-fanged vampires of economic disaster may do to us and our families.

"You know," he says, "if inflation goes on as it's going now for just six years, and if you're not earning *twice* as much then as you're earning now, well, man, do you know you're actually going to be sliding *backwards*?" I know, I know.

Our problem is that we belong neither to Big Business, nor to Big Labor, nor to Big Government. We fall under the unsung category of Big Miscellaneous. We are Miscellaneous Hustlers. There may be millions of Miscellaneous Hustlers in Canada but we don't get much press, and maybe that's our own fault. If we were not ornery enough to be miscellaneous we'd have a lobby, a research office, a spokesman with a speechwriter.

A Miscellaneous Hustler is an entrepreneur who never strikes it rich, a capitalist who never reaps a big capital gain. He's a general manager who never gets a bonus of company stock. He's a worker who never knows the comforts of job security, or raises that automatically click into place, or overtime pay, holiday pay and sick leave with pay, or strike funds, or company pension, medical and educational plans.

He takes risks, and never escapes the direct connection between his money and his effort. I used to think doctors in private practice were Miscellaneous Hustlers. No longer.

70

Nor are most dentists, lawyers and established architects. The Miscellaneous Hustler is self-employed but the moment his self-employment earns him big bucks, I kick him out of the hustlers' brotherhood.

He is not part of The Great Debate, which whirls futilely around the question of who's most to blame for inflation. Is it profiteering management, bloodsucking unions, or wastrel governments? The debate clatters along as though the Miscellaneous Hustler simply did not exist, and as a cause of inflation, perhaps he doesn't. He merely *feels* inflation.

A recent newspaper ad seeking a "doorperson" for a Halifax beerhall reminds me I'm flaunting my male pigginess. *Of course* Miscellaneous Hustlers come in both sexes. They include itinerant salespersons who survive on commissions, craftpersons, freelance writers, designers, illustrators, private detectives, actors, and the proprietors of corner grocery stores, laundromats, hair-dressing salons, small farms, small publishing houses, small massage parlors, and so on.

The Miscellaneous Hustler doesn't want to be a boss, or have a boss. You know the type. In corporations, he's a cynic or a sorehead. In armies, he's a disaster. What he wants is independence. He's the sort who sacrifices vacations to feed a retirement fund. The impulse that makes him quit jobs to escape a boss's thumb also drives him to work nights to escape a mortgage's thumb.

He does not crave fabulous wealth. He only dreams of a time in which he can afford to do nothing. It is a time in which he owes no one work, obedience, or money; and, surely, reaching it will be like arriving at the windy peak of a hill that's decades long. Up there, answers will at last be clear for miles in every direction. Life will be free, fearless and grand.

But what does inflation say about the dream? It says the Miscellaneous Hustler's retirement plans are a joke. It says his savings will end up so puny they'll mock a lifetime's effort. It says, moreover, that rising prices will soon wipe out all hope of his saving more. He is not in control. He hasn't enough control over his own income to gear it to a cost-of-living index. He has no control over electricity bills, fuel bills, food

71

bills. As he wrestles his mortgage to the ground, the tax bill on his house squirts upward like a helium-filled balloon. Bills are the new bosses, and he will do the obeying.

The Miscellaneous Hustler feels the sickening slip backwards, back downhill. He envies the rich. He resents the organized. He snarls at news of corporate profit and fat wage settlements. He can't celebrate the good fortune of others because their bonanza is his kick in the groin.

His heart shrinks, his courage falters. Was the whole plan wrong from the very beginning? Is he too old to crawl back into a union shop, too freaky to land a useless job in government? And if he tries to tough things out on his own, will the ogres of inflation see to it that he spends his last days at the bottom of the hill, still in harness, meaner than ever, knowing that the best he can expect from life is a fallen turnip?

Quest, May 1975

Confessions of a Seafood Junkie

"Stop the car, driver, stop the car," Malcolm (Mac) Parry ordered. "I see a fish shop." He's the lanky, English-born editor of *Vancouver* magazine, and though he now feels Canadian to the roots of his being, his accent is still Staffordshire and, in an emergency, imperious. So the driver stopped the car. We were in the heart of Edinburgh at the height of the evening rush hour. We were four Canadian journalists, one chauffeur, and one prissy, loquacious guide whose duty it was to show us not fish shops but such immortal Edinburgh ornaments as the superb streetscapes by the 18th-century Scottish architect Robert Adams, the gigantic monument to Sir Walter Scott, and the history-drenched Palace of Holyroodhouse. Our car for the day was a silky, black Daimler—a limousine of opulence fit for an Asian princess, an oil sheik, or an armaments manufacturer—and maybe that's why we got away with blocking traffic while Parry nipped into the fish shop. He gleefully returned with what appeared to be a tiny torpedo wrapped in the sports pages of the Edinburgh *Scotsman*.

He was excited. He tore open the package, and there she was in all her chubby, greasy, smelly glory: a foot-long smoked mackerel. "Ah," Parry said, "isn't she a beaut?" He gazed at the fish with all the awe and love of a cat burglar who's pulled open a drawer and found a nest of diamond rings.

"You have some first," he said gallantly, shoving the fish under my nose. I knew exactly what to do. I worked at it with my fingers till I got several fat, moist flakes, passed it on to the others. The guide shot an appalled glance at the chauffeur, who returned it with a shrug that seemed to say, "In this business, you meet all kinds." The Daimler's upholstery was pearl grey, perfect stuff to show off mackerel oil. "Don't worry, mate," Parry told the guide. "We'll look after the car, won't we boys?" And we did. As the car glided up The Royal Mile toward Edinburgh Castle, I wiped my fingers on the inside of my pants pockets.

No sooner had we finished the mackerel than Parry shouted, "I say, driver, stop the car. I see another fish shop." Though the groans from the guide were not audible, they somehow filled the Daimler. Our chauffeur, however, had apparently decided Parry was a seafood junkie, a fish fiend so desperately far-gone that the safest thing to do till we could get him to a treatment centre was to let him feed his habit. There'd be plenty of time later to impose a fish-withdrawal program on the poor blighter or, failing that, dreaded cold turkey. So the car stopped again, and Parry was off like a shot, his fine English nostrils twitching as the aroma from the fish shop mingled with exhaust fumes in the Scottish gloom, his long legs zooming him through the traffic with the speed of an ostrich.

I watched him go, and I understood him.

His home was the Pacific coast and mine was the Atlantic, but we shared the same insane and inexplicable passion. "Just to see he doesn't get into trouble," I lied. "I'd better go with him." When I caught up to Parry he was chatting up the two shopkeepers, young women with snowy aprons, soft Scottish accents, and friendly eyes that suggested they knew how to satisfy all the fishy needs of a certain kind of gentleman. Parry turned to me. "Ah," he said. "I thought you'd be the one to come, old man." (He'd seen how I'd wolfed down double my share of the mackerel.) The place had the mind-clearing fragrance of all good fish shops—it was almost as though the ocean were air and you could actually suck her sweet purity into your lungs—and some shucked mussels had just arrived, very fresh. Also cockles. "Shall we have cockles or mussels?" Parry said. "Your choice." Was any question ever easier to answer? "I think we should probably have both, don't you, Mac?"

We took them in little plastic bags to a discreet bar at the decidedly posh George Hotel and there, under the armorial insignia of all the great clans of Scotland we washed down the cockles and mussels with malt whisky. We exchanged memories of lobster-eating orgies, gluttonous behavior at oyster parties, the secret delights of humble salt cod, and countless Great Moments of Fish-eating in the years since we'd both become addicts. Soon the cockles and mussels had gone the way of the mackerel, and it was time for dinner. I ordered poached Scottish salmon in Hollandaise sauce and, counting the kippers I'd had for breakfast, that made the fifth variety of seafood I'd downed that day. It was wonderful, and that's the point: Your true seafood addict can eat meal after meal of fish for days on end, and never tire of it.

It was back in the summer of '75 that I realized my habit was both enslaving and incurable. After returning to Halifax from a three-day trip to New Brunswick, it dawned on me that I had eaten nine consecutive seafood dishes. For my breakfasts, I'd had creamed cod, finnan haddie and kippers; for lunches, fried clams, fishcakes, shrimp curry; for dinners, lobster one night, swordfish the next, then Digby scallops. And during the recent press trip to Scotland, that was pretty well the way I ate (even when Parry wasn't leading me on lightning fish-shop swoops).

I did eat venison one night; it was good but not as good as sautéed cod tongues. Nor could I escape haggis and boring beef at a Burns Night supper. I confess that after a ruddy, bellowing, gesticulating, bekilted Scot had delivered Burns's rousing address to the "great chieftain o' the puddin' race," and after he'd plunged his knife into its "gushing entrails bright," I lacked the courage to say, "No thanks. I'd prefer a shrimp cocktail, if you don't mind." The haggis was so dry that haggis-wise natives at my table doused it with Scotch whisky, and I followed suit. This trick helped but I'd still have preferred a shrimp cocktail, or clam chowder, or Portuguese sardines, or baby squid, or pickled herring with sour cream, or smoked salmon, or even a little morsel of raw fish in the Japanese style. Or better still, lobster, that great chieftain o' the shellfish race.

A fellow on the outskirts of Halifax knows my dirty

secret. He's an addict himself but he's also a pusher. He's not a rum-runner, he's a fish-runner. A faceless bureaucrat by day, he operates a mysterious fish-distribution business by night. Trucks pull up to his address and shadowy figures hustle cartons into his house, in which a freezer dominates the dining room. My friend is one of those men who can make "Good morning" sound as though he's just struck a deal with the Mafia, and whenever he calls, I wonder if my merely answering the phone won't somehow land me in the slammer. "There's another shipment in," he murmurs. Has he put a handkerchief over the telephone speaker? "It's beauteeful stuff, and it'll go fast. Better get your order in." Sometimes he's got live lobster from "contacts" in P.E.I. Sometimes he's got frozen bricks of snowy cod. At Christmas, he imports enough oysters to satisfy oyster fanatics all over town. I need him. His prices are good. He can give me a fix at odd hours. He's my local fishlegger, and if Mac Parry ever gets to the east coast long enough to discover the natural superiority of Atlantic salmon, I'll make sure those two meet. They'll get along. They both know what's important in life.

Epicure, Spring 1981

The Wrong Stuff

Watching the cockiness and cool of big-league ballplayers on TV, you'd never guess that some are nervous wrecks who need psychotherapy. They are the best and they know it. They get rich doing what they love to do. They are tanned, strong, graceful, fast and fit. Calm chewers of gum. Casual, spitting men. If *they* need shrinks, what about those of us who are pale, weak, awkward, slow and flabby? What about those who are not getting rich doing what they don't love to do, and know they'll never be best at anything? Actually, we may be luckier than we think.

For we never experience the murdering pressure of big-league ball. It can turn a demigod into a stumblebum, and drive him from the game forever, weeping and humiliated. The terrible tension is one reason why some baseball people believe every big-league team needs not only a manager, trainers and coaches, but also a Designated Shrink. His job, I gather, would be to help players conquer dreaded slumps; teach them to insulate themselves from the most destructive pressures; and promote in the quivering psyche of each emotionally fragile superathlete the correct on-field balance between relaxation and competitive fire. "Anybody who works at it can have a great body," says Mike Stanton, whose great body measures six feet two inches and weighs about 200 pounds. "Getting your head in shape is the tough part."

Stanton, a relief pitcher with the Seattle Mariners, had a so-so lifetime earned run average of 4.56 at the end of the 1983 season, but in order to do even that well he had needed a shrink to help him get his head into fighting trim. The doctor was Tom McGinnis, once a pretty fair athlete himself and later president of the American Association for Marriage and Therapy. McGinnis, Stanton said, "taught me relaxation and self-hypnosis—how to ignore a stadium full of screaming, hostile fans by focusing all my aggression on that hitter at the plate. It was amazing how that calmed me down, and made me throw with more control." I don't know whether McGinnis prefers pitcher counselling to marriage counselling, but I like to think his chest swells with pride whenever Stanton hypnotizes himself, bears down, and smokes fastballs past batter after batter. But what's the batter's shrink doing? Tearing his hair out?

McGinnis leaves no doubt that a slew of pro ballplayers need psychiatric help to make it through a season. "Fans have little comprehension of the stresses their heroes and goats labor under," he told Howard Eisenberg in *Sports Illustrated*. "I've had managers tell me that a player is homesick, hard to manage, immature, anxious, has marital problems, shows homosexual tendencies, is a hypochondriac or a compulsive drinker, or has threatened to kill the third-base coach. Authoritarian managers can be part of the problem, along with player rivalries, the endless nothing-to-do-on-the-road travelling, and worst of all, the daily pressure to win."

By the end of the 1983 season, Stanton had responded to the daily pressure to win by winning eight games for major-league teams—and losing 15. But without McGinnis's ministrations, it's conceivable he'd have done even worse. Stanton, on pressure, is as pointed as a base runner's spikes: "You play 162 games. There are quick ups and really bad downs. And the next day, everybody in the country knows what you did or didn't do. There are only 640 of us, and there's always someone bigger or faster coming up behind you. After the season, it takes me a good month to relax."

Rookies are especially vulnerable to pressures that make them perform in spectacularly embarrassing ways. Draft-choice catchers, for instance, sometimes develop a sudden terror not only of rifling the ball to second base but even of lobbing the ball back to the pitcher. Their minds have crippled them. Many rookies are barely out of high school. They're just kids who once played ball only because they loved it, then became minor-league aces, and must now cope with competition, money and publicity such as neither they,

78

nor their parents, nor indeed anyone back home has ever known before.

Some turn to booze and drugs. As Dr. Joseph Pursch told the *St. Petersburg Times*, "If you gave every 20-year-old small town or ghetto American male a penthouse pad in New York or Marina del Rey, with wall-to-wall girls, a $100,000-a-year salary, and millions of fans telling him he's the greatest, you would have a horrendous outbreak of drug addiction." An authority on addiction, Pursch argues that youngsters in the big leagues, by comparison with seasoned corporate executives, suffer "more intense and frenzied" demands on both their emotions and their bodies. Yet they have easier access to "the legal and illegal substances." It's scarcely surprising then that baseball, which author Roger Angell once called "an extremely difficult public profession," has nurtured not only heroes but also zonked-out has-beens still in their twenties with little to comfort them but memories of the afternoons when they had what it took.

Nobody has written better than Angell about the curse of the slump. In *Five Seasons*, a collection of his *New Yorker* essays, he said, "Pitching, it sometimes appears, is too hard for *anyone*.... The pitcher goes into a slump. He sulks or rages.... He asks for help; he works long hours on his motion. Still he cannot win. He worries about his arm, which almost always hurts to some degree. Has it gone dead? He worries about his stuff. Has he lost his velocity? He wonders whether he will ever win again or whether he will now join the long, long list—the list that awaits him, almost surely, in the end—of suddenly slow, suddenly sore-armed pitchers who have abruptly vanished from the big time, down the drain to oblivion."

Describing the agony, relief pitcher Dave Giusti told Angell, "I'd get right to the top of my delivery and then something would take over, and I'd know even before I released the ball that it wasn't going to be in the strike zone. I began worrying about making big money and not performing. I worried about not contributing to the team. I worried about being traded. I thought it might be the end for me." It wasn't. Giusti talked incessantly about his problem, and used his wife, teammates, just about everyone he knew as shrinks. He blabbed his way out of his slump, and survived 15 pretty good years in the majors, especially with the Pittsburgh Pirates.

Once in a rare while a pitcher suffers a permanent slump. To put it brutally, he doesn't merely choke, he chokes forever. Gerald Brandmeyer and Luella Alexander of the University of South Florida have, in their academic fashion, labelled this "psycho-social disability" as "Sudden Errant Throwing Syndrome"; and though it has sabotaged the careers of only a handful of notable pitchers in recent years, it is among the saddest phenomena in all sports. At the risk of indulging in Sportswriters' Exaggeration (a relatively minor affliction), I'd say the quick, mysterious and total disintegration of Steve Blass's pitching skill amounted to epic tragedy.

Blass was an established ace with the Pirates when the 1973 season began. He'd been in the majors nine years. In the 1971 World Series he'd pitched two superb wins to help the Pirates beat the Baltimore Orioles. In the season of '72, he'd won 19, lost 8, boasted an ERA of 2.48, pitched for the National League All-Stars. He was boyish, happy, funny, popular with fans and teammates alike. His fastball was not overwhelming but he had good, assorted stuff, and he was smart. Above all, he had control. "He was," Angell wrote, "an extremely successful and useful big-league pitcher, and was understandably enjoying his work."

Then early in '73, for no reason that he or anyone else has ever been able to explain, he simply lost the ability to do the one thing at which he excelled: getting the ball over the plate. It was as though a demon had laid a curse on him, or a witch doctor had made a Steve Blass doll and driven needles through its right arm. The sudden errant throwing syndrome struck him with such ferocity that during only one and a third innings in a hideously memorable game against Atlanta he threw three wild pitches, walked six batters, allowed five hits and no less than seven runs. "You can't imagine the feeling that you suddenly have no *idea* what you're doing out there, performing that way as a major-league pitcher," he recalled. "It was kind of scary."

Blass ended the '73 season with an ERA of 9.81. He lasted two more years in pro ball, spending much of the time humiliating himself in the minors. The harder he tried, the worse he got. With each ludicrously errant throw, he dug his career's grave deeper. He tried transcendental meditation, psychiatry, visual therapy, hypnotism, assorted coaches. None of them helped. He was incurable, and in 1975, at 33, he finally sent himself to the showers for good.

Another modern victim of sudden errant throwing syndrome was Kevin (Hot Sauce) Saucier, a scrappy, cocky bullpen star who had worked his way up through the minors to become Most Popular Phillie in 1980; and in 1981 with the Detroit Tigers racked up 13 saves and an ERA of 1.65. In *Sports Illustrated*, Ray Kennedy vividly described Hot Sauce at his hottest: "Highstepping off the mound like an ostrich in heat, hand-slapping and hugging every teammate within reach after a save, the "Flying Saucier" became the hottest attraction to land in town since Mark (The Bird) Fidrych flapped into view in 1976."

"I just know there's no son of a gun alive who can hit me," Saucier bragged. His motto was "Gimme the ball," and he loved pitching so much that "when I get close to the end... they're gonna have to rip this uniform right off me.... I want to play, I reckon, until I'm 45." That was in 1982. In the spring of '83, not at 45 but at 26, he himself ripped off his uniform for the last time. The wild-pitching curse had hit him with the same devastating force with which it had hit Blass a decade earlier, and Saucier quit baseball because "if I had stayed in, I would have driven myself crazy." He talked of "a strange feeling" that overcame him when he faced batters: "I just didn't feel right. It was like I was under a spell. It was a feeling of being lost, like trying to type with no fingers. What do you do? You're lost. You can't help yourself. You try, you try to relax, and you just can't."

Trying to type with no fingers. Hot Sauce hit a nerve there. What writer hasn't dreaded that he'll wake up one morning to discover that, for no reason he knows of, he's lost his winning ways? He can't put words together as he did only yesterday. His prose fastball has lost its hop. His change of pace won't change. His curve won't break. His slider won't slide. His screwball won't screw. He tries to send the ball low and outside. A critic belts it over the centre-field wall. Or it sails somewhere way off behind the critic's back, and arouses the hooting derision of all those who were once the writer's fans. He's lost. He can't help himself.

Surely such fears occasionally haunt not just writers and athletes but everyone who derives joy and confidence from performing well enough to earn money and respect. People who care about being good at what they do—be they surgeons, pulpwood cutters, tax accountants, hairdressers, corporation lawyers, dancers, preachers, salespeople, pizza chefs, or whatever—live with the possibility that some day, for no fair or understandable reason, they will no longer be good at what they do. A time will come when people who count will recognize that "he just hasn't got it any more."

Baseball hugely dramatizes this possibility. Like a Roman candle that amazes for a second and then prematurely expires, Kevin Saucier became a Designated Failure. If I'd seen Steve Blass let the Atlanta Braves score seven runs in one and a third innings on June 13, 1973, I would not have been able to utter the weakest of raspberries. I'd have thought, "There but for the grace of God go I." Blass and Saucier are worth remembering when you hear the fashionable bitching about the astronomical salaries ballplayers collect. Not one of those calm chewers of gum knows for sure that when dawn breaks he'll be any good.

Quest, September 1984

The Perfect Day

Ragged Head has been part of the seascape of my mind for nearly thirty years, and I believe it was part of the seascape of my father's mind from the first months he could see till the last moments he could think, and it was there, too, in both the plain sight and internal vision of his own father, and the fathers of other Bruces since long before the Battle of Waterloo.

It's east of the old farm, and from the beach—which is a great, slow, perfect three-mile curve of sea and wind-scoured gravel—you can see that Ragged Head is an arrow, flying a ribbon of wild spruce and shooting farther toward the heart of the big bay than any other effort of land along this whole shore. The French may never have bothered to label the Head, but long before them, the Micmacs, peaceable kings of the huge solitude, would stroke their big canoes up the bay every year and they could not have passed Ragged Head without giving it a name we'll never know now.

Even when you're not looking at it, it's somewhere there in your head, a kind of background music to whatever you've chosen to think about. I suppose, if I were to live here as long as I want to, the ceaseless change in the way it looks would tell me something about tomorrow's weather. Some days it seems much closer than it really is. Some days it is simply gone in fog. Other days, you can see the far, white smashing surf on the tip of the arrow. This is because, beyond the Head in the European east, Chedabucto Bay widens right out into the open ocean; and, since you can see the rainclouds gather and pass over Ragged Head, I remember some verse from a book of my father's poetry:

You can see the rainclouds gather and pass,
Over Hadley's Beach or the Artois Plain;

And dust on the grass is dust on the grass,
In Guysborough County or Port of Spain.

I was 11 years old, going on 12, when I first saw it, a kid from Toronto who'd come "down home" for the summer of '46; and, off and on, in the 27 years that have followed, I saw it in my head and from the real beach more times than I'll ever be able to count. But I had never, in all those years, actually gone out and sat down on the dust on the grass to discover what was *there*. There's no road to Ragged Head, and unless you time your hike to the low tide that opens a strip of sand along the long shore, the walk on the gravel is rough. Moreover, just before you get to the head, there's a tidal gut and you can never be sure how deep it's going to be. The right way to go to Ragged Head is by boat.

It took me a quarter of a century to put a sailboat of my own on Chedabucto Bay. I was 14 when I first knocked around Toronto Harbor in sailing dinghies and I remembered the Head, and I knew that it would be hard to find better sailing anywhere in the northern world than the sailing that Chedabucto Bay promised.

The far shore is a high purple cloud on the horizon, but rock really, and it disappears 20-odd miles out to sea in a jumble of deserted islands, the desolate town of Canso, warning lights, horns, whistles and generally violent water. Our shore is kinder to boats, men and farm animals. The bottom is a plain of immaculate rippled sand. It holds a boat well and once, in my grandfather's time—which was before I was born—the water just off our beach was alive with sail-driven fishing vessels. The moorings were wooden cages, filled with beach stones, and most years they served well enough.

It's been 28 years since the last one of those boats moved over the bay, and during all that time she's been gently shrinking into a pile of rotten timbers and planks a couple of hundred yards down the beach from our place. I played in her still-solid hulk the first year she was beached forever, and maybe she and the ghosts of the others, and the great,

84

reliable, mind-clearing wind around here, and Ragged Head, too, maybe they were all reasons why it seemed like such a good idea, for such a long time, to sail a boat of my own on Chedabucto Bay.

We trailed our own boat up from Halifax in the last week of August, and a fellow down the beach gave me a rusty, 100-pound hook; and late on the first day we arrived, I had our boat gently riding at anchor a couple of hundred feet off-shore. From our cabin up on the wild bluff behind the beach we could see both the boat and Ragged Head. They were the stuff of an old dream, and the next morning was hot and odd with the whole bay a sheet of dark, radiant glass, and a brilliant streak of silver mist lay all along the far shore, and it was time to find Ragged Head.

The water was slippery-looking, a deep, deep green, and so clear and spooky with glints of light that we could see right down to the bottom without even a glass-bottomed bucket. The three kids hung their heads out over our bows and kept them there—deep and quiet in the strangeness of starfish, sand dollars, crabs and nameless undulating growths—for the whole way out to Ragged Head.

The second we glided around the Head we felt in our stomachs the smooth ride of the long swell from the open ocean, and for all we knew, each heavy surge had begun to gather itself together somewhere off Portugal. I remembered that this day of hot peace for as many miles as anyone could see, was the hundredth anniversary of the historic August gale of 1873; and that, once, my father told me that *his* father had been a boy that summer and had said the gale had lifted the fishing vessels out of the water and hurled them into the trees and fields.

At the Head, there were two, small crescents of fine pink sand. The rocks that broke the surf and the boulders that framed the sand were like none I had ever seen in that part of Nova Scotia. They were red and foreign. There was a knoll of feathery grass, and the sunlight filtered to the grass through a perfumed maze of spruce and fir saplings, old giants and fallen wrecks. Along the shore a way stood an old capstan for hauling nets and boats out of the water, a splintered, grey table for cleaning fish, and the broken skeleton of a fishhut. They were the only evidence we saw that anyone else had ever set foot on Ragged Head; and finding them was like finding drawings on the walls of a jungle cave.

Something else about that day was strange. Normally, if you put your bare foot into Chedabucto Bay, the water seems icy enough to turn polar bears chicken-hearted. Now, however, you could flop around in the bay for hours, and snorkeling among the hairy red rocks was like swimming off the last of the clean islands in the Caribbean Sea.

We sang and shouted and explored the woods and the huge, calm pond behind the Head. We saw exotic birds and, once, the black bulge of a seal's head. We stuffed chopped egg sandwiches into our mouths, and plums and oranges, and my wife and I downed a couple of cold Mooseheads and a bottle of Italian red, and late in the afternoon, shadows began to move on the bay, the heat of noon was gone, and a big, clean breeze blew down on us from over the hills in the far south, and it would be a beam reach all the way home.

We didn't go straight home. The sailing was too good for that, and how long had it been since Bruces had sailed a boat of their own on Chedabucto Bay? We took a long, looping curve right out under the diving sun till the two shores were the same size, right out to the middle of the bay, and then we turned her to starboard, eased sheets and rolled home on a roller-coaster run.

By six that night we were back up in the cabin, eating wieners and beans by the gallon, and listening to the rattle and crash of the bay below, and the sailing wind in our trees, and I kept going out to the edge of the bluff to see the boat strongly accept her buffeting and to see, too, the tiny white explosions on the far rocks that I now knew were red, and I set all this down now simply because there are only so many perfect days in any man's life.

Quest, November 1973

Christopher Pratt:
Magic As Reality

Christopher Pratt, a lanky, articulate Newfoundlander who believes in his own self-control the way some people believe in God, may well be the finest realist painter in Canada. It's still a matter of opinion. What is indisputable however is that, out on the coast of Newfoundland, Pratt has discovered a private rhythm of peace, a life and place that are as close to a Canadian paradise on earth as most of us are ever likely to find. He does not relish leaving home, and if it's true that home is where the heart is, he never really does.

At a seething and pretentious arts conference in Ottawa last spring, Pratt was as impatient as his great white sloop at her mooring in Conception Bay; and, if you'd once seen him alive and calm near the seals and the magic geese and the unknowable caribou of Home, you might have understood why. Home is an endless song, and his wife, Mary. Everything else is merely ordinary, though an arts conference may be even less than strictly ordinary.

At this one, the Cultural Vanguard of the Nation had at last discovered Participatory Democracy, and hundreds of artists, art administrators, art hucksters, art bureaucrats and art angels had come to Ottawa to hammer out for all time a cultural policy for Canada. It lasted two days, ample time to fashion destiny, but Pratt was there for only one of them. Farewell, Chateau Laurier. Farewell, corridors of culture. See the silver bird on high. She's away. And eastward bound.

Pratt may be a great painter. It takes a while for the rest of us to decide who's great, and he's only 38. East coast Canada has a curious corner on what the art world sometimes calls Magic Realism. At least half a dozen highly skilled Magic Realists have either studied in the Maritimes and moved on, or studied in the Maritimes and stayed to do their work and make their lives there, but according to some art experts the supreme blossom in this regional flowering is Pratt.

Dorothy Cameron of Toronto, one of the country's leading authorities on contemporary art, says, "Of all the realists who've come out of that area, I've always thought Chris had the most intensity, the most mysterious quality in his work. He always has this extra quality, a quality beyond the object. There's something extra he always gives you. To me, Chris...well, he's just our finest poetic realist."

A dozen years ago, before Pratt dared to believe a Newfoundlander could ever survive by painting alone, he sold copies of a silk-screen print called "Boat in Sand" to fellow students at Mount Allison University for $15 (and to one guy, for 50 cents). Now, if you could find someone willing to part with "Boat In Sand," it might well cost you $1,000. His current price for a new oil painting is $8,000.

His work shows you things you can recognize: windows, stairs, shelves, wainscot, haunted shops, barns, doors, barn doors, a shed, a bed, blowing bed-sheets on a clothesline, a kitchen stove, ice, snow, cold trees and often, stretching across the whole canvas or just lurking there in a corner, a stretch of mysteriously calm sea. The sea tells you something about billions of years. The things tell you about someone you cannot see, someone who has just gone away, for a few seconds, for a week, perhaps for ever.

Someone will be back. Or perhaps he won't. Either way, he left something there in the curious glow of the room, in the waiting air over the brown ground, in the shadows beyond the shutters. There's a strange, careful simplicity in Pratt's work. His lines are somehow straighter than anyone else's. He makes and sells unearthly calm and, to some people anyway, sitting alone with a Pratt painting is the beginning of wondering why you exist.

The art world calls him a Magic Realist. But you would not take him for a painter of any kind if you met him at one of the cocktail parties he tries to avoid. You would swear he was an army officer in civvies or an engineer, a man with a lifelong faith in his slide rule.

He's six feet tall, bony, straight in the spine, balder than any of the bald eagles that still cruise the sky above his wilderness home. The word "Prussian" flickers inaccurately in your mind, and there's something monkish about him, too. His talk is efficient. It has that odd Newfoundland mix of primness, lyricism, precision and flashing simile. He closes his mouth on each word, and icebergs will turn to wine before anyone will ever hear Chris Pratt describe anything as either "right on" or "groovy."

In Ottawa, there was a crust in his voice. A bunch of us were sitting around a table wondering how to convince politicians and bureaucrats that we deserved lots of money. Someone said that well, after all artists vote too, you know. Pratt cut in. We would be naive beyond belief, he suggested, if we allowed ourselves to think for half a second that artists, as artists, had an ounce more grass-roots political clout than a pile of fish guts. We looked at him. What was he? An artist, or a backroom boy?

Many artists are more inclined to accept government money than to root around among the square people who fight to get governments elected. Pratt worked for the Conservatives in the last two provincial elections, the ones that upset Joe Smallwood, and he discovered that making speeches was "an hypnotically satisfying experience. I could imagine Hitler getting his kicks from it."

He worked in his home district of St. Mary's (voting population: 2,700) for PC candidate Gerry Ottenheimer, who is now Minister of Education in Newfoundland. "Smallwood spent three nights here," Pratt recalls. "He had every man on public works. He was giving out gravel and culvert contracts like it was Christmas. There was liquor galore. In our campaign, there wasn't a thimbleful. We won that election by 78 votes, and it was a miracle. The second time, it was a walkover for us."

Pratt, as a painter, has other unlikely preoccupations. Perhaps they are not unlikely in any profound sense. Perhaps they are unlikely only in the light of a superficial but still pervasive image of the modern artist as a creature of the city whose character and creative obsessions surround him with broken marriages, neglected children, faith betrayed, civic irresponsibility, dirt, disorder and narcotic indulgence. Perhaps artists aren't like that at all.

Pratt, however, is *less* like that than any artist you're likely to meet. His passion for efficient equipment, for control, for cleanliness, for order in all things amounts to a religion. He believes that, simply as a human being, he's a custodian of millions of years of development and that he therefore owes it to a universal order to function as well as he can.

Matter, he speculates, may be a refinement of something like electricity; life is a refinement of matter; self-awareness is a refinement of life; and self-control is a refinement of self-awareness. And whether or not there is a God, Man himself, Chris Pratt himself, through self-control, may be a stage in the evolution of God. Pratt thinks about his participation in Time; it astounds him to realize that, in just 15 years, the flesh of his own hands has smoothed the edges of a 12-inch wooden ruler. Like the sea on rock. Minute by minute, habit by habit, vision by vision, brush stroke by brush stroke, he obeys his belief.

He has never in his life had a shot of booze (which, in Newfoundland, is enough all by itself to make him a freak of nature) and, though there are ancient personal reasons for his abstinence, they all come down to his belief that drink wrecks efficiency. He takes no drugs. He smokes nothing. He collects postage stamps. He keeps a diary. And each day, in the blackness of winter and the gathering dawns of the Newfoundland summer, he rises at five-thirty.

He has served on the town council of the tiny community of St. Catherines. He sits among the business suits, quiet neckties, and the talk of dollars, sales volumes and production capabilities at Newfoundland's Regional Development Authority, which loans money to farmers and sawmills and fishermen.

He's the major shareholder (his father and a young brother are the others) in a chic, deep-sea racing yacht, a beautiful, white charger of the sort you associate with stockbrokers, advertising executives and beer tycoons. She's an Ontario-built Cuthbertson and Cassian 35-footer, worth at least $35,000, and under way, such sailboats are a supreme marriage of human technology to the old forces of nature. From the tip of her masthead wind indicator to the ocean-floor range of her depth-sounder she *works*. There's a heavy supply of paper towels aboard. No random drop of diesel fuel, nor muddy smear from a crewman's foot, escapes instant elimination. He named her Lynx, not really because "The Lynx" was one of his earlier and finest prints but because he liked the clean order of the lines of those four capital letters together—LYNX.

(On a luminous evening in June, Pratt took the sloop out for only the second time, to try out some of her eight Hood and two Elvström sails; and, as she loped down Conception Bay, out toward a glowing blue iceberg, he stood behind her silver wheel, and she put her rail down, and his pleasure was as warm as the air was cold. "Just think," he said, "Van Gogh nearly starved to death.")

Pratt hikes with his children, cross-country skis with them, plays hockey with them every afternoon there's ice on the Salmonier River. He writes poetry with a sharp pencil, in a small, neat hand, and keeps it in an 80-cent hardcover notebook. Some of the verse is for his wife. He tells you, with a conviction that seems to come out of another age (and another profession) that no one on earth is more important to him than she is: "Mary is important to everything I am. It was she who gave me the encouragement to abandon all those other things and be a painter. For 10 years here, I've been with her constantly. She is my closest friend *at every level*. We have the usual man-woman relationship. I mean we have four kids and, but for the luck of the draw, we'd have a lot more.... But she's also my friend. You know what I mean. She's my *friend*."

Most of the year, they rise before the sun and their

91

children are up. They eat breakfast alone, and together. Chris is at work in his studio by 7 a.m. He joins her for coffee at ten. He returns to his studio. He joins her for lunch at noon. He returns to his studio. He joins her for coffee at three-thirty in the afternoon, and when the kids get home from school he fools around outdoors with them. He joins her for supper with them at 5 p.m. He watches the news. He returns to his studio. He joins her at nine-thirty or ten and they are alone, and together.

They met at Mount Allison University, Sackville, New Brunswick, in the mid-Fifties; and for a while, in that whole romance-ridden little place, there were few more troubled romances than theirs. Mary was Mary West of Fredericton, daughter of the attorney-general of New Brunswick. Would-be seducers found her less than satisfying. Oh dear, she'd say, what am I going to do about poor Chris? Chris is *so* unhappy. Chris is so miserable. Chris is so confused. Chris just doesn't know what to do with his life. Let's talk about Chris. What can I do for Chris?

She had curly dark hair, brown eyes, glasses, an elegant little shape. There was a powerfully appealing air of innocence about her. She was bright, funny, popular. And Chris was a walking lump of young gloom. "I was wretchedly unhappy," he recalls. "I simply didn't know what in hell I wanted to do."

Mary was an art student, and she knew what he should do. Lawren Harris Jr. and Alex Colville, who taught art at Mount A, knew what he should do. Everyone in Sackville who saw what he could make with the box of water colors he'd brought from St. John's knew what he should do. Everyone, except Pratt himself, knew he should be a painter.

The urge, if not the hope, had been in him for a long time: "I remember very clearly, I was only about 10 or 12, and I saw a little girl walking along Waterford Bridge Road at home, and she was carrying a handful of water-color brushes, and I remember very clearly *resenting* her. I hadn't even done any painting myself, but even then, I considered it my trade, my territory or something."

92

But both on his mother's side, the Dawe family, as well as his father's, Pratt was part of Newfoundland's establishment (even though a couple of his harder-drinking uncles may have "had the arse out of their pants"); and in the St. John's of the mid-Fifties, painting pictures as a career for a young man of distinguished ancestry probably ranked just below knitting. There were few, if any, full-time artists there. There was no art gallery. There was no formal art school, no Art Scene.

There were no artists' factions, gossip, feuds, openings or hairy parties. There was nothing in town to inspire anyone to Be a Painter and even now, the social aspects of the art world bore Pratt. The Canada Council invited him to an opening in Paris last June but, he says, "I couldn't bear the thought of it. There's only one part of me that I want to see participate in the art world, and that's my work."

The other result of the artistic desert in St. John's, however, was that it took Pratt till 1963, when he was 27, to commit himself totally to living off what he could earn alone in his studio. He messed around in engineering for a year at Memorial University. And at Mount A, he messed around in biology, he messed around in the general arts course and majored in English, he messed around in pre-med to try to pick up enough biology to prepare for ocean studies. "I don't think I ever really considered the horrendous possibility of looking at someone's liver."

His confusion made him feel guilty. His guilt made him feel confused. His refusal to drink prevented him from ever becoming one of the boys. Not once did he hitchhike across the New Brunswick border to guzzle beer at the Legion in Amherst, Nova Scotia; and that little trip, for perhaps thousands of Mount A freshmen, was as traditional as fertility rites in the South Pacific. It's doubtful if any Newfoundland fish ever felt so far out of water.

Many of Newfoundland's blushing young feel they're terribly unsophisticated when they leave their island home for the first time; and the social atmosphere at Mount A fed Pratt's confusion over what in God's name he was doing there, anyway. He left after two and a half years. In all that

93

time, he had cracked his books for about four hours. He had no degree, but he had a friend.

They married in Fredericton on September 12, 1957, and on September 14, they boarded the *Nova Scotia*, an 8,000-ton freighter-passenger vessel. They were bound for Scotland and the Glasgow School of Art, where Chris would study for two years. They returned to Mount A, and in 1961 Chris and Mary graduated together with Bachelor of Fine Arts degrees. The news of his work began to spread. Sales, recognition, prizes and job offers crept up pleasantly, but still, his Newfoundlander's suspicion of his own talent held him back. He wondered if the national cultural authorities at Ottawa were interested in his work simply because they couldn't find enough other Newfoundlanders to fulfill somebody's idea of appropriate regional representation.

He wondered, too, if he could really feed his family simply by painting pictures, and he took a job that instantly plunged him into the despair he'd known in Sackville in the mid-Fifties. The job involved running an art gallery for Memorial University and teaching painting at night, "mostly to women whose husbands had booted them out of the house on poker night." He recalls that, "quite literally, I almost went insane." He paid regular visits to a doctor for a condition that felt suspiciously like stomach ulcers. He'd lost most of his hair. He was 26.

The Pratts lived in what he calls "a CMHC box" in a part of St. John's in which "the moving vans came by as often as the milk trucks.... I can't even bear to think of the place. It's all I can do even to drive up that road now."

Then, in the spring of '63, he quit Memorial, he quit St. John's, he quit security. He said he would now be a painter, and he took Mary and the kids out to this rangy old summer place at St. Catherines that his father owned, and he thought they'd try to live there happily ever after, and they'd scarcely completed the hour-long axle-threatening drive out from the city, they'd scarcely unpacked their stuff and got some food on the table and the kids settled for the night, when a great wind came up and the trees roared, and the sound told Chris something he'd waited a long time to hear. It said that he was home.

The most silent and vivid moments of his boyhood, the magical seconds that he still dreams about, had occurred on weekend fishing and hunting trips to beautiful corners of the Avalon peninsula, and usually at dawn. Few events are as clean as a Newfoundland dawn. Years later, he'd dream of riversful of trout and salmon, and skiesful of geese and partridge and ducks, and long before he moved to St. Catherines, he had dreamed once about a flock of eider ducks.

The drakes were white and black, with a dusty gold headdress. The hens were dusty brown. There must have been 50 of them, and they all rose together, through a fog at dawn, and flew up the river.

"That was the dream," he recalls, "and on the second or third day we were here, I suddenly woke at five in the morning, and I went to a window, and there was a flock of eider ducks. The drakes were white and black with kind of dusty gold headdress. The hens were sort of dusty brown. They all rose together, and there was a heavy fog. They flew up the river. There must have been 50 of them. I've never seen so many together, before or since. And quite honestly, I accepted it as an omen."

The place is on the banks of the Salmonier River, where the river joins St. Mary's Bay, and the Pratts live there under Canada geese, eagles, bitterns, gulls, ospreys, black ducks, golden ducks, mergansers, "practically every bird in Newfoundland."

Seals cruise and otters romp in their river pond. Their four kids boat there, swim there, skate there. Mary can call them home for supper from the kitchen door; and supper, on any summer day that anyone feels like fishing, will be trout caught just off their lawn.

Moose sometimes amble in among the flowers, the pretty hardwoods, the blackberries, gooseberries, the vegetable garden, and the loose toys and sports gear that surround the house. A stone-lined creek splits the sloping grass, and rattles down to the river.

The house is really two houses joined together. It is low. It stretches, like an old ranchhouse. It's got six bedrooms and one-and-a-half bathrooms and, in separate buildings, Chris and Mary have studios of their own. Mary is an accomplished painter in her own right, in a style that's sometimes labelled Photo Realism; and, lately, her independent reputation has been growing. By the nature of their work and gentle preferences, the whole family is together there in their coastal wilderness almost all the days of their lives. There are no property taxes in rural Newfoundland.

Across the river, the Pratt family owns 250 acres of black spruce, fir, birch, witch hazel, mountain ash and the odd willow. Beyond that, stretching across the lunar barrens there's a herd of hundreds of caribou. "Sometimes," Pratt says, "I have to go to some smoky cocktail party in St. John's, and I have my customary ginger ale, and I come home late. I like to stand by the car for a moment and think that, if I were to walk straight through there, I would find the caribou ground before I'd ever find a road. It's romantic, I know. But it's *not* romantic, because they're there."

He goes on. "I guess what I'm saying is that I really like it here. I've learned to live in the present here. I've overcome that greener-pastures thing that plagued me for years. The actuality here always exceeds the anticipation, and that's a damn good way to live. I wake up in the morning, and I'm actually *glad* to be here."

There's a work of art on the outside of the old white garage at Pratt's place. A child has painted a huge, smiling face and the words, "Be Happy." It's a cheerful order, and in the case of Chris Pratt, it seems at last to be entirely unnecessary.

Maclean's, December 1973

96

The Joy of Conversion to Pure Scottish Schmaltz

My family name has resounded through Scottish history for seven centuries, but Scotland never fascinated me. During the whole year that I spent in London as a college boy, I didn't take one train up there to see the lochs, burns, scars, scroggies, and wee lassies. I dismissed Scotland as the grey northern home of a penny-squeezing, pinch-faced people, of second-rate castles in a second-rate culture. Naturally, when university closed in spring, I turned my back on Scotland. I plunged instead into Denmark, Switzerland, Germany, the perfume of romance in Paris, and the hot elegant decadence of Rome.

During the next quarter-century, my indifference to Scotland actually turned to distaste. As a junior reporter for the *Ottawa Journal*, it was my boring duty to cover maudlin Burns Suppers where tears burst from the eyes of ruddy, chubby, Canadian bureaucrats who discovered once a year that they were born-again Highlanders. On the way to these banquets, I imagined, each one had ducked into a telephone booth, stripped off his flannel suit, and emerged in kilt, velvet tunic, silver buttons, lace at the throat, sporran, buckles, scarlet garter tabs, and knee-high socks with bejewelled dirk. Is it a bird? Is it a plane? No, it's MacSuperman!

These weren't "professional Scots." They were enthusiastic, amateur, colonial, *imitation* Scots, and with the quick intolerance of most young reporters of my time, I lumped them with Shriners, Knights of Columbus and other buffoons who paraded around town in silly costumes. As someone who'd majored in English literature, I thought Burns's verse was sentimental doggerel in a bastard language. As someone with a normal palate, I thought haggis was boring at best,

97

disgusting at worst. As someone who believed in being Canadian first, last and always, it was enough to know that my paternal forbears went back to a certain James Bruce who'd settled in Guysborough County, N.S., in the 1790s. What part of Scotland he'd once called home was of no more interest to me than the recent and utterly useless news that the chief of the house of Bruce, Lord Elgin, possessed two of Robert the Bruce's teeth.

I learned about the teeth in a press release from the British Tourist Authority which, along with British Airways, had suddenly invited me to join a gang of travel writers during a five-day junket to Edinburgh and Glasgow. The BTA, you see, had proclaimed 1981 "The Year of the Scot." Moreover, this year it's Scotland's turn to hold the International Gathering of the Clans. (Nova Scotia, you'll remember, had its turn in '79, and will have another in '83.) The idea is to get people of Scottish descent to come home from all over the world to look up roots and relatives, feel the auld sod under their feet and, quite incidentally of course, pump zillions into the auld sod's economy.

To help make all this happen, Gathering promoters invited us press to the opening event of the 1981 program: The International Burns Supper on a Saturday night in dear old Glasgow town. It was in the City Chambers, a gloriously pretentious Victorian edifice, lined with acres of marble in patterns of swirling caramel and cream. The whole adventure was free, and as proof there's a trace of Scottish blood in my veins after all, I offer the fact that I cannot remember ever having turned down a free airline ticket to anywhere. (The other proof is that despite my earlier reservations about Scottish culture, I've always had an embarrassing reaction to any good bagpipe band. I have to hide my tears.)

I suppose you've already guessed what happened. Five days of seeing Scotland wiped out every sour misapprehension that I'd nursed during a lifetime of *not* seeing Scotland. From the moment I left Prestwick airport, I had the classic Brigadoon reaction. *Haven't I been in this misty countryside before? In another life perhaps?* Nowhere outside Canada have I felt so thoroughly at home as I did in Scotland.

I won't forget the silver-grey light over glowing moors on a late afternoon; the fierce steely beauty of the wind-whipped Firth of Clyde; the castles, cottages, croftlands, country lanes and mellow stone fences; the burns, the tythe barns and bonny, sheep-rich braes; the wit of Glasgow people and the risible lilt of their voices; and Edinburgh, dear Edinburgh, easily the finest small city I've ever explored. I didn't even get up to the Highlands, but nevertheless, I fell for Scotland so hard that, like a Lothario who has at last found the girl he desperately wants to marry, I wondered why I had ever squandered affection on the likes of Greece, Portugal, Barbados, California, Indonesia, Hawaii.

Scotland even taught me to like Robert Burns. "He was a poet and patriot of the first standard," Lord Birsay, a beloved judge, declared in thundering Scottish syllables at the International Burns Supper. "Without Burns our language would have died, and our culture with it." Without Burns, I'd never have made it to Glasgow. What a night! "The Germans don't get stinko on Goethe's birthday," someone proudly observed. "The English don't have a Keats Carry-on." Lord Elgin, my chief, led more than 400 of us in a strange series of toasts. And there was I, the unabashed convert to Scotland the brave, standing on a table with my whisky on high, wearing a Bruce kilt, velvet tunic, silver buttons, lace at the throat, sporran, buckles, scarlet garter tabs, and knee-high socks with bejewelled dirk. MacSuperman himself!

I'm going back. I'm going back in August, and most of my family's coming with me. If further proof of my new-found love of Scotland were needed, it's that this time I'm actually paying my own way. Or most of it anyway. I mean we may try to sponge off Lord and Lady Elgin for a couple of days. Family roots, you know. Anyway, the chief promised he'd show me two fascinating objects: teeth that actually grew in the mouth of the Bruce who demolished the English at Bannockburn a mere 667 years ago.

Atlantic Insight, April 1981

Pete Seeger, the Bible and the Byrds Close a Generation Gap

Did you find what you needed for your party?" I ask our 15-year-old after he's sorted through our old recordings.

"Oh sure," he says. "I got lots of classics."

"I didn't know your friends liked Bach and Mozart."

"Not *that* stuff," he retorts. "The Beatles, the Doors, the Byrds, the Mamas and Papas. You know, the *classics*." Ah well, it's only a dozen years since a renowned sociologist predicted future generations would recognize the Beatles as having exerted as much influence on the music of the Western world as Beethoven.

"My father's so old," I heard one girl confide to another, "that he can actually name the tunes on the Muzak in the supermarket."

A friend swears he overheard a girl on a bus marvelling, "Did you know Paul McCartney once played for another group?" Poor child. Her classical education is sadly deficient. Actually, I find my friend's story hard to swallow, but it does force me to face the dismal fact that time zooms so fast there are already millions of Michael Jackson freaks who were born not merely after the Beatles' heyday but after the Beatles broke up. Moreover, at the first sounds of Gordon Lightfoot's guitar, most of these kids would doubtless get up and leave the room.

My younger son, he who appreciates the classics, also likes video music on TV. Once, when I asked him what strange crap he was watching, he witheringly replied, "Don't you know that's one of the greatest videos of all time?" His flair for hyperbole will come in handy if he wants to pursue a career as a sports announcer, but I do not doubt his judgment.

If he said he was watching one of the greatest videos of all time, he was indeed watching one of the greatest videos of all time. What do I know? What does any 49-year-old know?

He is fair about who gets to watch what. On a night when he craved his regular fix of video weirdness, he tolerated my watching a documentary about the Weavers. Now if the Beatles were classical, the Weavers were prehistoric. Their leader was Pete Seeger, and in the primeval McCarthy era they sang stuff that reflected leftwing attitudes that got Seeger into political trouble. But they also amazed themselves by delighting much of North America's grubby capitalist society with commercial hits: "So Long," "On Top of Old Smoky," "Wimoweh," "Kisses Sweeter than Wine," and the song that's since ended a million dances, house parties, and campfire singsongs, "Good Night, Irene."

The Weavers were a quartet, and a superb example of the whole being more than the sum of its parts. Seeger played banjo, sang in a split-tenor wail, chopped logs onstage, and exuded so much love for what he was doing that it was a cold crowd indeed that didn't forgive him for being a shade arch. Ronnie Gilbert had a bronze, imperative contralto. Her voice soared like a challenge to the whole world to wake up and do right. Fred Hellerman played guitar, sang high, sang low. Lee Hays boasted what Seeger called "a big gospel bass." And now, in 1984, coming at me from Bangor, Me., here they all were, together again, and for the last time.

Ronnie was now a chubby, grey-haired doll, and Seeger a scraggly stripling of only 64 or so. One of the others was in a wheelchair. They were shaky, bitten by age and disease, and they smiled into one another's eyes. They lifted their cracked voices together one more time, and belted out the old songs. "If I Had a Hammer." "Where Have All the Flowers Gone." Short time passing. Good night, Irene, good night. Good night, Weavers.

I was near tears.

"Can we watch 'New Music Magazine' now?" my son asked.

A decade before he was born, my wife and I saw these

same codgers perform in Ottawa; and that fact, I'm sure, confirmed his opinion that we were not only elderly but also guilty of ludicrously quaint taste in music. It was 1958 when we saw the Weavers. Only three years had passed since the House Un-American Activities Committee had investigated Seeger. He was convicted on 10 counts of contempt of Congress (charges that were not dismissed till 1962), but he and the other Weavers still had a following in Canada. Of course, their work was not as popular as "Diana" by Ottawa's own Paul Anka, then 15, or "Catch a Falling Star," or that revolting Christmas ditty, "The Chipmunk Song."

When I recall such crud, I know I'm not on good ground to knock the music that now ent. aces teenagers. After all, it was my teenage years that gave the world such gems as "Sentimental Me," "A—You're Adorable," "I Saw Mommy Kissing Santa Claus," "Somebody Bad Stole de Wedding Bell," and the dreadfully unforgettable "That Doggie in the Window." The one with the waggly tail. Or was it "waggeldy"?

I still cringe to recall that, at 17, I confessed to a cynical buddy that the Teresa Brewer version of "Till I Waltz Again With You" was "probably my favorite song." My friend, who'd studied classical piano, exploded in such derisive hysterics we had to leave the restaurant before I could summons from the jukebox either "Little Things Mean a Lot," in which someone was urged to "touch my hair as you pass my chair," or "The Naughty Lady of Shady Lane," in which the singer keeps the cute secret till the last line. The naughty lady, it turned out, was "only nine days old," and they can't take that away from me.

I wish they could. That's the trouble with having the sort of memory that causes you to wake up one morning in 1984 knowing that, more than 30 years earlier, you hung out with teenagers who thought it was killingly funny to change the song "Rags to Riches" to "Bags to Bitches." Somebody'd sing, "I know I'd go from bags to bitches if you would only be my own," and we'd all break up. The way we were.

By the mid-Sixties, which were my early 30s, I'd put

away childish things and learned to love the Byrds. The title song of their album "Turn! Turn! Turn!" was a variation of verses in Ecclesiastes: "To every thing there is a season, and a time to every purpose under the heaven... A time to be born, and a time to die... A time to rend, and a time to sew; a time to keep silence, and a time to speak... a time to love, and a time to hate; a time of war and a time of peace...." Now the man who adapted the words and wrote the music for "Turn! Turn! Turn!"—and he did it years before anyone had ever heard of the Byrds—was none other than good old Peter Seeger. The thing was, you put Seeger and the Bible together with the Byrds and you got, well, a *classic*. What's a classic if it isn't something that occasionally bridges a generation gap?

Atlantic Insight, July 1984

Twenty Years After the Bump

I suppose you have heard of the earthquake we had out here. Not much damage, but it sure was scary. The only bad results we had in our house was the following morning when my husband opened the cabinet door and some of my crystal goblets came tumbling out and crashed in a million pieces. When the earthquake hit, the first thought in my mind was bumps in the mines. So I guess I've still got Springhill in my heart. Can't make it home this year but....
—from a recent letter to the Springhill and Parrsboro *Record* by Mrs. Alan Dorman of Sidney, B.C.

Why, Mrs. Dorman? Twenty years have passed since the first

of the modern disasters that promised to destroy Springhill, Nova Scotia. How come you've still got Springhill in your heart? What's Springhill, anyway, but a synonym for sorrow and horror, a catch-basin for misery? The floodlights at the pithead burned all night, and night after night. The women and children waited. The press waited. The world waited. The ambulances, the hearses, the Hillside graveyard waited. And the trapped miners waited, where night would never turn to day. Out came the bodies, on canvas stretchers. The living, the dead, the unrecognizable, the broken; and no man less than a hero.

Springhill...A crucible for the refinement of every kind of human suffering ranging from mere depression or a work-worn body or the loss of a job all the way down to unspeakable grief, terror, agony, sudden death and, worse, a lingering death—among scampering rats and the gathering stench of dead friends—in a hole blacker than anything Calcutta ever knew...Springhill. If there's a community worth forgetting, surely it is Springhill; and yet, the Springhill and Parrsboro *Record* has hundreds of subscribers all over North America, and like Mrs. Dorman, they refuse to forget.

There were always miracles in the bad old days of the bumps, explosions and fires, miracles of rescue and survival to arouse the wild joy of wives who'd lost hope for their men; miracles to cling to the next time the ground shook, windows cracked, lights flickered, dishes tumbled to the floor, telephones died and a distant clap of something that was not thunder knocked the cigarette right out of your mouth. The miracles shone amid the general horror, like the lights worn by the draegermen rescue crews discovering those who were still merely half-dead. They were the stuff of perfect headlines, grist for microphones and cameras to make the most compelling Canadian news footage of the Fifties, the reason why Springhill could keep the world on the edge of its chair for days at a time.

But those days did end. The last corpse emerged into sunlight. The last interview with the last dazed survivor sputtered to a halt. Prince Philip came and went, and, boys, it was time to move out. Springhill drifted into journalistic history as the top Canadian story of one more year and, now, a quieter sort of miracle could take shape. It was simply the fact that, despite everything, Springhill would not dry up and blow away.

The explosion of November 1, 1956, was the first of three orgies of devastation that swept the townsfolk in 1956–58, but not the first disaster in Springhill history. The very first (and very worst) was the "Springhill Horror" of February 21, 1891, an explosion that killed 125 men and boys, and 17 horses. Four years later, a fire demolished the commercial heart of the town. Then typhoid fever hit Springhill, and in 1910, there was a strike of such bitterness that, according to *Springhill* (1926) by Bertha Isabel Scott, "a company of militia was sent from Halifax. It was a disturbing thing to see a gun drawn to the top of our hill." The strike lasted almost two years, and if the horror of '91 and the fire of '95 were previews of the disasters of the Fifties, the years 1910–11 were early proof of the miners' ability to live on wit, pride and scraps.

Nothing sensationally bad happened after that for almost half a century, though mining accidents continued to kill roughly two men a year. Most miners never failed to kiss their wives as they left home for a shift down below. Some succumbed to miners' lung diseases and died early, but despite all the death and grief, Springhill was proud to be a coal town, proud to be the giant of mainland coal production in Nova Scotia, proud to be the birthplace of bluenose coal unions and the site of the first mining school in the province.

Coal was to Springhill what fish were to Lunenburg and apples to the Annapolis Valley. By the 1950s, men had been mining Springhill's superior bituminous coal for 125 years, and the big Dominion Steel and Coal Co. collieries had been open for three generations. Now, they were among the world's deepest shafts. On the slope, the miners travelled almost three miles underground to reach some coal seams; the distance, straight down, was 7,800 feet, a depth roughly equal to the combined height of two Eiffel Towers, two Empire State Buildings and two Toronto CN Towers.

"There wasn't any choice," Bill James, a draegerman, recalled. "You didn't go to college. You couldn't afford it. You followed your father into the mines. You were supposed to be 18, but as soon as you were big enough to lie about your age, you went into the pits. I started in '40 or '41. I was 14, but I was big. I got $3.41 a day. That was big money. If you worked all day in the woods you only got 50 cents."

Most miners owned their own houses. "Those fellows were smart," said Charles Allbon, the retired Springhill newspaper publisher. "They'd help each other. They just wouldn't have had houses if they hadn't built their own. The miners were remarkable people. They could do anything." Allbon's son Jack, the town's industrial development officer, searched for a word for the independent air of Springhill miners. "The miner, I guess you'd say, was a very self-reliant type of individual.... He was a bit of an electrician, a bit of a carpenter, a half-arsed plumber.... They'd help each other build cottages, too. A fellow'd have a nice little cabin down on the Northumberland Strait or the Parrsboro Shore, among old friends, *plus* a hunting and fishing camp on a lake. They couldn't have gotten the same sort of life on a salary of $25,000 or $30,000 in Toronto. Not for *any* salary."

No, these were not the sort who pull up stakes easily and move on to the next hole-in-the-ground where there's a buck to be made. Some were third-generation Springhill miners. Con Embree, who saved the lives of 50 gas-trapped men in 1956 by teaching them to breathe through holes in a compressed-air pipe, had already lived through two mine mishaps and his father had survived the tragedy of '91. Several victims of the disasters of '56 and '58 were descendants of men who'd been Springhill miners in the 1880s. Springhill people enjoyed spending their lives among neighbors and relatives, and when the horrors came, there was scarcely anyone in town who did not lose someone so dear that, for a while, the grief was prostrating.

The miners, needless to say, were the town's economic

106

backbone. By 1956, Springhill's population was 7,348; more than 1,425 were on Dosco's payroll. Beside coal, all other industries were measly. All the shops—and by 1951 there were more than a hundred—fed off miners' salaries. The town was there on the surface of Springhill, because the coal was *under* the surface of Springhill, and Canada needed it. But what would happen when Canada did not need Nova Scotia's coal?

By the mid-Fifties, clouds of economic doom were already gathering above Springhill, and in the years to follow the skies would unleash on the little town three awful thunderbolts.

November 1, 1956. Shortly after 5 p.m. six cars, loaded with coal, climb toward the top of No. 4 colliery. Mysteriously, they break loose and as they hurtle downhill backwards, raise a blizzard of coal dust. They slice through an electric cable and the arc from the cable ignites the dust. Thirty miles away, people feel the explosion. The blast kills some miners, traps others, spreads deadly methane gas among still others. By midnight, the known dead number seven, including two gassed draegermen. There are 118 men still underground. Three-and-a-half days later, the last of 88 survivors emerge. The gas is still so dangerous that the company seals up the colliery and, with it, the bodies of 26 men. On January 18, 1957, 11 weeks after the explosion, miners bring out the last of their dead friends. The final count: 39 dead. "I'll have to go down again," says Chesley Harrison. "What else can I do?"

December 26, 1957. A black gift for Boxing Day, an echo of 1895, a fire guts Springhill's business and shopping district. Meanwhile, Dosco has announced it will never again open No. 4. More than 450 miners are without work. Some drift away to Cape Breton, Ontario, the U.S., the Prairies. Some work from day to day at farms or lumber camps. About 150 hang around town, wondering. And now, as '57 rolls down to '58, the company complains about wildcat strikes and absenteeism in the huge old No. 2 colliery, and threatens

107

to close it, too. It employs nearly 900 men, and it's all that's left of coal mining in Springhill. United Church minister William T. Mercer speaks for much of the town when he says, "If No. 2 closes, there'll be nothing here . . . Springhill will be a ghost town."

October 23, 1958. Since March, six big "bumps" in No. 2 have injured 14 miners. (A bump is an unpredictable, inexplicable and explosive compression of an excavated coal seam, like an underground earthquake. It crushes men and machinery and releases poisonous gas.) Now, on this golden, Indian summer evening, the worst bump in Springhill history shakes houses 10 miles away and, once again, sends hundreds racing out of their homes, into the streets and up to the pithead. This bump, the last disaster in the last Dosco colliery, traps 174 men and kills 75. It is memorable for horror, heroism and two miracles. The first occurs six-and-a-half days after the bump; 12 living men emerge from the depths. The second occurs almost nine days after the bump; this time, seven men come out. Reporter Dick Andres sees a connection between the miracles and Springhill's fame as a baseball town. "Players discarded their pit lamps for baseball caps at game time and thrilled Maritime senior leagues with the never-say-die spirit so evident during the past two years of tragedy."

There was no pattern to the future of the survivors. When Herbert Pepperdine, one of the last to escape No. 2, emerged in November of '58, his ailing mother, who'd lost a son in the explosion of '56, said, "I'd give everything I have to keep him out of the mines from now on." But when businessmen reopened an ancient shaft on the outskirts of town, Pepperdine went underground once more to do the work he knew best. Hugh Guthro was trapped for three-and-a-half days in '56 and for six-and-a-half in '58. "I don't care if we starve to death," his wife said when he came out in '58. "Hughie will never set foot in another mine." But he did. He joined Pepperdine in the reopened shaft and, for a while, travelled 25 miles each way every day to work in a coal mine at River Hébert.

Douglas Jewkes, who'd craved 7-Up during eight-and-a-half days of hell in '58, went to Toronto—appropriately enough to a job in a soft-drink plant. The governor of Georgia sponsored a two-week holiday on a Georgian resort island for the survivors who'd been trapped longest in '58, and Levi Milley liked the South so much he stayed down there. Others went to mines in Alberta, to a watch factory in Maine, to new lives in Ontario. Hundreds drifted away. Shops failed. The population shrank 25 percent. And yet, there were many who just damned well wouldn't leave town. In December 1958, Canadian National Railways published an industrial survey of Springhill in which the authors marvelled that, despite everything, "there had been no indication of any general migration...." Springhillers were sticking to Springhill the way rockweed sticks to rock.

But the air was grim. Sorrow and hopelessness left the town lethargic for months. "I'm going to tell you, it was pretty bad here for a year or two," Bill James, ex-miner, remembered. "You owned your own home. You didn't want to leave, but there wasn't any work. You just didn't know what to do."

"Both higher levels of government felt the town couldn't possibly survive," Mayor William Mont recalls. "They felt the people would just gradually fall apart and it would become a ghost town. But this didn't happen. There *was* a state of shock for a year or two but it wore off, and the people rolled up their sleeves...."

Governments helped. They built institutions of their own and encouraged small industries to settle in Springhill which, if it had nothing else, had a ready supply of men who understood the relationship between sweat and wages. A battery factory opened. A frozen-food plant. A manufacturer of plastic containers. A carpet factory. A building-supply outlet. And in about 20 small mines, secret coal-digging continued. These clandestine mines failed to meet legal safety requirements but they at least kept a few old miners busy bringing up about 60 tons a day for both their own use and a steady local market.

It was these "bootleg" miners who discovered the productivity of the old "Syndicate" shaft. A Nova Scotia syndicate had opened it in the 1880s, run it for a couple of years and closed it after a fire. Now, more than 70 years later, the Springhill Coal Co. Ltd. took over the shaft the bootleggers had reopened and, in the Sixties, employed more than 100 miners, produced more than a million tons. Flooding closed the shaft in the early Seventies, but local entrepreneurs opened it yet again, this time as the Springhill Miners' Museum. Eloquent guides, all of them ex-miners, show the shaft to as many as 600 summertime tourists a day.

Other ex-miners, and Mayor Mont (who had worked on the surface for Dosco) got solid jobs at the $12-million medium-security prison that the federal government built on the outskirts of town. It employs close to 300 people, and miners make good guards. "It's their attitude, I guess," says Jack Allbon, the town's development officer. "Nothing scares them."

Allbon, as devout a positive thinker as you're likely to find in any town, can rattle off Springhill's other assets like an auction salesman: the "lovely industrial park with its lawns and ponds"; the curling club, built on the backside of what used to be a United Church; the 26 miles of streets, "all 100-percent paved"; the elementary schools, all within easy walking distance of the kids' homes, none more than 10 years old; the new $1.1 million high school; the new Cumberland County Vocational School; the new sports centre, the new fire hall, the new hospital. And the friendliness of a people who think nothing of turning out, 300-strong, for a surprise party to honor the part-time janitor at the curling club.

By 1975 Springhill's most vehement boosters were so sensitive about what the town's dramatic past might do to its economic future and so proud of its unsung, lilac-blown prettiness that they were still sore about the way Upper Canadian journalists had arrived in the Sixties to get photographs of the ugliest shacks they could find, to confirm in print the grim image of Springhill that the outside world had known for a dozen years. Why didn't those creeps expose the slums in their own towns? How could you attract industry with that sort of stuff going out across the continent?

The odd story, however, did stress "the amazing economic recovery" of the once-blighted town. Ah, sweet rebirth. "It's a pet theory of mine," says Mayor Mont, "that the town economy is really only about 15 years old. Considering the lack of tools, the tools of wealth, the people have made remarkable progress.... I really think Springhill people are a special breed." By 1975, Springhill was hardly a boom town but it was at least no worse off than dozens of other small towns in the Maritimes. And if there were a law of averages governing the frequency with which disasters strike communities, Springhill should have been safe for centuries. It now proved, however, that there is no such law.

July 20, 1975. A Sunday. Around 3 a.m., a fire breaks out in a restaurant kitchen at the bottom of the Main Street hill. The wind's blowing at 40 m.p.h. and, as the fire skips to the old Knights of Pythias Hall and across the street to a clothing store, the big breeze snatches it and whips it up the slope as though the whole business district were a chimney. Propane tanks explode, paint cans pop, tar-paper roofs burst into flame. Firemen pour into Springhill from 10 towns, some more than 50 miles away. But long before dawn the fire is so hot they can't get close enough to fight it. The heat is unbearable even 300 feet away and the incineration of downtown Springhill lights the sky for miles into the hills.

By the time Springhill churches open their doors for morning services, 80 percent of the main business district is a smoking dump. Twenty buildings, housing 34 businesses, have disappeared. The fire has damaged nine more. Ten families have lost their homes. Nearly 100 men and women have lost their jobs. "When the town hall went," Mayor Mont later recalled, "when that old tower was all aflame, you could feel the heart of the town going.... We'd just remodelled the inside, and it was now one of the best town halls in the province. I had insisted the time had come for a real mayor's office. The mayor had always just borrowed the town clerk's desk. Anyway, I got it. I got the office, with a shiny new desk,

111

a shiny new leather chair and a shiny new filing cabinet with the keys in a plastic bag. Then the fire came. You know, I never even got to sit in my fancy leather chair. Not once."

There is a somewhat happy ending to this story. It involves what may well be a Canadian record for speedy government action to relieve distress. Red tape withered. Decisions blossomed overnight. For once, the phone worked to get big, fast, dollar commitments out of government. The political and bureaucratic effort to rejuvenate the town after the fire of '75 was the last of the Springhill miracles; and it began when Guy Brown, the local Liberal in the provincial legislature, got some of the most powerful Grits in Nova Scotia to come and see for themselves a scene that "looked like pictures of cities bombed during the war."

"I knew right where Bags was," Brown said. "Bags" was Environment Minister Glen Bagnell. "He was over at a cottage at Northport, and I had him here at 10 that morning. The fire was still smoldering. Bags had a mobile unit in his car and we used that to talk to the premier. He came in by helicopter." It took only 24 hours for Senator Al Graham, a Nova Scotian who happens to be president of the provincial Liberal Party Association, to arrive beside the ashes of what had once been downtown Springhill. Immediately he started to prod federal agencies to stretch the rules of their programs in Springhill's favor. "We played everything right," Brown said happily a year later. Within 72 hours of the fire, federal and provincial governments had committed themselves to a fat program of goodies for Springhill. "They never had a chance to think."

Here's what Springhill got: special assistance from higher levels of government to build 100 new houses, a senior citizens' home and an $800,000 town hall-cum-provincial office building; more special assistance to replace the sewer, water and street services the fire had destroyed and to complete construction of the town's sports centre; still more special assistance in the form of loans to help destroyed businesses re-establish themselves, to give Springhill its own industrial development officer, and to buy a market survey that would help the town lure chain stores; a $460,000 renovation program at the federal prison; acceleration of plans for a $3 million town water-delivery system; acceleration of exploratory coal drilling by the province; a $300,000 DREE grant to help the new owners of the defunct carpet mill establish themselves; and, to clean up what was left of Main Street, a $500,000 grant from the Local Initiatives Program. And, incredibly, the money began to arrive in Springhill within 30 days of the fire and without Springhill itself even having applied for it.

And now? Well, Springhill is not yet as healthy as its faithful would like it to be. Caleb Rushton (who's too modest to volunteer to strangers that his calm advice kept his companions from cracking during the six-and-a-half-day entombment in '58) runs the Manpower office in Springhill these days, and he says that, no, there still aren't enough jobs to go around. But in Springhill, optimism springs eternal.

The rebuilding of Main Street began this fall. Soon, the town would have a new motel, a new restaurant and cocktail lounge, a new complex of offices and shops. Everywhere a positive thinker looked, he saw promise. A lawyer had moved into town for the first time in 20 years. Springhill was building a medical centre, too, to lure young doctors. Shacks were falling, new houses were blossoming and surely, any day now, men would exploit the golden opportunities Springhill offered to a jeweller, an optometrist, a dry-cleaning business. Moreover, the miners who'd left town years ago were now growing old and they'd be home soon, not just for summer weeks but for good. They'd bring money with them.

Rod Fisher, chairman of Springhill Industrial Commission, has done so well as the local Honda distributor that the Honda organization awarded him a 15-day trip to Tokyo. "I've been all over the world," Fisher says, "and I don't think you can beat this community anywhere.... I don't dwell on the past. The only thing to do is look ahead, keep going ahead." Spoken like a true Springhiller.

Maurice Ruddick is 64 but he doesn't look much older

than he did in 1958 when he earned world fame as "The Singing Miner" whose hymns had bolstered the spirits of six entombed men. After that, he appeared on "Front Page Challenge" and, by gathering some of his 13 children in groups called "The Singing Miner and the Harmony Babes" and "The Singing Miner and the Minerettes," managed to pick up a few hundred bucks a year. He's bounced around from construction work, to the carpet factory, to odd clean-up jobs. Sometimes, even though his house has an oil furnace, he still goes out by the Miners' Museum to scrape coal into a shovel with his hands. He burns it in his kitchen stove. The times have not been soft for "The Singing Miner" but he has never seriously considered leaving Springhill for good. And what if exploratory drilling results in the opening of a new coal shaft? Would he report for work? "Yes," he says quickly, as though he were half a century younger. "Yes, I'd go down." And that, too, is spoken like a true Springhiller.

The Canadian, October 1976

Coastal Visitors on a Moonless Night

In the utter darkness just before dawn on the first night I slept there alone, a log in the stove thunked into place on its own, and it shook the whole cabin so that I almost came awake, and then I heard someone breathing in the room with me but the sound was not frightening, and in a few seconds I knew it was only the ocean surf. The tide was so low it had opened up a great width of sand beach below the gravel, and now the little rollers were sliding up the sand, and sighing, and sliding back as surely as the breath goes in and out of a sleeping woman.

Sometime in recent years, the loneliness of travel had begun to outweigh its romance, and I now thought there could be few more desolate experiences than travelling by yourself near Christmas. The ocean sound helped, and so did the memory of the men on the beach, and I went back to sleep.

I had arrived the night before. I had driven 180 miles to do five minutes' work. Our sailboat weighs half a ton, she's open, and she'd been sitting on her spine down on the beach ever since we'd hauled her out in October. She would collect water in her bilges and the water would turn to ice, and decades ago they said around here that a man who did not look after his boat was lazy.

I phoned from Halifax at noon and asked Rose to get Clayton to meet me on the beach at seven that night. I reached the cabin at six, and it felt as though its whole foundation had become an iceberg. It took me an hour to get a fire snapping away in the stove and the candles and coal-oil lanterns nicely flickering.

By 7:20, Clayton had not showed up, but I heard a strange bump outside. It seemed to come from the beach, which is below a steep cliff of spruce and balsam fir. I pulled on my boots, grabbed a flashlight, clambered down to the beach. The night sky there is usually brilliant with an amazing display of stars or a cloud-wreathed moon, but now the whole world was inky beyond belief. You could not see your hand before your face, and the huge bay was not the glittering vision it usually is. It was only a presence.

Flashlights moved near my boat. I walked to them. I could hear low, easy talk. There were two young fellows, two older fellows, and Clayton. He introduced them to me, and we shook hands without seeing one another. They were too polite to shine their flashlights in my eyes. "We thought we'd surprise you," Clayton said. The boat was already upside down, resting on logs they'd gathered from the beach and, now, her hull was like a turtle's shell, protecting her innards.

They came up to the cabin, and for an hour or so they sat around and helped take the chill off the place, and they told me who some of my ancestors had been around there; and one said that in the Twenties there was a storm like none he had ever seen before or since but his father had told him it was just a breeze compared to the August gale of 1873. A couple had a rum or two, the others had coffee, and then they all filed out into that cold nightful of relentless blackness and, since I was grateful in ways that words nor money could explain, I shook hands again with each one as he passed through the door.

"Sort of like going to church," one of the younger ones said. A gentle edge of mockery pops out of these people at moments you can never predict.

I ate a can of mussels in hot Spanish sauce, and braised chunks of veal in beef broth, ketchup, bay leaf and curry powder. I ate alone. I listened to the clicking of the stove, and every once in a while the surf startled me, as though strangers were on their way up from the beach.

Around midnight, I poured dishwater down the cliff and into the lacy wall of meshing branches. The trees are so thick there you'd think a squirrel would have trouble getting through, but I heard something with big haunches stirring

116

below and when I turned on the flashlight I picked up two eyes, and they glittered not like the reflectors on a bicycle but more like orange diamonds with secret energy sources of their own, and then I saw the creature's shape. A raccoon. The first wild one I'd ever seen. Christmas, for one traveller, was off to a fine start.

The Toronto Star, December 1973

Shoot That Puck, Grab That Briefcase

The real function of organized kid hockey is to teach corporate values to tykes, to mold their little personalities so that when they grow up they'll fit smoothly into the solemn machinery of Big Business. Today's peewee is tomorrow's vice-president of management services. Mom and dad—even as they rise at 4 a.m. to drive peewee through a blizzard to a rink where he skates hard with other tiny, applecheeked potential vice-presidents—are only vaguely aware that the outfit in which they've enrolled their kid is not only a hockey team but also the kindergarten of corporate life. Not that they'd mind. But dad secretly dreams his boy is bound for the NHL, and mom just thinks it's good for him to enjoy himself when he's young, have nice chums and help beat the piss out of a team coached by the husband of a woman she detests.

"Kill 'em," the moms screech at their boys. "Kill 'em, kill 'em!" This was when things got rough along the boards during kid hockey in a small town I once knew. The hockey moms had a bloodthirsty streak that made the hockey dads look like flower children. Wearing curlers and kerchiefs, bundled up in duffle coats in the unheated rink, sucking on coffee and cigs, they'd perch near centre ice and shriek at small boys. One mom was already turning her kid into a semi-pro. She gave him two bucks for each goal he scored, and since her husband coached the team, the kid got lots of ice time. I don't know what she gave him when he missed the open net, but he was as tense an urchin as you're ever likely to meet. One night, a goalie allowed eight goals in one period. He wept in the dressing room. No one consoled him. No one would even talk to him. I wondered if anyone would talk to his mother.

Though teams from other communities played against the locals, the town itself had only two teams, and as everyone and his dog well knew, the coaches had hated each other's guts for years. During games between the town teams, the rink's mood was therefore nasty but zesty. Both coaches were poor winners. They were gloating needlers, and the boys played their hearts out to save those fat, steaming, puffy-cheeked and red-faced middle-aged men from the violent humiliation of defeat. Such games were "a learning experience." You see, company presidents sometimes hate other company presidents, and it's just as well that the little fellows learn about such unpleasantries early on. After all, as someone once said, "The road to the boardroom leads through the locker room."

Others make the same point. Some argue that the reason why women haven't gained their rightful place in the corporate world is that as little girls no one tore them from their dollies and shoved them into team sports. "The traditional boy's games are far from pointless, childish pursuits," Betty Harragan wrote in *Games Mother Never Taught You: Corporate Gamesmanship for Women*. "They are training grounds for life, preparation for adult imperatives of working with others, practical education for the discipline of business.... Baseball, football, and basketball are all team sports, and a structured, organized team is a well-defined social unit.... Each player knows exactly what his duties are and how they dovetail into operations of the rest of the team...and each player knows that he has to perform smoothly and cooperatively with the others if he wants to retain his place on the team."

Fathers, when they face the fact that junior will never be a Gretzky, recognize that team sports do teach boys useful business attitudes. Gai Ingham Berlage of Iona College, New Rochelle, N.Y., described a recent survey of 222 fathers of boy hockey players and soccer players in Connecticut and New York. Most fathers thought the most important values that hockey and soccer taught their boys were teamwork and self-discipline. Now hear Michael Maccoby, author of *The Gamesman: The New Corporate Leaders*. He describes "the new corporate top executive" as "a team player whose centre is the corporation. . . . Thus he thinks in terms of what is good for the company, hardly separating that from what is good for himself. . . . He has succeeded in submerging his ego and gaining strength from this exercise in self-control." More-over, he's the organizer of a team, and, like any good coach, he's not interested in stars, prima donnas, locker-room loud-mouths or guys who think they're so good they can skip practice. What he wants is total dedication from everyone on the team. If you can't give that, you're out on your ear.

An eight-year-old, first-string player for a hockey team that travels already has much in common with, say, the 45-year-old marketing chief of an outfit that manufactures inter-nationally known photocopying machines. As company obligations dominate the man's life, hockey obligations domi-nate the boy's. Wives and children know daddy's job comes first, and must inevitably clash with dinner hours, vacations and other family pursuits. But in the Berlage survey, 80 percent of the *fathers* said their *boy's* hockey career messed up dinner hours, 44 percent said it disrupted vacations, 72 percent said it threw family activities out of gear, and 28 percent said it even interfered with the kid's schooling.

Why do parents put up with this? "The reasons," Berlage states, "are similar to why company men let the corporation interfere with their family life. . . . As social prestige for the father revolves around his work, for the child social prestige at school and in the community often is a product of his sports participation. As families bask in the reflected status of the corporate husband, parents bask in the reflected status of having an athletic son." Moreover, as the boss calls the shots not only for the marketing manager but also, to some extent, for his family, so the coach calls the shots not only for the eight-year-old but also, to some extent, for the boy's family. Parents plan family trips to accommodate their little left-winger's schedule. Among all 222 hockey and soccer fathers, Berlage reported, "No one expressed the idea that family trips, even at Thanksgiving or Christmas, took precedence over travel games."

If parents refuse to arrange their lives to suit the coach, there are always more cooperative parents waiting in line. In hockey, as in business, there's always another boy on the way up. No one is indispensable. Bosses fire fractious adults. Coaches fire fractious tykes. Those who work for bosses or coaches quickly learn to obey commands or get out.

A sad sidelight on kid hockey as a prep school for corporate life is that it teaches children that winning justifies cheating, if you can get away with it. In organized sports for the young, sociologists Lewis Yablonsky and Jonathan Brower argue, it's now okay to use "all 'reasonable' tactics to win. Getting away with undetected rule infractions...and taking advantage of an umpire or referee's mistakes has become institutionalized as 'all part of the game.'" Some day these pint-size sharpies on skates may be able to arrange secret price-fixing deals, collaborate on rigging construction bids or bribe politicians. It'll make the bribing go especially smoothly if the politicians, too, are graduates of boys' hockey teams, where they first absorbed the fine old lessons about teamwork, obedience, sacrifice, dedication to a corporate cause and spearing a guy when the ref's not looking.

Finally, Berlage's report on the New York and Connecticut fathers revealed that "favoritism sometimes exists, whether it be for the coach's child or that of a large contributor.... The expression, 'It's not what you know, but who you know,' although not the case most of the time, has some basis in reality." The boys, in short, were already learning a bitter truth of corporate life: The best man does not always get the job. One father told an interviewer, "We think that instead of providing a focus for development and happiness during the important years between eight and twelve, youth hockey quickly becomes a harbinger of events that probably would occur in adult life." Actually, most kid hockey players start at six or seven. Too bad their childhood couldn't last a bit longer. But what the hell, it's a tough old world out there, and they might as well learn to pitch in like everyone else. After all, as no less a figure than ex-president Gerald Ford has said, "Few things are more important to a country's growth and well-being than competitive athletics." Shoot that puck, kid. Grab that briefcase.

Quest, October 1982

"*Here, Pussy, Pussy, Pussy!*"

His real name is Chedabucto, but when he bothers to answer at all he answers to "pussy." He was born 14 years ago in southern Ontario, and by heritage should be an Upper Canadian Tory. He is, in fact, an independent killer. While a kitten, he slaughtered a pigeon his own size, dumped it on our doorstep as an offering. His toll of birds and mice is unknown. I've caught him having a rare, old time with a dying garter snake in his claws. I saw him drag a baby rabbit under our cottage to kill it in his own good time, and I once found a tiny pair of bunny's ears in the nearby grass. I knew where the rest of him had gone. On the advice of vets, we've often fed Vaseline to our darling pussy so the bones of his little victims would pass through his system without tearing his insides.

Now that he's old, he sometimes traps a live mouse in his

mouth, stands outside our bedroom door at 3 a.m. with the creature's tail switching among his whiskers, and tries to meow without losing his prize. The noise is weird, both beseeching and sinister. My wife jumps up, grabs cat and mouse, rushes the package downstairs, fumbles with the latch on the front door while praying that the cat will not drop the mouse on her bare feet, then dumps the whole cargo outdoors. By 4 a.m., she's downstairs again, begging "poor pussy" to come in from the cruel night to the safety of our warm home. I'm not very good with animals.

We recently thought he was dying but a vet diagnosed him as being allergic to his own fleas, and prescribed medicine that restored him to such health that he resumed all his cute little habits: shedding, scratching, vomiting throughout the house. "Do you have a pet?" a doctor asked while examining an itchy red spot on my right biceps. "A cat," I replied. "Ringworm," he snapped. "I'll prescribe a cream." It cost me $9.50 for a thimbleful. Still, in the eyes of my wife and daughter, Chedabucto can never, ever, do serious wrong. He is too beautiful. They suffer from an incurable condition that's more common among women than men: cat addiction.

Like victims of other personality disorders, cat addicts frequently pass unnoticed among normal people. You have doubtless stood in line-ups at banks, supermarkets and theatres without once suspecting that the woman behind you— so close you could feel her feverish breath on your neck—was in truth an incorrigible cat-lover. Such people can answer the phone, make rational conversation, drive cars, even hold down a responsible job. Their workmates seldom recognize their condition because cat addicts are masters at faking normalcy.

But no victim of this affliction, which is peculiarly virulent among the more affluent, industrialized nations, can hide her craving indefinitely from her husband. Sooner or later, while they're strolling near garbage cans, she'll spot a grey kitten scampering on white paws that remind her of "adorable little spats." Or maybe the creature that triggers the woman's ecstatic hysteria is a pulsating blob of orange fur with nasty yellow eyes. But whatever the style of cat, the addict swiftly abases herself in public. Smirking strangers witness her strange performance. She assumes an ingratiating pose and, in high-pitched, squeaky, inhuman patter, actually tries to communicate with the beast. She is on a cat "high," and for a while no power on earth can bring her back down.

She pays the brute absurd compliments, interrogates it, caresses it, gets it slithering round her calves. "Ooooh, you're so friendly. What's your name? How are you today anyway? How've you been? Just fine? That's good. Ooooh, what a baby. Yes, you're very handsome. Yes, yes, you're very pretty, you really are. I'd like to take you home. Would you like that? You would? Awww. Isn't that sweet?" In extreme cases, the addict demands that her husband also converse with the cat. "Nice pussy," he mumbles, hoping no one he knows has heard.

Before proposing to a woman, a prudent man finds out about her religion, family, home town, economic status, job prospects and previous husbands; but if he's like the Newfoundlander who told me, "I hates cats," then he'd also be well-advised to determine if she's a cat addict. Here's a simple, pre-marital test: Sit her down before a TV show sponsored by a cat-food manufacturer. When fluffy pussies march in squads, play the piano, dance the can-can, or otherwise strut their stuff on the commercial, does your beloved switch channels? If so, feel free to pop the question. But if her eyes gleam unnaturally and she emits simpering vowel sounds, if she asks you to guess which pussy she's chosen as the absolutely darlingest of them all, then get rid of her. Just tell her you've been meaning to surprise her with the news that you've got the friskiest old Doberman in a compound out back, and that as long as you keep him chained and muzzled, why, he'll be cuter than any cat a girl could ever want to stroke.

Only rarely does a man such as myself come along, one who loves a woman with so monumental a passion that, *even though he already knows she's a cat addict*, he proposes to her. Such commitment, surely, is as inspiring as a death scene

123

in Wagnerian opera, and yet it is not more touching than the battle for cat custody that a Toronto couple recently carried all the way to the Supreme Court of Ontario. In this rare case, the man, too, was a cat addict. To spare the principals the further pain of publicity, let us call him Roger, the woman Alice, and their two cats Mutt and Jeff.

The cats were brothers, and inseparable. But Roger and Alice, a childless couple, were not at all inseparable. They separated. Each one wanted both cats. They hired lawyers, went to court. An interim court order gave them shared custody. Roger got Mutt and Jeff for a while, then Alice got them, then Roger again, and so on. This routine was heart-breaking for both Roger and Alice, and no one could get straight answers from Mutt and Jeff about the harm that a severely unstable home life might be doing to their psyches. Was Alice teaching them to hate Roger? Was Roger filling them with poison about Alice? Roger declared his "need" for Mutt and Jeff, but did they need him? Did Alice want them for her own sake, or for theirs? When a marriage collapses, why must it always be the little ones who suffer most? One could only thank providence that, throughout this ordeal, Mutt and Jeff at least had each other. (Marriage break-up is such a traumatic experience for "the only cat.")

Surely it behooves the court to consider what's best for the future well-being and psychological health of Mutt and Jeff. They're only three-and-a-half years old. They have their whole lives ahead of them. If King Solomon could make a shrewd ruling in a similar situation nearly 3,000 years ago, I'm sure the Supreme Court of Ontario will do the right thing by Mutt and Jeff. Meanwhile, the case stands as further proof that cat addiction, if left uncontrolled, can turn normal human beings into creatures who do strange things whenever the moon is full and something's yowling on the back fence.

Atlantic Insight, June 1984

What Part Are You Playing Now, Eric House?

No magazine man who sets out to write a story about someone else ever knows quite what he's getting from his victim. The victim considers the penetrating questions. Perhaps they are odiously familiar questions. He sees the magazine man nod his sly encouragements: *Yes, I think you're dead right there, that's extremely interesting, what an odd coincidence that you should say that, yes in my business too, and you know I never thought of it that way before but of course you couldn't be more right, and don't you think that...?* The victim is not fooled. The enemy ballpoint moves across the notebook that's beyond his vision, and he thinks before he answers. He works on his phrasing. He decides how little of himself he wants the magazine man to have. He must impress in order to bare little. He *performs*. They all do it a bit. Politicians, businessmen, cops, doctors, athletes, clergymen, housewives, pensioners, even kids...they listen to the question, observe the notebook and, when they speak, maybe they move their hands more than they do when they're talking to people they like.

The acting always gets in the way of the magazine man's rightful pursuit of the Truth in a Personality. He tries to see through it. But what is he to do when the Personality is no mere politician, businessman, athlete or housewife but, rather, someone who really *knows* how to act? What if the Personality is someone who has spent almost a quarter of a century as a professional actor; someone who may just be intensely sensitive to the ways magazine publicity can shape his public image; someone who knows in his devious heart that few things in life are finer than tricking strangers into believing that one is other than the man one really is; someone who is shrewd and magical? Eric House is in town today, magazine man. See if you can corner him for an hour or two and find out what sort of bloke he is. Let's reveal the *real* Eric House. Okay? Right.

It is a rich, blowing, blue-and-golden August morning in Halifax, and already, there's an old, disturbing autumnal snap in the air. House has been playing at the Neptune—in *What the Butler Saw* and *The Miser*—for most of the summer, but the season is about to close and pretty soon he'll be back home in Toronto. Before this summer, he had never played in Halifax. The nice thing had happened here, too. Strangers recognized him. They stopped him on the street, as they've done in Vancouver, Winnipeg, Ottawa, Charlottetown and a lot of smaller burgs, and they said, "I know you, how do you do, you're Eric House, aren't you? I saw you in something on the CBC." That is a great thing, *to be known as a Canadian actor*.

"It's a great life in some ways," he says. "It's marvellous to be able to travel all across Canada, to be offered work all over the country, to get to know Canada, to feel you're part of Canada." Being recognized does not merely please the ego; it makes House feel he belongs in this country.

It is hard not to believe that Eric House deeply means what he says, but then surely all skilled actors bring great conviction to whatever roles they're playing. Already, House has been kind enough to warn the magazine man about actors. "A good enough artist can say, 'Let's pretend that I'm a star actor,'" he said. "He can *pretend* he's good at what he does, and you believe it." Instead of playing the part, the actor plays the part of a star playing the part, and you go home wondering what it was about this marvellous production that left you a bit dissatisfied. A long time later it may occur to you that the flaw lay in that fellow's acting. It was bad. The good he was trying to do himself hurt everything else. House, in the interview hurts no one; but the thought lurks there in the suspicious head of the magazine man: what House is *this* anyway?

He appears to be a soft-spoken, intelligent, concerned, sensitive, thoughtful, generous, humorous and serious middle-aged single man. The press has referred in the past to his "appealing wistfulness" and his "talent for under-playing." Does he carry modesty to a fault? On the phone, he kept asking, "What's the angle?" As though he were part of a cheesy newspaper drama. What's the angle? House worried about it. Surely it must be derogatory. What have I to say? What's the angle?

As though it were not angle enough that, ever since before the Korean War, he has been performing Shakespeare, Gilbert and Sullivan, Leacock, musical drama, comic acting, song-and-dance, clowning, tragedy, Canadiana, historical skits, parodies, everything from *Charley's Aunt* to Jean Genet's *The Balcony*, everything from *Hands Across the Sea* to *Murder in the Cathedral* to the c.n.e. *Grandstand Show*. As though it were not enough that he has performed for the Queen, that he has earned good reviews in the West End, Broadway, Boston, Washington, Edinburgh, Chichester, Los Angeles, Expo 67. As though it were not enough that he has played in more radio drama than anyone can remember, that he has appeared in nearly 300 different theatrical productions on literally thousands of the nights of his life, that he has played in more than fifty major CBC television productions for literally millions of viewers. House has been in movies, as well. He's directed revues and plays in Canada and the States. Except for ballet, grand opera, and the night-club circuit, he's done it all. Still, he says, I hope we can find an *angle* for you. It is an apparently naive and truly becoming concern.

Eric House has played Uncle Harry and Uncle Willie. Back in the 1950s, he played the father of his good old friend Ted Follows so often it became a favorite joke of theirs. He has played cops, Cockneys and Ko-Ko, Mergenthwirker, Morgenthau and Morgan. He has played Snobby Price and Archie Rice. He has played Joe Gargery and William Lyon Mackenzie, the Prince of Aragon and the King of Eldorado. He has played Casca, Iago, Fluellan and Milton Cross, Scoop Davis, Brother Orchid, Kid Conner and Papa Barrett. He has been soldiers, sailors, generals, admirals, headmasters, mur-derers, judges, convicts, cooks, mayors, professors, psychiatrists, photographers, producers, barbers, dancing masters, intruders, clergymen, wizards, and a lot of drunks. He has been Peter, George, Fred, Clark, Jake, Reggie, David, Oscar, Emmett, Hubert, Herbert and Augustus. And a hundred more ordinary and amazing people as well.

But who is he today? Is he, by any chance, The Great Canadian Journeyman Actor who has, in a most gracious and totally likable way, agreed to be interviewed by the local representative of a small national magazine in the middle of a magnificent day in a port on the Atlantic Ocean? The magazine man must dismiss the thought. It is childish. How absurd to assume that an actor performs during every second that he is not alone!

Eric House was staying on the twelfth floor of Fenwick Towers, a high-rise apartment house that Dalhousie University bought as a student residence when the building's financing collapsed just before the developers had finished construction. Canadian actors, as they move about the country, do not stay in the best hotel in town. This was a pretty good spot. A couple of men students came in regularly to clean the apartment.

House opened the door. His face was more theatrical, stronger than it was supposed to be. Why was the magazine man expecting a mousier person? House's eyes reminded him of someone else's. They were large and dark. The eyebrows, too, were large and dark, and so was the moustache. Could someone look like Adolphe Menjou and Zachary Scott at the same time? Probably not. The magazine man had seen House's recent and terrific performance in *What the Butler Saw* and had simply assumed the moustache was a fake. House was wearing sandals, olive slacks, a bulky navy-blue sweater with a thick knit. He was supposed to be smaller than this, too. Old press reports had suggested House had become an actor partly as compensation for his tiny physique and that, even as an adult, he'd resented the word "little." Now, however, he appeared not so much small as neat. Contained.

He was forty-nine or fifty. He'd seen more of the country

128

than any governor general had. Some years, he was home in Toronto only a few weeks. He travelled the way professional athletes travel, but not among busloads and planeloads of team-mates. More like a ski-bum, or a tournament golfer. Usually he was alone in his car. Ted had married. Ted Follows had a house, a wife, a bunch of kids. House had not married, it was 11:10 a.m., he fixed his breakfast in a glass. A couple of eggs in Ovaltine. His doctor had said that, since he insisted on skipping real breakfasts, this would do. At least he'd get his protein. He had a lot of pills with him, white, pink, orange vitamin capsules. He'd been feeling a bit funny lately, and wondered if maybe it wasn't possible to take in too many vitamins.

Some things are too personal to talk about with a magazine man. To marry or not to marry, to stay in Canada or not to stay in Canada, the money one earns, the money one does not earn, maybe an ambition that's too precious to defile with casual revelation. No, there was no specific and supreme role that he yearned to play. Yes, those fantastic and perfect and indescribable moments of magical union between audience and players occur only a few times in an actor's lifetime, but let's not spoil them with analysis. Could we talk then about immediates? Sure. An agent had offered him a part in a Broadway musical, a terrible musical but a very good supporting part, and he had not yet bothered to reply.

"I'd go to New York if I thought it would *lead* to something, to bigger parts, to a great part where I could really *do* something, or a lot of money. But this is just a good part, it's something I could do, sure, but it's not worth going to New York for. The damn musical may be a great success but *I don't want to live in New York! I don't want to live in New York just to work!* This happens all the time. They, of course, think every actor wants to work in New York. I think they're a bit shocked to learn that you'd rather make less money working in regional theatre in Canada. They probably put you down as a peasant or something....

"I used to think that one thing led to another. You know, that you *build* a career. But Broadway, parts in Hollywood

129

movies, things like that, they don't necessarily *lead* to anything any more. I just don't feel relaxed in the States. I don't care to put myself under that additional pressure to be on guard all the time. In 1971, I had a marvellous supporting part in Washington, in *The Ruling Class*. You know, it was like a military campaign to go home from the theatre. Every step in the parking lot. It's all everybody talks about at cocktail parties. What happened to you today in the way of violence? Who do you know who's been assaulted lately? Where on earth did you park your car? That sort of thing. . . .

"You know, getting a part in the States used to lead to more respect in Canada. You had only to say you'd played in London or New York. That doesn't work so much any more. Directors, theatres in Canada are more confident now, a lot more sophisticated. There's new experience and knowledge here. They've seen some of New York's theatre standards, and they just aren't all that high. If some New York productions came here, I think people would walk out on them. And there's good and bad in the West End. The batting average for Canadian regional theatre may be as good as any in the world. . . ."

Is all this not a healthy sign then? We hear a lot these days about the growing audiences for live theatre in Canada, the boom in the writing of Canadian plays, the birth of vigorous new theatres all across the land. But is it not a possibility that the real evidence of a maturing Canadian theatre lies in this intangible, this new willingness to coldly assess those who come to us from what we once thought were the Big Leagues?

"Yes, but it's all of us in the theatre, we're *still* the last stronghold of the old attitude!" House got up and began to walk, as though he could not express strong feelings unless he were pacing somebody's boards. "It's us, the actors, the producers, the directors, all the people in the theatre, we're the greatest con artists on earth, we con ourselves, we're the ones who refuse to believe in ourselves. We're the ones that, too often, approach the theatre as if to say, you know, 'I'm only learning, I'm just a Canadian, I'm getting there.' Instead of saying, 'I'm there!' Instead of that swagger. I don't mean an artificial swagger. It's more than confidence. It's assuming you're *there*."

You yourself appear to make that assumption, Mr. House.

"I try to. In some plays, most of the time."

The others seemed to come easily to his mind. The old gang. They'd all been green and young together, and bright as hell. "They were all people who could be found any night in Diana Sweets or Chez Paris." Most of them graduated from the University of Toronto in 1949 and 1950. Most were academically superior in such subjects as psychology, English literature, philosophy, political science, art and archaeology. A lot, including House, got training and inspiration from Robert Gill at the Hart House Theatre; and all of them, in one way or another, ended up selling their souls not to psychology or political science or whatever it was they'd studied formally but, rather, to the theatre. Donald and Murray Davis, Ted Follows, Dave Gardner, George McCowan, William Hutt, John Howe, Chris Taylor, Henry Kaplan, Barbara Hamilton, Kate Reid, Araby Lockhart, Anna Cameron. House had served four years with the RCAF. He was a bit older than the rest.

In the summers of the late 1940s, House and some of these friends formed the Straw Hat Players in the Muskoka resort district of Ontario, and during 1951 and half of 1952, he revelled in what he still calls his "baptism of fire" at the Canadian Repertory Theatre in Ottawa. The old CRT operated on a grinding schedule. It produced a different play every week from September right through till May. With the CRT, the Straw Hat Players, and a winter season in Bermuda, House appeared in nearly seventy plays in the space of two years. Just as television arrived in Canada, and just at the moment the Stratford Festival was born and Toronto's Crest Theatre was preparing its first winter season, Eric House was ready. He was already an accomplished actor. His passion for acting and his talent conspired with the new opportunities, in the happy way that circumstances sometimes do for people,

131

and the 1950s were a good young time.

"I just wanted to act. I did it because I loved it. I think it's tougher for the kids now. They've all got to go through theatre schools. I've always been sort of a dilettante in the theatre. I enjoy myself in theatre. I go from one part to another, really spreading it around, instead of doing one thing. I've had a lot of fun. I wanted to try it all, and I *have* done."

He had always loved his work, and that was more than most middle-aged men could say. And yet, to the magazine man (who was admittedly as fallible in his perception as any audience) there was still a bewilderment in House about where things were leading him. House could not forget the triumphs of the others. McCowan was now a Hollywood producer. Kaplan had made it in television and film production. Kate Reid was not only a famous actress, she must also have made a killing out of "Jalna." And Hutt. He'd known Bill since they were kids together at North Toronto Collegiate. House and Hutt. Tyrone Guthrie had called them "two very good residences." Now, Bill seemed destined for further glory at Stratford. The old gang. "I'm the only one that... well, just look at the successes in there. But there I go with the loser bit again...."

What do you mean?

He did not want to complain. You remember, there was the matter of the actor who acts as a Star acts. Well, there's often a similar and more defensible process at work off the stage as well. Stars do not publicly mope about how little money they're earning. It damages the image, and in House's business, the image is no joke. If we must talk about it, it is better to generalize.

The magazine man gathered from what House was saying that since Canadian television drama had abandoned shooting live productions, since everything was now on film the technicians and the cameras had come to overwhelm the actors' performances. Actors no longer mattered to the total production as much as they once had, and their declining significance reflected itself in declining pay. Many competent actors were therefore returning to the legitimate stage, to the regional theatres, where the pay was not so hot either.

This contributed to a depressing situation for the middle-aged actor. There seemed to be a kind of plateau, a permanent level of income, and it was somewhere near a good schoolteacher's salary, or maybe an army officer's pay. But the teacher and the lieutenant-colonel each had fat pensions and retirement funds waiting for them. The middle-aged actor was in something the same sort of spot as a tired old pro-hockey player in the early 1950s. You play as long as you can, you hustle endlessly about the country, just to earn enough to keep you going. And then what?

The magazine man was drawing his own conclusion but it seemed to confirm an odd habit of ambivalence in House's thought. House liked to see Canada and to let Canada see him, he liked travelling. But he was sick of travelling. He wished there were year-round employment in Toronto. He wanted to stay home in the high-rise apartment in the district where he'd grown up. House had a kind of envy without rancor for old friends who were doing well; he came close to suggesting that, by comparison, he was a failure. And yet, "I like to think I can stand up to English-speaking actors anywhere in the English-speaking world." (And he can.) House says he has no regrets, but his face wonders about the other routes he might have taken.

The magazine man had forgotten his suspicions. They were not important. Eric House was a middle-aged man who was worrying about money, wondering about the meaning of his career, considering the content of what was left of his life. Or he was merely a brilliant middle-aged actor who was playing the part of a middle-aged man who was worrying about money, wondering about the meaning of his career, considering the content of what was left of his life. That was no longer conceivable, but in any event, it didn't matter. Either way, the lesson was clear. The magazine man, too, would be there soon. Any day now.

Saturday Night, November 1972

133

Down the Drain with Hopeless Inc.

Hopeless Inc., the only outfit that's ever offered me a directorship, was a small, doomed firm with an embarrassingly high profile, and when our lawyer told the board to consider "factoring our receivables," I pretended I actually knew what he meant. "Good idea," I harrumphed, "but before making a move like that we'd better consider the pros and cons." Later, I consulted *A Dictionary of Canadian Economics* and discovered that a factor is "a financial institution that takes over the accounts receivable of a firm, at a discount, and collects the money owing." So that was it. A collection agency. Next time, I'd know.

That was my style on the Hopeless board. Mostly I kept my mouth shut, but I'd occasionally say something to hide the fact that it would be easier for me to master Sanskrit than interpret a financial report, become "a good man with a balance sheet" or, indeed, extract even a grain of meaning from the reams of numbers in the monthly reports and projections.

All I knew was that more dollars were leaving Hopeless than were coming in and that some of my desperate fellow directors represented outfits that were picking up the difference. In business parlance, these other companies and a bank or two were "taking a bath." The directors included the lawyer, a bank executive, two advertising men and a whiz accountant from a major supplier.

We were not happy people. We met in a small smoke-filled boardroom and twitched in a mist of gloom. On fragrant summer days when the sailing breeze was seductive, we were as miserable as children who'd been ordered back to school in August. We were a gallery of furrowed brows in a foundering executive suite.

The meetings all had the same unwritten agenda: grim agreement that Hopeless was becoming more hopeless; grim interrogation about where its revenue was going; grim analysis of "the cash-flow problem"; grim decisions about what debts to pay off and what debts to risk putting off; grim suggestions about "financial restructuring"; and, finally, grim reports about the sudden cooling of potential investors. We'd dreamed they'd come galloping over the horizon, with bugles blaring and millions in their saddlebags, to rescue the virtuous Hopeless and make it forever "viable." But a time always came, just as we appeared to have sold investors "a package," when they sounded a retreat. It became hard to reach them then, even by phone.

Board meetings ended with unanimous agreement that, barring a miracle, someone would "pull the plug." I heard that horrid prediction so often I imagined a monster who'd cackle fiendishly and pull the plug while we were still sitting in that same fetid room with the black-and-yellow plaid carpet, and suddenly we'd all be thrashing about in a huge whirlpool, waving our tiny arms and screaming "cash-flow problems" and "restructuring package" and "factor the receivables."

Something like that finally did happen to Hopeless. It went into receivership, and I haven't been on a board since. But strange to say, I actually miss that secret brotherhood of despair. I miss the sense of conspiracy. As a journalist, I try to worm information out of people and curse those who hide it. As a director, I finally understood why business people are close-mouthed. Bad news in business is a self-fulfilling prophecy, and spreading the truth about Hopeless would have reduced its already puny resale value and hastened its death.

I also miss the language. When business people make formal speeches, they tend to be boring. Moreover, if a company is successful, its directors' meetings may be satisfying, but dull. It took looming disaster, the hand on the plug, to inspire the expletives, metaphors and appropriate clichés that gave the Hopeless board meetings such spice. We had one woman director, and she knew she'd finally been accepted as an equal when our most imaginative master of cursing quit saying, "Excuse me," to her before uttering an obscenity. Excuse me, but it was he who warned us that when two representatives of a Toronto investment group came down to Halifax to investigate Hopeless, they'd "have their arseholes boarded up."

One of our directors described a man from a bank that had loaned Hopeless money as "a dropout from the Attila-the-Hun Charm School." The dropout had attended one meeting to deliver a scathing lecture on our plight and to warn that his people had had enough of Hopeless and would certainly pull the plug. With that, he left. But his bank's loan, unlike the investments of others around the table, was fully secured. So one of our directors broke the ghastly silence that followed the dropout's departure with this superb summary of the situation: "He's messing his pants, but the rest of us are sucking air."

I took notes on stuff like that. I hoped my note-taking suggested to the others that I was conscientiously trying to sort out Hopeless's problem, but I was, in fact, preserving such strange assertions as: "We'll have to have a trigger mechanism that also has some muscle in it.... When things are in the cookin' stage, he's got to come up with some crunch numbers.... We just haven't got enough hoses to put the fires out."

The representative of one creditor warned that if Hopeless passed over his firm while paying off another debt, he'd start to "make noises." The dim possibility that we'd strike "a doable deal" with new investors often raised our hopes. Ah, yes, that would be "the bells-and-whistles part of it." In the end, however, Hopeless yearned to be taken over, even though the buyers we had in mind would "certainly take a whack at where we are." Worse still, they might "just come in to pick the bones."

The doable deal was never done, and the bells and whistles never sounded. A year after Hopeless went under, I returned to the old boardroom. It was now a hair-dressing salon with two chairs and shampoo sinks. The pine furniture was gone. Only the black-and-yellow carpet remained. "I guess a lot of people have been clipped in this room," I said mysteriously as a comely woman clipped my hair. She looked bewildered and explained she'd been there only a few months. I gave her a fat tip. "There you are, my dear," I said. "I hope that improves your cash flow, so you won't have to factor your receivables."

Canadian Business, September 1984

Big News: Bruces Spot Seal

On the eighth day we saw the seal and he was the major news event of the whole fortnight we spent on the coast. We'd wrestled the little yawl across the gravel beach and into the water and now we were three miles out in the cold bay and, down in the east, the open Atlantic surged along under half the sky and, just astern, the seal's head—it was as big as any horse's—appeared and disappeared and kept on appearing again.

We were making four knots, and he followed us for an hour. He was bigger news than the gulls, the hawks, the jellyfish, the clams, the return of the great blue heron, or the story the old storekeeper told us about an even older man, a fellow of 81, who shot a black bear in his farmyard about five years back. The seal was even more sensational news than the map that yet a third old man drew on a piece of cardboard in his garage to show me how to find the Halfway Cove shoal. And the map was a genuine news leak. Even around here, a lot of people can't find that shoal. They do not know its virtues as a place to jig for cod.

I bought a chain saw from the old man at the garage, too,

but in the front page of my mind it's still the seal that gets the dominant headline. "Bruce family spots huge seal." Below that somewhere, I'd play the other stuff: stories about amazing moons, shooting stars, the growth of the woodpile, intrepid voyages to Queensport and Peas Brook, overflowing rain barrels, candlelight and lamp oil, the terror warfare that our black cat conducted against the voles, the storms that wheeled in over Ragged Head, and the nights that the crazy, shifty, moody bay silently turned itself into a black mirror for a hundred square miles.

My sports pages would list the tallies of matchsticks after the nightly poker games, and the attendance figures would always be five. That's how many of us there are, and day after day went by without our ever seeing anyone else. We began to know one another better than we had before. There's no phone up there. There's no radio, no television, no newspaper, no magazines. But I knew there'd been a federal election. At noon on July 9, I walked through the birch and balsam fir to the spot on the dirt road where we'd left the car, turned on the radio and discovered who the Prime Minister of Canada was.

Juan Peron had died, and Dizzy Dean, and Earl Warren. I hadn't known. Phlebitis, doctors said, had threatened Nixon's life in the Middle East, and it had sent General Franco to hospital. Premier Chou En-lai, it turned out, had suffered a heart attack. I hadn't known any of that. And Richard Burton, divorced from Elizabeth Taylor, had arrived in England with a blonde named Ellen. Frank Sinatra and his goons had infuriated a lot of Australians, and how had I possibly survived 14 days of my life without knowing a tittle of these weighty events?

Gold prices had plunged, and bond prices risen. The dollar had declined, and petroleum stocks dipped. Food prices had jumped and the Queen Mother had ended her sixth visit to Canada. Riots in Bangkok, a coup in Ethiopia, a coup in Cyprus. And the grass seed we had sewn in May had become a field of shiny, green fur. Spring had been wet.

Brezhnev had said his talks with Nixon were "weighty

and constructive." Nixon had said his talks with Brezhnev promoted "our goal of a permanent peace for all people." Then, Nixon's U.S. and Brezhnev's Soviet Union had both set off nuclear explosions. So had the United Kingdom. So had France. I had known nothing of any of this. The wild strawberries were impossibly sweet.

When I'd left for the coast, the FBI was searching for Patty Hearst. When I returned, the FBI was searching for Patty Hearst. Polls still showed that news coverage of Watergate irritated the American people. Israel was still insisting the Arabs were preparing more war. Bombs were still going off in Belfast. The Expos were still two games out of first place. Andy Capp was still in the tavern. Mandrake and Lothar were still invisible. Maggy was still mad at Jiggs, and something was still on my mind. It was the seal. I'd like to see him again.

The Toronto Star, July 1974

George

I met George Chuvalo and Irv Ungerman out at Irv's chicken-plucking emporium in west-central Toronto, and at first I thought maybe they're putting me on. Or maybe they think I'm Damon Runyon or something, and they're trying to help me out with my little write-up. Or perhaps those stinky old movies about "the fight game" were not stinky after all but serious art imitating nature.

George is the heavyweight boxing champion of Canada. He is a creamy-skinned youth of 31 with a broad, bony face. His dark hair is neat and generously slick. He does not say "duunnhh" or come out bobbing and jabbing every time the telephone rings, but there is something about the heaviness of his face that makes you think he's glowering all the time. He doesn't say much. Chuvalo can't remember exactly how many pro fights he's been in, but he's sure it's either 66 or 67, and that he's won either 54 or 53 of them, mostly by knockouts. He is famous internationally for having refused to fall down after speedier and more artful pugilists (the speediest and most artful being Muhammad Ali) had pummelled him about the head and shoulders till their hands turned puffy.

And Irv? Irv is George's manager. He's something else, too. It is tempting for writers to dismiss Irv as "Irving Ungerman, the chicken plucker" but so simple and pungent an identification does great injustice to Irv's achievements. He is a veritable Axel Springer of the poultry-packing business in Toronto. He's the president of Royce Dupont Poultry Packers ("Killed on Premises Daily") and he is also the president of Irving Investments Ltd., Robindale Developments Ltd., Apollo Promotions Ltd., and, not surprisingly, Irving Ungerman Ltd. Royce Dupont has its own farms, and distributes no fewer than 1.5 *million* chickens a year to restaurants, supermarkets, hospitals, airlines and just about any other institution that's prepared to go along with the idea that "For Choice Call Royce." Royce Dupont has 51 employees and Irv, when he pleases, can watch many of them on the closed circuit TV screen in his office.

Only the ghost of a smell from all that chicken killing, chicken drawing, chicken plucking and chicken freezing finds its way out to Irv's main lobby. The lobby contains a photograph from a newspaper ad. It shows, left to right, former world's heavyweight champ Rocky Marciano, with his friendly, famous and hammy face; little Irv, clearly happy; and George, who also has a fair grin going for him. Irv is holding a chicken (dead, plucked, ready for the broiler) and Rocky and George have heavy-fisted grips on the legs of the same bird. The chicken appears to be a bantamweight. The caption says, "When you say 'chicken'—smile.... Take a tip from Rocky Marciano and George Chuvalo. Try some of Irv Ungerman's Royce Dupont chicken and you'll smile, too.... Makes you smile, don't it?"

140

Irv is middle-aged, tanned, stubby but not fat, and he's got sideburns. His brown eyes are shrewd and friendly, and on the day I went out to his place, he was both genial and cordial. He was wearing a black, short-sleeved shirt with red and gold trim. He had a big purple ring on his cigar hand, a sparkly silver one on his telephone hand. "You mean," he asked the phone incredulously, "you mean you haven't got a couple hundred light fowl to spare? Yeh, yeh, light fowl, light fowl. I don't care if they're red, black or green...." And then, "Hullo, Teddy? (Teddy is the matchmaker at Madison Square Garden in New York) Yeh, Teddy, look, so who? Mathis! I'm talking George into Ramos. I thought maybe we'd go with a Ramos." Irv frequently uses the indefinite article when he's talking about fighters. He wants, or does not want, *a* Ramos, *a* Mathis, *a* Jerry Quarry, *a* Sonny Liston.

Irv was busy, so I nosed around. He is not the sort to let some pushy, artsy-crafty, interior-decorator type destroy the personality of his office. I mean, you *know* that this is Irv Ungerman's spot, and no one else's. Above the TV screen, which happened to be concentrating on one of Irv's chicken trucks, there were photographs of Rocky and George and Joe Louis, and middleweight champ Nino Benvenuti, and one from Muhammad Ali himself. It was dated November 14, 1966, and the message from Muhammad Ali was "To my dear friend Irving....Keep Chuvalo in shape. We may meet again." There were a lot of fat, silky prize ribbons for Royce Dupont poultry at the Royal Winter Fair; a huge model of a three-masted squarerigger; a metal sculpture of a big, snorting bull; and, all over the joint, little models of poultry, and wall cutouts of wild fowl and flying fish. On one table there was a book entitled *Did Man Get Here by Evolution or Creation?* and, just as I was about to open it to find out, Chuvalo himself got here, by evolution I guess, jaunty and late.

Chuvalo's last big fight was more than a year ago. He was beaten by Joe Frazier, who is now recognized in New York state as the heavyweight champion. The fight had to be stopped because something repulsive had happened to one of

Chuvalo's eyes. The way he explains it, he'd been badly butted in a fight about a month before the Frazier match. The eye kept swelling up in training, and never quite got a chance to heal. The whole eyeball protruded a bit. In this position, it was not properly protected by the brow and cheekbone that nature provides to guard eyeballs from damage. Frazier, I gather, delivered a left hook in the second round that burst a blood vessel, pushed a whole lot of blood in behind the eyeball and thereby forced it out even farther. Then, he whacked at it every chance he got. I imagine that—even by the standards of pain thresholds among professional boxers—it hurts something awful to get punched right on the eyeball. Chuvalo's was punched so hard, or so often, that it dropped right through the "floor" of the facial cage that encloses it.

There was serious doubt whether George would ever fight again and Irv who, to use the sports announcer's imperative, *has* to be one of your Good Guys among fight managers, helped set him up as the host and resident celebrity of a Toronto nightery. Rocky and Joe Louis attended the gala opening in January (I'd long been puzzled by Joe's, and particularly Rocky's, interest in George's welfare. The way Irv explains it, they act as "advisers" and lend a certain stature to the Chuvalo camp. This helps Irv when he's dickering with the big fight people in the States. In return, Irv helps them out financially now and then, and they knew that if Chuvalo had beaten Muhammad Ali, Irv would have taken care of them very nicely indeed. By now, it's quite possible that Joe and Rocky also have a friendly, personal interest in how George is making out. Anyway, the relationship does not really have a great deal to do with chickens.)

Early this summer George won a couple of cheesy fights in western Canada and he is, as they say in *Ring* magazine, on the comeback trail. Ever since George's valiant survival of the night on which Muhammad Ali pounded him almost as though he were sitting there in a chair, fight fans have honored him for his courage, and Irv is quite right—one victory over a highly ranked heavyweight would put George right back in the big money. "We haven't fought in that place since it's the new one," Irv said. He was referring to the new Madison Square Garden. The use of "we" struck me as quaint since George is the only one who gets his eyeballs batted around, but among fight managers, I'm sure it's far from peculiar to Irv. "I'd love to see George in there."

I asked George about the eyeball. He said that if other fighters "try to make the same accident happen again, it's ridiculous. Because it can't. Now there's a piece of plastic, a piece of plastic silicone they call it. It's under the eye to replace the optic floor."

A little later George, too, talked with Teddy at the Garden ("Yuh, I'd like to get something going, I'd like a little action,") and it looked very much as though he, I mean *they*, would get a fight against Jerry Quarry late in September.

That night, I dropped around to George Chuvalo's Ring-side Club, which is upstairs at George Chuvalo's Caravan Club. I had a pretty good filet mignon and some not bad red wine. I watched "two bumptious exotics" take off their clothes and one female impersonator do the things that female impersonators do. (Previous shows have included French Without Dressing and the Burly-Q-Capers.) George came in, a bit later than I suspect Irv would have liked, and he sat near the back of the club. His suit was dark and tight, and there was something about the amount of gleaming cuff he was showing, something about the arrogant and gracefully heavy way that he walked. It had something to do with an old bullfight movie starring Anthony Quinn. He looked bored. There are worse things than the ugly glories of the ring, even if you do have a wife and five kids and a piece of plastic under your eyeball, and maybe one of them is watching a female impersonator every night. I hope George takes a Quarry.

The Star Weekly, August 1968

Rocks of Ages: In Scotland the Noble and Ancient Sport of Curling Endures

When on the rink we take our stand,
Each with a broom-kowe in his hand,
We fix our cramps, our stanes arse-clean,
We bend our knees, and raise our chin...
                    —1805 Scottish poem about curling

He is a clan chief, a ruddy-cheeked Scottish lord who has inherited duties he cannot escape: the duty to buy his many children a proper education; the duty to make his cavernous mansion burglarproof; the duty to maintain it, as his ancestors have done for centuries; the duty to write letters to editors to defend those ancestors against occasional insults in the press; the duty, in a time in which impertinent but powerful tax bureaucrats do not look kindly on the landed gentry, to look after an estate numbering thousands of acres; the duty to preserve a titled family's great past and, at the same time, perform public services to prove the title's value to the present. The duty, too, to entertain as a lord should entertain. Many envy him. They do not understand. Moreover, his roof leaks and his ankle hurts.

Two dozen people attended his Christmas dinner, and now it's Hogmanay. Champagne flows on New Year's Eve. Elm logs crackle in massive fireplaces. Food and wine vanish down 50 gullets. The dancing begins. Intricate, graceful, wild Scottish reels. With brandy, port, red wine, spices and oranges bristling with cloves, he concocts a fragrant, steaming grog and, limping a little, serves it to every guest. It's fine stuff at a fine party. Then he and a Glasgow businessman, both standing straight and jolly, sing a few rousing Scottish songs. After "Auld Lang Syne" the dancing resumes. The young folk stay up all night. A dozen are houseguests. Twenty of us gather for breakfast, and his wife, a countess, again does all the cooking.

His ankle still hurts, but he remains outwardly merry. That, I think, shows considerable class. Since I sometimes suffer gout, I know how sourly one's disposition reacts to any nagging pain in what Fats Waller once called "your pedal extremities." I know what I'd have done if I'd been in milord's shoes. I'd have holed up in the remotest corner of my castle. But a good Scottish lord always holds up his end.

What's bothering him, it seems, is an old war wound. It has chosen Scotland's most festive weekend to start throbbing. He straps a metal brace to his calf, grabs a stave, heads outdoors. I tag along. Huge oaks and mighty beech trees, their mottled trunks wearing a green blush of moss, loom in the mild mist. Curlews screech. Edible pigeons scatter. Rabbits bound for safety. Pheasants cruise his low and beloved hills. But he's not after game today. He doesn't tell me what he's after. He climbs a wire fence, negotiates a soggy field, descends on a clump of willows and sycamores. Within the clump there's a dark, secret pond with a wooded isle.

This place is the pool of his desire. He disappears inside a ramshackle shed constructed of poles, then emerges with a plank. He sets it on the frozen pond, walks out, thumps the ice with his stave, returns to the shed, lights a kerosene lantern, gestures toward a cache of curling stones. They are arse-clean, and there must be 100 of them. "Take your choice," he says. Let the spiel begin.

Now I witness a miracle. It is not on the scale of the raising of Lazarus or the parting of the Red Sea, but it is an impressive little miracle all the same: the Curing of the Ankle. He takes a small wooden "tramp," a launching platform for curlers, and he sets it on the ice near the shed. Then he paces out a couple of hundred feet and places another launching pad at the far end of what he has now defined as a curling rink. As he paces, his limp vanishes. His stride is pure. He

145

turns. With his face full of controlled ecstasy, with his broom as a target, he bids me deliver a stone.

I have never lifted a curling stone in my entire life (since I'm a middle-aged Canadian male, he finds this fact incomprehensible), but despite my sensationally awkward style I manage to hurl that blob of granite, which weighs 40-odd pounds, to within a few feet of his broom. In 1715 a Scottish poet wrote, "In time now when the curling stane/Slides murmuring o'er the icy plain," but my particular stane neither slides nor murmurs. It bounces, clatters, leaves an ugly wake of white dints in the black ice. It stops just a bit short. "Eat more porridge, boy," milord rejoices.

His children and their friends join us, two dozen youngsters in all. The stones zoom over the ice. Here in the cold air over the pond in the dale, the sound of their clunking together mingles with the chime of jokes, laughter and the glad roars of a Scottish lord whose ankle has mysteriously stopped aching. His spotted bird dogs giddily skid round the action. The wind blows soft and clean. Cheeks redden. Trees sigh. Birds call. The day wears on, and at last I have an inkling about the charms of this weird sport.

The lord and his lady tell me later that impromptu curling sessions are their favorite winter amusement. I say, "impromptu" because their playing is entirely dependent on the natural formation of ice, the precious ice. Historically, the sudden formation of a sheet of curling ice was so important to Scots that they cancelled all mere work to enable parish to fight parish in joyous bouts of "the roarin' game." If the ice was right, clubs fined members for failing to show for a match. A typical 19th-century club ruled that any member was "bound to attend and play, except he can give a satisfactory excuse that attendance will be to the hurt of himself or family."

Ice was God's gift, and never to be disdained. After a long frost in 1841, the secretary of the Kilmarnock club wrote, "All are frozen out, or at least *out* all must go, out of respect to their much beloved and Illustrious visitor, Ice. Ice is all the cry. Indeed, to presume to be Buzy just now would argue one's ignorance of society. Every Idea of Business is totally frozen, the Curling alone excepted."

So far as the birth of curling in Scotland goes, the printed evidence peters out in the 1500s. In his 1890 *History of Curling*, the Reverend John Kerr concluded, "We leave the origin of curling where we have to leave other origins, in the mist and haze of an unknowable antiquity." We do know, however, that by the early 1600s, the game was already a seasonal epidemic in the Lowlands, and that it soon inspired poets to celebrate its joys in lusty verse. "It cleares the Brains, stirrs up the Native Heat / And gives a gallant appetite for Meat.... From ice with pleasure he can brush the snow / And run rejoicing with his curling throw."

Curling poets continued to churn out such zesty stuff right into the 20th century. (I found a lot of it in *Curling: An Illustrated History*, by David B. Smith, a Scottish sheriff who's so nuts about curling he researched his book for 15 years.) But the point about the verse, no matter what its century, is the exuberance with which it invariably glorifies not only the sheer joy of simply being alive in frosty weather but also a brotherhood that momentarily demolishes class distinctions. "How amiable, here, to see / All ranks dissolve in social glee."

Curling brings out the peasant with snot frozen to his sleeve, which is therefore "glaz'd with blue-brown ice"; but "Even titled Grandeur flings aside / The stiffness of Baronial pride." My friend did just that, whilst also flinging aside the pain in his ankle. He is not really "aged," but I thought of him again when I read some curling lines written in 1809: "Aged men, / Smit with the eagerness of youth, are there, / While love of conquest lights their beamless eyes, / New-nerves their arms, and makes them young once more."

A curling poem usually ended just where a day's curling ended: in a warm pub. "The bonspiel o'er, hungry and cold, / They hie to the next ale-house." They convened "o'er a bowl of nect'rous juice," ate beef and greens, remembered brilliant shots, raised their glasses to one another. May the hinges of friendship never rust. The game, the weather, the camarade-

147

rie, the rituals of friendship—these were what counted forever. The fact of who actually won the match counted only for a moment, and even then not for much. These priorities, I gather, are still in order on a few outdoor rinks in Scotland.

When the ice is right, the lord and lady of my acquaintance take a cauldron of thick soup and some good grog over to their pond. If night has fallen, which it does as early as 3:30 p.m. during Scottish winters, they switch on a string of lights. They use a handy spike to scratch out the target rings that form the two "houses." Word has spread. Neighbors and villagers magically materialize in the mist, go to the shed, carry their favorite stones down to the ice.

> Then to the loch the curlers, hie,
> Their hearts as light's a feather,
> And mark the tee wi' mirth and glee,
> In cauld, cauld, frosty weather.

Older Scots lament the long death of outdoor curling. They acknowledge Canada's mastery of the sport, the superiority of Canada's curling palaces, the role Canada has played in turning the game into a big-time, televised, International Event. When the Air Canada Silver Broom occurred in Moncton two years ago, Roma Senn said in *Atlantic Insight*, "For a sport that columnist Allan Fotheringham calls 'lawn bowling in slow motion,' curling has put Canada on the international map almost as much as hockey." Sponsors, flacks, airlines, batteries of press, hotels, all manner of deals, they're all part of the new curling; and despite the notorious conviviality of major bonspiels, it's winning that matters more than anything else now. Scots recognize all this as inevitable, and because it promotes interest in the game among youngsters, maybe even good. Still, some regret the withering of the game's soul.

A gang of so-so curlers from New Zealand arrived in Scotland in 1973. They'd never played indoors. They'd never played on artificial ice. "At a time when many Scottish curlers were getting worried at what they saw as the commercialization of curling because of Canadian influences...the attitude of the New Zealand curlers was an inspiration," David B.

Smith wrote in his history of the game. "To some of us who had the good fortune to play against them, the experience was like a breath from the past. They personified the simple virtues of friendship and brotherhood, both on and off the ice, which we had been brought up to believe were the hallmarks of curling, but which . . . seemed threatened by the win-at-all-costs philosophy which tough competition and big prizes engender."

"Why don't more Canadians curl outdoors?" the lord asked, just before I left his estate. "It's so much more fun, you know, and you have a veritable infinity of natural ice over there." In a world of suffocating artificiality, he could not understand why we passed up such a fabulous chance to revel in natural freedom. I could not enlighten him. I only knew that although I wouldn't walk round the corner to witness the Silver Broom, his kind of curling was glorious. I remember him out on his own ice with the kids on New Year's Day in the morning, and I think of two sentences by an American philosopher. "Do you know what a holiday is?" Sebastian de Grazia asked. "A day to dance in."

Quest, May 1982

Rugger Ranking: Mount Allison's Once and Future Glory Days

To avoid the indignities of initiation at Mount Allison University in Sackville, N.B., I joined the rugger squad. The team commanded such awe on that intimate campus that just turning out for practice granted me immunity from the humiliations sadistic sophomores inflicted on freshmen and "freshettes." (First-year students are doubtless "freshpersons" now, but let's not get into that.) There were other perks. Filthy, smelly and occasionally a bit bloody after practice, players barged in at the head of the supper line-up in the men's cafeteria. This was their ancient right as heroes. They sat at their own table, like the more honored guests at a banquet, made twice as much noise as everyone else and got twice as much milk.

But it is ludicrous to use the word "banquet" in the context of those old-time Mount Allison meals. A player once found his glutinous pork and beans so disgusting that he turned the plate upside down and marched it back to the kitchen. Not a bean dropped. At Mount Allison in the mid-Fifties that was a daring act of student protest. Before week-end dances, which the administration rightly suspected increased the campus horniness factor, hundreds of dishes of applesauce remained untouched. Saltpetre, don't you know?

I was built like a stork's leg. I weighed 132 pounds and quit rugger after one week. It was a blond, bony pre-med student, now a Halifax physician, who helped me make up my mind. He had a jaw like Fearless Fosdick's, shoulders like Steve Reeves's and knees like a blacksmith's hammer. He ran like Jim Brown, and during one of the games in which the senior varsity habitually beat up the junior varsity, I suddenly found myself horribly alone. He was coming at me with the ball, and I was the last guy between him and the junior varsity goal line. Now, rugger is a masochist's delight. No one wears pads. To avoid getting your nose and collarbone broken you're supposed to approach the enemy ball carrier not from the front but from the side. You jam your cheek against his hairy thigh and squeeze his legs. With Fosdick-face that would have been like dancing with a cement mixer, but I couldn't just stand there and let him go by. I'd be branded as a chicken-shit jerk. So I just fell prostrate at his feet and lay there like a trembling lamb awaiting the knife. He tripped on my torso and down he went.

The coach was mightily pleased with my brilliant, unorthodox defensive move, I can tell you, but the future doctor had clouted my dainty rib cage with his boots. I couldn't breathe comfortably for two weeks, and decided to take my lumps—comparatively gentle lumps—from the mad sophomores. The worst part of the initiation hysteria was over anyway, and I really didn't need all that milk.

As the rugger season continued, head bandages, arm slings and leg casts proliferated among the beefy fellows at the team table in the cafeteria, and I knew that if I'd stuck it out I'd have celebrated Christmas on crutches. Some of those guys could have served as models for paintings in the federal war museum. But they had immense status. Since rugger required no expensive gear, it suited tiny athletic budgets, and at most Maritime universities the game was big stuff right down to the mid-Fifties. Moreover, thanks to such bruisers as Fosdick-face and Les Davies—an ace-hot dropkick specialist from Wales who lived in Pictou, N.S.—Mount Allison, in my time, had championship teams. It excelled at rugger and a related extracurricular activity: donating blood. Mount A, during Red Cross drives, routinely led all Canadian universities in the proportion of its students who gave blood.

The reasons for this curious distinction were, first, that there were only 700-odd students and, second, virtually all of them lived in university residences. Mount A was a boarding school, and few escaped tremendous doses of what the psychology prof called "peer-group pressure." Mount A must surely have been the most rah-rah college in Canada, and anyone who refused to donate blood risked being sent to Coventry. Not giving blood took more courage than falling down in the path of a rampaging, 200-pound rugger star, and pressure to support the team was almost as intense.

The students hired entire trains to go to games against, say Acadia University in Wolfville, N.S. Since Mount Allison was affiliated with the United Church and frowned on drink, it was just as well that its president, an affable clergyman, did not come along for the ride. Two hours south of Sackville, at Truro, N.S., the booze was already running short. Truro was a station-stop, and Robert Stanfield's hometown now witnessed a mob of hammered teenagers, wearing garnet and gold Mount A sweaters, charging to the local liquor store to stock up before the train pulled out. Drinking at Acadia, run by Baptists, was an even graver offence than it was at Mount Allison, and the condition of our chaps astounded Wolfville. Students there believed Mount A was a marvel of freedom and sinfulness. At least once, Mount A kids pretty well wrecked an entire train from the inside out.

It's odd the way affection for Mount A clings to its alumni. You never really shake the place, and in the 28 years since I graduated, I've dismally awaited the return of its glory in autumn. Canadian football arrived on the campus the year after I left, and it launched the dear old garnet-and-gold on a seemingly endless era of utter humiliation. Year after year after year, in Ottawa, Toronto and Halifax, I'd turn to the fine print on Monday morning sports pages, and find scores like these: Acadia 63, Mount Allison 5; St. Francis Xavier 58, Mount Allison 9; St. Mary's 49, Mount Allison 0. The Mounties were a regional joke, the doormats, the pussycats of the Atlantic Universities Football Conference. They were as aggressive as a punching bag. Other Maritime teams included not only the best in the region, but in some years the best in all Canada. I imagined them on the buses that rolled toward Sackville. They'd be relaxed, giggling, horseplaying around, happily anticipating another afternoon of belting the inept Mounties all over the field and completing touchdown passes whenever they felt like it.

The worm turned at last a couple of years ago. The Mounties actually began to win more games than they lost. Last October, I ambled from my Halifax house to the St. Mary's University stadium where, for the first time in more than a quarter-century, I watched a Mount A team in action. I found a seat beside an accountant who'd been a friend back at Mount A when we were as young as the screaming kids who now surrounded us. The only flamboyant drunks were two guys with red plastic bugles. They wore Mount A jackets. But of course. They'd come 136 miles to cheer for the garnet-and-gold. I had a flask of rum, and my friend packed a small bottle of Chivas Regal. We quietly sucked away at our booze on this warm, windy, autumn-fragrant Saturday and watched with utter satisfaction as our boys came from behind to whup the St. Mary's Huskies 22 to 15. The game wasn't rugger, but the glow was just as it had been when we were very young.

By November, little old Mount A, with a student body of only 1,600, was ranked seventh in the nation and had earned the right to play against the powerhouse from St. Francis Xavier University at Antigonish, N.S., for the conference championship. Each team had defeated the other in close games. Could the Mounties possibly go all the way? Could Mount A actually win a national championship at something other than giving blood? My summer cabin is beyond Antigonish. I decided to drive up there with my wife, catch the game, spend two nights at the cottage, then close it for the winter. I figured you couldn't plan a better late-autumn weekend in Nova Scotia, but we left late and it was halftime before we reached Antigonish. The car radio said the Mounties had blown a one-touchdown lead, and were now losing 17–8. We could see the St. FX stadium from the highway. The crowd looked bored. "I've a hunch," I told my wife, "that the X-men will slaughter them." We drove to the cabin. O me of little faith!

I missed the closest, weirdest, most thrill-packed game in the history of the conference. Mount A came back, St. FX came back. They both came back again. The game ended in a

153

35–35 deadlock. They went into overtime for 10 minutes. Nobody scored. They went into overtime for another 10 minutes. Mount A scored a field goal. St. FX scored a field goal with 43 seconds to go. Night fell. Score: 38–38. Game called on account of darkness. "I've never felt so empty in my life," said St. FX Coach John Musselman. "It was like I was in a vacuum. We had played 80 minutes of football and nothing was decided. . . . It was little short of unbelievable. That game had everything—the mistakes, the exciting plays, and unbelievable execution at times." Doug Mitchell, the burly Mount A coach, had played in three Grey Cup games, and now he said, "I was emotionally drained. That was probably the best game of football I've ever seen played."

They settled things three days later, again in Antigonish, which meant that for the second time it was the Mounties who had to do the travelling. The distance from Sackville to Antigonish is 155 miles. The second game was a grinding duel, fought on a sea of icy mud, amid a welter of costly penalties for dirty play, mostly against the Mounties. Their quarterback Jim Tierney—he's from Deep River, Ontario, and he is as brilliant in his studies as he is nervy in football— had suffered a knee injury in the 38–38 thriller, and with seconds left in the first half of the second game, St. FX smeared him so successfully that he left the field on a stretcher. Mount A was still leading 11–8. In a scene out of the corny, pulp sports fiction of my childhood, Tierney returned to the game from hospital with 12 minutes on the clock. He was limping. He was wearing a brace to support his twisted neck. Alas, this was not pulp fiction. Time had run out. The garnet-and-gold lost 26–16.

I wish I could report that St. FX went on from there to win the Canadian championship, but only four days later they faced the University of British Columbia Thunderbirds in the Atlantic Bowl in Halifax; and I'm bound to admit that even if the Mounties hadn't pounded the X-men into exhaustion in those two recent and murderous games, St. FX could not have handled the awesome Thunderbirds. After X-men supporters had greeted the strangers from the west coast by chanting, "B.C. sucks," the Thunderbirds whomped St. FX 54–1. Oh, well, you can't win them all, though the Thunderbirds did. A week later they beat the University of Western Ontario Mustangs 39–16 in Toronto to grab the national title. The Thunderbirds were, as they say, something else.

But so were those youngsters from Sackville, in their own tenacious way. As a Toronto-born graduate of Mount A, I may be the only guy in Canada who roots for both the Argos and the Mounties. It wasn't a perfect football season for me, but it was nevertheless the best since Elvis Presley first recorded "Heartbreak Hotel," since Floyd Patterson knocked out Archie Moore to win the world heavyweight title, since Khrushchev told a bunch of Western ambassadors, "History is on our side. We will bury you." Wait'll next year.

Quest, April 1983

No, My Fellow Canadians, You Have Not Heard the Last of John Diefenbaker

It is 8:50 in the morning, and 12 below, and white smoke curls sharply out of the chimneys of central Ottawa and onto the hard sky. The fur hats are out, and all the proud old cold-weather jokes; and the temperature and the wind factor have been on the front pages for days, and so have the politicians. Kierans, Sharp, Martin, Hellyer, Winters, Stanfield, all the boys, all the old names in the papers...again yesterday afternoon, again this morning and again, most certainly, tomorrow. It is just another mid-winter in Ottawa. But where is that *other* name, the name that—in mid-winters that stretch all the way back to the ancient regime of Louis St. Laurent—

155

was the biggest of them all? Where is John Diefenbaker, The Great Performer himself, and what's he up to anyway?

He is up in his little brown office in the Parliament Buildings, and if there's even one stranger with him, he is performing. The office is only a few dozen feet from the huge room he used to have—Robert Stanfield is in the big one now—and because it is really too small for Diefenbaker's personal museum, it has a cluttered atmosphere, as though he were still moving in. Or as though he felt he might not be staying here long anyway, so it doesn't really matter *where* he puts the busts, the statues, old photographs, piles of mail, the short totem pole, the Shevchenko Freedom Award from the Ukrainian Congress Committee of America, the pretty blue casting flies that some sporting goods firm has just brought out and named "The Dief," and all the other things that matter to him, and that he can hold. The thick, Tory-blue drapes are drawn against the winter morning. On his desk there's a tape recorder, and one of these days, he'll start making speeches to it so that it can keep for publication all his thoughts about his long and fantastic life.

Diefenbaker has been puttering around his desk since 7:50. Now, just before 9, his secretary has not yet arrived for work, and seated at her desk, there's a tall, thick, gentle fellow in his late 60s. There's something familiar about this man, with his slightly dishevelled look, and the shadow of rural shrewdness behind his honest amiability. "I'm Elmer Diefenbaker," he says, offering his hand. Then, after a comment about Ottawa's "western" weather, he pokes his head inside his older brother's office, says something softly, and out comes John. John Diefenbaker looks the wrong way for a second or two, and fiddles with something on a shelf. Then he turns and extends, at the same time, both his hand and the force of his tailoring, his importance and his *impressiveness*.

He leads the way back into his office and, because his hearing has declined, guides his one-man audience to a chair that's close to his better ear. Diefenbaker still dresses as though he were Prime Minister. His suit is a deep grey with a suspicion of a lighter grey pinstripe. His shoes are plain and black; his socks are dark blue, wool; his tie is dark blue, silk; his cuff links are rectangular, gold. When he sits with one knee crossed over the other, he reveals a couple of inches of pale, hairless calf, and on this particular morning, one lens of his glasses is cracked. But nothing in his appearance or manner betrays that he believes he is any less important than he was last year, or 10 years ago.

His famous tremor is barely noticeable this morning. His face is smooth, shiny, faintly brown. He still has that trick of telegraphing with his eyes that he is about to say something that he thinks is very funny so that his audience will be ready to laugh, and *will* laugh, even if the joke turns out to be terrible. The audience remarks that several of the Liberal leadership candidates are resting in hot parts of the world. "They're all down south," Diefenbaker says. Heh, heh. Twinkle, twinkle. Get ready. "They're all trying to find a place in the sun." But, oddly, it still works. The audience finds himself laughing a bit, following John, though he's not sure why.

And what about the Commons, Mr. Diefenbaker? Will we be hearing much from you in there, now that you've got your memoirs to write, and a dozen visitors still drop in to listen to you and *see* you every day, and there's this endlessly pleasurable activity of reading your fan mail, and pushing things around on your desk? Will you be saying anything in the Commons about, well, special status for Quebec, and this two-nations idea?

Slap! The long fingers come down together on the corner of the desk, and with all the old quavery ferocity, he spills the familiar words: "I stood in Toronto to bar that concept.... It was then I spoke and, finally, stood as a candidate.... No other Prime Minister, from Macdonald to me, entertained that false and dangerous concept.... The day there's any reference to this in the House, on the part of *any* party, will be the day I speak. The concept of two nations I will oppose to my *last hour*, with all the force I can bring to the task...."

He leans back, panting very slightly, and the conversation turns to The Younger Generation of Today. They're generally pretty idealistic, he thinks, and more knowledge-

157

able and sensible than youngsters were in his day, and among the hundred or so that write to him every month, they are "greatly disturbed by this two-nation idea."

"And these Beatles," he is saying. "What's the other one, the other group...?" He is snapping his fingers, trying to remember, and for a second or two, he looks older than he did even five minute ago. He looks 72, which he is.

"The Monkees?" the audience offers.

"No, no, no. Yorkville, Yorkville."

"Oh, the hippies."

"Yes, that's it, the *hippies*," he says. "Well, they've found an answer to the age-old problem of living without working. But I don't find them as unattractive...no, don't say that... I don't find them as *unique* as some people do. They're a manifestation of a passing fad."

He gives the audience a bit of Sir John A., a bit of Churchill, a bit of Scottish history, a bit of fishing talk. He appears to be feeling extraordinarily well.

"One of the things I very much treasure is the Jewish people of Vancouver giving me an award they call the tree of life. It's supposed to permit, or provide for your living to be 120." The eyes flash out the signal again. Joke coming. Now. "*That* ought to create some interest among some people."

Clearly, the "some people" are his enemies, the internal enemies of Canada, and Diefenbaker, without saying much of anything, manages to give the impression that he possesses a great deal of information about them—secret, factual, indisputable evidence that relates to specific events of the past decade; evidence that he has so far been too ethical to disclose; information that will vindicate him in history and cover his enemies with shame; information that he may just decide to publish in his book, not in the last chapter but in the first. "Some people" are going to get theirs some day fairly soon, and though Diefenbaker is not yet ready to name them or to describe their sins, his smile, when he considers the first chapter of his memoirs, is beatific.

The Star Weekly, February 1968

Oh, Those Devious MacDonalds!

In "My Short, Grisly Career as a TV Superstar," I told a million or so *Maclean's* readers that one reason I lasted only five months as host of "Gazette," CBC Halifax, was that I could never overcome the awesome popularity of my predecessor, Marilyn MacDonald. I said she had had a grossly unfair advantage because 76 percent of all Nova Scotians were MacDonalds, McDonalds or Macdonalds. A *Maclean's* researcher, whose job it was to guarantee the accuracy of the magazine, pored through telephone directories and insisted I was wrong. How could Canada's National Magazine print such a lie? "It's not a lie," I said. "It's a joke. It's uh, hyperbole, you know? Deliberate exaggeration for humorous effect." I won. The lie survived, but only after I'd promised to take "full responsibility" if tens of thousands of McNeils, MacIntoshes, Frasers and others complained about this egregious error. (Actually, none did.)

Ah, the MacDonalds. It's their fault that I recently found myself in Toronto. I didn't want to be there. I'd have preferred to have spent the entire winter enjoying the semi-tropical delights of Canada's Ocean Playground, but here I was in Hog Town, imprisoned by a blizzard that might have put Murmansk to shame, not to mention Moncton, and my misery was entirely the fault of a mess of manipulative MacDonalds. What have they got against me? So far as I know, we Bruces haven't a drop of Campbell blood in our veins.

Here's what happened:

Don MacDonald, reporter for the *Herald* newspapers, was chatting in the Halifax Press Club with Ron MacDonald, executive assistant at the Nova Scotia Teachers Union. Ron

159

MacDonald is the brother of Flora MacDonald. (Flora Mac-Donald is MP for Kingston and The Islands and, in that capacity, she's a successor to Angus L. Macdonald and Sir John A. Macdonald.) Now if it weren't for the fact that this same, sly Ron MacDonald had manoeuvred me into covering his sister's bid for the Tory leadership in 1976, their relationship would be beside the point. But that earlier MacDonald conspiracy had landed me in Ottawa for a full week of the kind of weather that we now know inspires prime ministers to quit their jobs. The complexity of the conspiracy may be seen in the fact that the aforementioned Marilyn MacDonald, Ron MacDonald's wife in those days, was writing speeches for Flora MacDonald, speeches that I was dutifully working into my story. That Ottawa adventure resulted in my suffering a crippling attack of gout in our nation's capital. I had no medication except pain-killing booze that Ron MacDonald, in his fiendishly persuasive way, had conned out of backroom boys in Premier Richard Hatfield's hotel suite.

OK. Eight years later in the Halifax Press Club, Don MacDonald tells Ron MacDonald that his (Don's) uncle is none other than the Rev. Donald C. MacDonald, moderator of the General Assembly of the Presbyterian Church in Canada, and a true son of the Green Hill neighborhood of Pictou County. Not only that, Don MacDonald tells Ron MacDonald that the moderator of the United Church is the Rt. Rev. W. Clarke MacDonald and, get this, he too comes from Green Hill. Ron MacDonald phones Marilyn MacDonald, his ex-wife, to tell her what Don MacDonald has told him about the Rev. MacDonald and the Rt. Rev. MacDonald. Follow me?

I work for Marilyn MacDonald. She's the editor of *Atlantic Insight*, and she tells me what Don MacDonald has told Ron MacDonald about the two clerical MacDonalds. She orders me, an unsuspecting member of the House of Bruce, to hustle my agnostic butt up to the Toronto offices of the MacDonald clerics and get this terrific religious scoop for her magazine.

Within minutes of my arrival, the blizzard drops like an avalanche. Office towers close early. Screaming secretaries walk backwards against the lashing wind to reach subway stations. Motor traffic dies. Chipper TV newswomen happily flash their teeth while the film footage behind them shows transportation chaos. Ain't blizzards fun? For some they are. Hotels offer special deals to thousands of businessmen and businesswomen who phone their spouses to explain they cannot possibly make it through the night. "Storm parties" make huge impersonal hotels seem as intimate as ski lodges, and rock the buildings from the inside while the snow-laden wind batters them from the outside. The Reverends MacDonald would not entirely approve of these goings-on, but I know other MacDonalds who would not object at all.

In the morning I ride the subway to its northernmost limit, miraculously find a cab, and—even more miraculously—reach Donald C. MacDonald's snow-smothered shieling in a remote Toronto suburb. He's as gentlemanly a Presbyterian moderator as you'd ever want to meet, and in the Nova Scotian way, we exchange family information. "Perhaps you know my nephew, Donald," he ventures. "He's a reporter for the *Herald* newspaper in Halifax." The *Herald* building is within a caber's toss of the Halifax Press Club, and the goodly reverend has let the plot slip. Now, for the first time, I know why I was wrenched from the bosom of my loving family, forced to ride a blizzard-racing jet, sentenced to a term in storm-throttled Hog Town. It was because a Mac-Donald boasted about MacDonalds to a MacDonald in the press club. To think that they stood shoulder-to-shoulder with us at Bannockburn. And now this. My turn will come. We Bruces may be gullible, but as any reading of Scottish history will show, we are exceedingly patient and our memory is long.

I leave Donald "The Presbyterian" MacDonald, and struggle through the storm to Clarke "United Church" Mac-Donald. In 1943, when he was 23, the telephone directory for New Glasgow alone listed no fewer than 109 MacDonalds, McDonalds, and Macdonalds (and that's a fact, not hyperbole). We chat for an hour about such vital matters as the challenges facing Christianity the world over, but just as I'm leaving I remember the basic sort of question that the Ottawa *Journal*'s city editor—Art "Black Mac" MacDonald of Cape Breton—taught me to ask 30 years ago. "By the way, Dr. MacDonald, what was your wife's maiden name?" He smiles angelically, and says, "Oh, she was Muriel MacDonald of Prince Edward Island." I should have known. After downing a quarter-pounder at a nearby McDonalds, I light up a Macdonalds cigarette, and remember the well-known fact that 76 percent of all Prince Edward Islanders are MacDonalds, McDonalds, or Macdonalds.

Atlantic Insight, May 1984

Old Beer Habits Die Hard

A magazine fashion of our time is the series on The Pleasures of. . . . Magazines are forever getting writers to dream up for readers the unparalleled joys of marathon auto rallies, sliding, jogging, backpacking, hunting mushrooms, shooting pool, massaging your feet, growing vegetables for midgets, hurling yourself out of speeding aircraft, swimming among icebergs, mountain-climbing in the nude, or whatever. In family magazines, of course, one does not write about *that* (the first pleasure that leaps to many minds), and this may be understandable. What's more mysterious is the failure of our writers to express in print their own mellow, hearty, satisfying, deep-down, long-lasting passion for the simple Canadian pleasure of slurping beer.

Another cliché of Canadian editorial attitudes is the blockbuster story on some eternal regional grievance or distinction. *What Quebec Really Wants . . . Cape Breton Won't*

Bite Bullet... Trouble in Lotusland: B.C. Bubble About to Burst?... "DREE's a Drag"—Outporter Opines. Again, however, it's one of the most baffling mysteries of contemporary Canadian journalism that, despite this undying preoccupation with regions, reporters rarely investigate the regional idiosyncracies of drinking beer.

Drinking beer in Place Ville Marie is *not* the same as drinking beer in a Prairie legion hall. Drinking beer at Bloor and Avenue Road is *not* the same as drinking beer in Parrsboro, Nova Scotia (which once boasted the only tavern between Quebec and Halifax). The texture of the experience is entirely different, as silk and flannel each have virtues of their own. The differences lend to our most ubiquitous national pastime the sparkle, the zest, the effervescence and kick of variety. They contribute to the cultural mosaic. They are one reason why this country is what it is today.

Take, for instance, the prosaic matter of labels. Actually, they are only superficially prosaic. Actually, they gleam with the romance of travel. They are subtle and irrepressible reminders that, as you travel across Canada, you are moving from jurisdiction to jurisdiction, from culture to culture, from mystery to mystery. They are like the posters on a Parisian kiosk, or the symbol of the London transit system, or a Russian cigarette package. They tell you where you are. They remind you you've left home.

You see a white schooner sailing a golden ripple across an eternal blue sky on your bottle and, friend, you know you're not in downtown Winnipeg. "I will list ten of my favorite beautiful wholly Canadian things," the poet George Bowering wrote in *Maclean's* in 1972. First on his list was a Montreal Canadien sweater. Second was the label on Moosehead Ale. My affection for local history inclines me toward the elegant little stag's head on the label of the old Halifax brewing house that gives us traditionalists Alexander Keith's India Pale Ale; and, if it were still around, I know I'd treasure the Newfoundland dog on Newfoundland's Old India Beer.

Speaking of Newfoundland, nothing could better illustrate the ornery character and sheer perversity of regional loyalties than the beer-label situation in that country. (But it's not a country, you say, it's a *province!* Well maybe, but when a Newfoundlander talks about going out to the west coast he's not referring to B.C. He means Cornerbrook or Bonne Bay.) Let me explain. When Newfoundland joined Canada, one of the terms of the union was that Newfoundland trademarks would remain valid. There was an outfit named Bavarian Brewing in those days, and it had a product it called Black Label. Then the Labatt's interests bought Bavarian Brewing, so that although Black Label is Carling's Black Label to most Canadians, it's Labatt's Black Label in Newfoundland.

For similar reasons, India Pale Ale may be Labatt's I.P.A. to millions of Canadians, but among Newfoundlanders it's Molson's I.P.A. Moreover, though Black Horse Ale has gone into limbo across the country (across Canada, that is), it continues to thrive in Newfoundland. Newfoundland is also the home of perhaps the most happily blatant exploitation of local patriotism in the history of Canadian beer commercials. The commercial, which some say has the emotive power of "The Ode to Newfoundland," shows a bunch of worthies in a tavern. They're drinking Blue Star. The chorus of their song which ends with a rousing toast, goes like this:

> *Blue Star, Blue Star*
> *The finest in the land.*
> *You can drink a toast*
> *To Newfoundland*
> *With a Blue Star in your hand*

And then, all together now, and beer on high:

> *Up she comes!*

The brand names of beers arouse provincial loyalties that are as mysterious to fathom as religious fervor or the noblest expressions of nationalism. There used to be a New Brunswick ale that almost all Maritime beer-drinkers knew was not only distinctly uninspiring to taste but also generated the strangest bubbling action in the lower reaches of one's digestive system. And yet it had its defenders. They loved it as

164

though there were some enviable distinction in living in a place that could produce such an abominable brew. It was part of their regional identity.

National breweries, when they take over a local brewery, do not tamper recklessly with the character of beloved beers. One does not tromp on the old flag (and, indeed, the label on Old Scotia Ale bears a suspicious resemblance to the flag of Nova Scotia). The result of this respect for the local loves of beerdom is that, almost everywhere in Canada, we have the national personalities and, at the same time, the provincial personalities. They vie for prominence, and public admiration. They are the beer student's parallel to the federal cabinet on the one hand, and the proud, powerful, and locally knowledgeable provincial leaders on the other. This relationship, of course, is as thoroughly Canadian as was the good, right (drinking) hand of Sir John A. Macdonald himself.

Beer-drinking, in my own case, is like hearing bell buoys at dawn, and black-backed gulls; it's a piece of the East. How does the poem go? Ah yes. *We give you ships and tides and men/Anchors a-weigh and a beer-filled gut.* For me, beer-drinking in Atlantic Canada has all the nostalgic power of the memory of first love....

I see a golden, humming, fall-fragrant Saturday afternoon in October of 1952. I am in a room in the men's residence of Mount Allison University, Sackville, New Brunswick. There are four other young guys with me and we're drinking brown quarts of Red Ball. No one I ever knew in Toronto has ever heard of Red Ball. Up there, back home, you can't even buy beer in quarts. Just puny pints. I'm no longer homesick for Toronto. I'm feeling good. This afternoon I can hitchhike to Moncton. I can stay out all night. In the whole eighteen years of my life, I have never before been so free.

The window is open, and there's an unseasonably hot breeze lifting the curtains and bringing the sounds from an English rugby game in the field below. There are about 250 Mount Allison girls in the stands, and they'll all be at the dance tonight. Maybe Moncton can wait.

165

So. Me and my buddies put some Red Ball in a haversack, and we walk up a sun-dappled avenue in the hot, funny, dying season to a place called the quarry. The quarry is merely a big, dark, and faintly sinister pond with steep, wild shores. It's been a trysting place for the more sinful young Allisonians since before any of us were born. Anyway, we sit down in the grass among crisp yellow leaves, and we snap open some Red Ball and, after a while, we're all singing country music. Mostly Hank Williams.

How strange! I never liked country music in Toronto. University life is so broadening. Warm beer out of quart bottles. We're not supposed to drink beer at Mount Allison. It's best to be clandestine about it, and outdoors. That's a good way to lose your virginity, too. Ah, Red Ball. Sing us another one. *If you loved me half as much as I loved you... How you laughed when I cried each time we saw the tide take our love letters in the sand....* Yes, I think I'll go to the dance tonight. I think I'll go up to Moncton tomorrow. I think that, after that, I'll live forever....

A long time later, I worked in Toronto and Ottawa. For more than fifteen years. I didn't drink much beer up there. In my memory, of course, beer was still dear but, in practice, liquor was quicker. Moreover, a kind of elitism crept into my drinking thinking, and beer seemed rather grubby, don't you know? People who couldn't afford psychiatrists drank beer. Smoky Scotch was the proper potion. Or British gin. *An extra-dry martini on the rocks with a twist of lemon, if you please, Harold?*

The martini shops—where one gathered with the bright, the beautiful, the upwardly mobile, the would-be eagles of assorted Toronto professions—were high on hotel rooftops. Beer halls were aptly low-down. Indeed, many were underground, where worms, moths, and centipedes lived. They were sad, sour, lethargic joints and only confirmed my undemocratic conviction that, if beer was good for anything, it was as a Saturday-morning palliative against the penalties of Friday night's indulgence in socially superior London gin. You took it furtively.

166

But four years ago, and almost twenty years after I first drank a quart of Red Ball at the quarry, I came back to Atlantic Canada. The bell buoys clanged. The black-backed gulls cried again. The schooner was upwind on the label, and I began to drink beer again.

I had to. If I wanted to keep in touch with what was happening in business, politics, sports trivia and the less serious pursuits of the big men of our time in Atlantic Canada, I had to spend my noon hours drinking draft beer. Going to cocktail lounges and drinking martinis would have kept me in touch only with junk television and lonely bartenders. In my crowd in Halifax, the smart money was not on martinis. Only fools and Upper Canadians (and, my cronies generously admit, there's often a difference) shelled out the kind of money it took to buy satisfactory quantities of hard liquor in bars. Beer was good enough for any man. It was, as the makers of Newfoundland's Jockey Club liked to argue, "the honest, uncomplicated" brew.

At noon in Halifax taverns, class barriers do not vanish. But they fade. You can begin to see through them. The tavern I frequent often reminds me of something the New Brunswick writer Alden Nowlan said about life in the Maritimes: "It's wonderful for me as a journalist and fiction writer to be intimately acquainted with people who are farmers, professors, soldiers, senators, and garbage collectors.... There have always been poor people in the Maritimes. But the best of them ... don't feel at all inferior to the middle class or upper middle class. You couldn't find a subservient, good chauffeur in New Brunswick."

There's an air of freedom, equality, independence, respect, wit, and sunny celebration on the best days in a tavern down here. The beer is not Red Ball, of course (for which I thank whatever divinity rules the affairs of brewers), but the spirit sometimes reminds me of the quarry in Sackville. It makes my friends feel younger than they are, too. Up she comes!

Saturday Night, June 1975

The Mellowing of Max

You may know Max (Rawhide) Ferguson as the most beloved character in the entire history of CBC radio, but these days—and now here's Max!—he's really just a skinny, 59-year-old country gent who vacuums his rugs, washes his dishes and floors, fixes his chimney, lays tile in his bathroom, cooks for his young wife, concocts his own sausages, makes his own wine, plans to get his own cow and chickens, keeps honey bees, grows vegetables, harvests fiddleheads and maple syrup, plants fruit trees and, like some legendary granny, makes Christmas cakes for the young folks, and gathers wild berries to whip up memorable jams and jellies. If actor Paul Newman can market Paul Newman salad dressing, I imagine Max Ferguson could easily peddle Ol' Rawhide's Elderberry Jam, or Apple-Thyme Jelly. I also imagine he's so happy he'll never bother trying. "Ah yes," he says, surveying his nine acres in southern Ontario, and remembering Neil's Harbor, Cape Breton, "if only I had the ocean here, this place would be Shangri-La." He points to a gully, and adds, "Maybe I'll get a great big pond scooped out there. That'll be next best."

If the pudding of Ferguson's contentment is his domestic life, the whipped cream is that, every Sunday morning now, he's back on network radio with his own show. His fans have waited seven years for this. When he retreated to Neil's Harbor in 1976, ostensibly forever, he didn't just quit working for the CBC, he excoriated its management as being—among other loathsome things—"cheats, drunks and incompetents." He was scarcely the first to make such observations, but he was the first to state them to the half-million readers of *Maclean's*. Nobody ever left behind him so many furiously burning CBC bridges. When he returned to Toronto in 1977, "my name was mud." In the years that followed, the only CBC work he landed was the odd spot on this show or that. Now, at last, he's once more host of "The Max Ferguson Show" (Sunday mornings).

Even this came about not because the return of Ferguson excited CBC management but because the return of Ferguson excited listeners. He got letters. The show began merely as a nine-week summer replacement. Indeed, the CBC had other shows ready to go in the same time-slot for its fall and winter programming. As the summer rolled by, however, the trickle of letters became a deluge. Then, on the eighth Sunday, Ferguson's curmudgeonly crony and ancient ally among CBC announcers, Allan (Big Al) McFee sorrowfully (and craftily) reminded listeners that, alas, this was Ferguson's second-last show. The deluge became a regular Niagara.

"No radio program in CBC history ever drew so much unsolicited mail," John Dalton said. He's the young executive producer from St. John's who puts together Ferguson's show, and oversees McFee's "Eclectic Circus," and "The Royal Canadian Air Farce." The letters came from across Canada, from the States, and from a Ferguson cult in the Maritimes that stretches back nearly four decades to his irreverent invention of "Rawhide" at CBC Halifax.

"I've loved you for a long, long time, Max," a Toronto woman wrote. "Live forever." One listener said, "Despite his being on at such an ungodly hour, two hours is nowhere near enough of him." A Nova Scotia man wrote to say the show gives "exquisite pleasure. By golly, there's hope for the CBC yet (but not very damn much)." A housewife told Ferguson by mail, "You have to be the sweetest person on radio, or anywhere else.... Hug your dogs for me. Thank your wife for sharing you with all of us."

And so it went: "The best thing to happen to summer listening since the swallows returned to Capistrano"... "That comfortable voice, the always interesting and often piquant commentary, and the amazingly varied collection of records—just a real joy to have it all back"..."That you would overstay your welcome is about as likely as the CBC's stopping you from heating sandwiches on the transmission tubes!"

When the CBC dithered about the show's future, an irritated listener asked, "Why make such a cliff-hanger of the affair? Why not come right out and guarantee that [Ferguson, with McFee] will be around for as long as they can be persuaded to totter to the microphone?" And something like that guarantee soon came about. If any lingering resentment remained among CBC brass over Ferguson's seven-year-old insults, the cascades of adoring letters smothered it. Just before the final show of the summer, Dalton said, "The order came down: 'See if there's any way to keep it on the air.' We'd already taped the last show with McFee doing a farewell. We had to bring him in to do a new bit.... Now, officially, it's set till next March 31, but judging from the mail, I'd say Max can do it just about as long as he wants." For Ferguson, how sweet it is. How vindicating, and how convenient.

His Shangri-La-without-the-ocean is 128 km east of Toronto in rich farming country near Grafton, but since he tapes two shows at a time he need report to the CBC studios in Toronto, a city he does not like, only once every two weeks. On the Wednesday night in late September that I saw him taping, he brought along Barney, his Airedale. "Barney's bored stiff," Ferguson explained to the control room as they emerged from the studio after the first session. "He's been in there sighing and wheezing and licking his dink. I'd better take him outside for a minute." Barney exploded down a CBC corridor, slithering as though he were trying to chase a rabbit over slick ice. Ferguson followed him, and Dalton turned to set me straight on what a consummate pro Max was.

In the first place, Dalton explained, Ferguson brings in the records for each show but never times the selections. He just *knows* that the couple of dozen cuts he's chosen, plus his patter, will fill two hours, and "he's dead on." Ever since 1949, when the CBC moved "Rawhide" to Toronto in order to give him to the nation, rather than just the Maritimes, Ferguson has been borrowing records for his shows from the main shop of Sam the Record Man. "Sam Sniderman used to say, 'Give me challenges,'" Ferguson recalled. "At a conservative guess, he's lent me $50,000 worth of records. He gets some of

170

them back with fingerprints and jam all over them."

Dalton showed me the line-up of 26 tracks for the first show they taped that night. It included stuff from Sweden, Spain, the Ukraine, Greece, Poland, Scotland, England, Ireland, band music, dance music, boating songs, loving songs, BBC satire, the whole mixed bag of Fergusonian preferences that so many listeners love and cannot get from anyone else. "That's what stereo radio is all about," Dalton said.

He'd been a producer eight years. He'd seen a lot of radio talent, and what astounded him most about Ferguson was that "he does everything ad lib. He has just an incredible mind." Aside from some hen-scratching on the typed schedule of music, Ferguson used no script. He linked pieces with his own ludicrous memories, tidbits of musical trivia, opinionated historical asides (Bonnie Prince Charlie was "that incompetent man"), offbeat political information ("Silesia is divided into three parts, Black Silesia, Green Silesia, and White Silesia") and, as part of an old on-air game, insults to McFee ("If my muscles were as hard as your arteries, McFee, I'd be in superb condition.... For a man in whose breast the milk of human kindness lies in clots, it's amazing how McFee can get that nice, warm, sincere, resonant quality in his voice"). All of this, Dalton says, flows from Ferguson "just like he's sitting down across the table from you, and talking to you. I think that's why people like it so much. He doesn't seem to be trying."

As a matter of fact, when Ferguson's at work he is sitting down across a table from Dalton, who's behind glass in the control room, and he's talking to him. They have a bit of that magical producer-performer rapport that's essential to the best radio. Dalton laughs at the right time, signals delight, behaves like the president of a Max Ferguson fan club. Besides, he's shrewd enough not to mess with a good thing. He spends much of his time trying to dream up new shows, with new ideas, writers and performers. "But here's a man just spinning discs all by himself, and talking. It's the fucking personality. They just love Max out there."

What would they call the show? Why, "The Max Ferguson Show," of course. And what would the theme music be? Why, the good, old "Clarinet Polka" by the George Barnes Octet, of course. Hundreds of thousands of Canadians would never be able to hear it without thinking of Ferguson. If it sounds scratchy on Sunday mornings, that's because the CBC was so sure Ferguson would never be back to stay that someone tossed the record out, and Dalton had to tape it from the introduction to one of Max's ancient shows. As the familiar tune bounced along to begin yet another Max Ferguson show on the night I was in the control room, a woman came in from the corridor and sat down.

"I just heard the music," she said. "Oh God, it gets me in the gut. I first heard him when I was a little girl." McFee's intro had been taped, and though you'd never have known it just by listening, Big Al wasn't there. As Ferguson slid into his opening rebuttal of a McFee put-down, the woman said, "Those two guys are still the best in the business. Just the best. Ferguson's wonderful. You know, I come in here after what I think was a good day's work, and he makes me feel inadequate." The good day's work was with CBC radio's top public-affairs radio show, "As It Happens," and this girlish Ferguson fan, as it happened, was none other than its co-host, Elizabeth Gray.

As it happens, Gray isn't the only Ferguson fan on the staff of "As It Happens," not by a long shot. Producer Pauline Janitch is his second wife, and if he'd met her before his celebrated escape to Neil's Harbor, rather than after, he might still be there, and his show might therefore never have been revived. For after all his talk about trading the idiocies of the CBC and the hypocrisies of Toronto for "creative stagnation" by the sea, it wasn't the Cape Breton weather or his enslavement to cutting firewood that convinced him he could not, after all, live out his life at Neil's Harbor. It was simply loneliness.

He loved the local people. He'd been coming to the house with his family (he has five children by his first marriage, and two grandchildren) for summer after summer, but he'd never toughed out the isolation of an endless winter there. "I was

172

going to stay forever," he explained, "but I was between marriages, and it's all very personal but it was just damn lonely." Indeed, it was so lonely even his two dogs, his only companions, began to act strangely, and in the spring of '77 he returned to Toronto, not exactly with his tail between his legs because he's a proud man, but certainly to a chorus of we-told-you-so snickering. Few gave him credit for having had the moxie actually to try doing what so many Torontonians only talk about doing: escaping the rat race.

While filling in for Don Harron as host of CBC radio's "Morningside," he met a young CBC staffer who'd recently come up from Halifax. Her name was Pauline Janitch, and they had a fair bit to talk about. Halifax, after all, was the city in which Ferguson had spent the happiest years of his life. Janitch had written for the city's alternate weekly, *The 4th Estate*, and then joined the CBC. In the Fall of '77 these two ex-Haligonians got married. The Neil's Harbor adventure was only a few months behind Ferguson. "We almost went back," he said, "but there was Pauline's job to consider, and we decided to make a compromise here [the property near Grafton]."

Pauline drives 128 km to work in the morning, and 128 km to get home at night, but the house is a fine place for her to relax after a hard day at the office. They found it in late '82, and moved in just before Christmas. It would be difficult to find a more picturesque house for a yuletide party. It was once a holding jail, then a country inn. One section dates back to 1860. Its white stucco hides three layers of brick. The house is therefore cool in summer, easy to heat with wood in winter. Surrounded by pine, spruce, cedar, poplar and maple trees, it sits on rich soil where the growing season is longer than it'll ever be at Neil's Harbor. "I love gardening so much," Ferguson said, bragging pleasantly about his first vegetable crop at his new home. "I got a beautiful yield of tomatoes, carrots, peas, beets, cabbage, onions, potatoes, watermelons. . . . I'm just delighted with the returns."

"You're looking very fit," I tell him.

"Well, I've got no worries on my mind."

173

It occurs to me that he's at last got what so many people ridiculed him for seeking at Neil's Harbor seven years ago: peace of mind beyond the city. In fact, he's got *more* than he sought in '76. He has Pauline. He has "The Max Ferguson Show." I think he knows he's got everything that any man approaching 60 has a right to expect out of life. He misses the ocean, sure, but do you want to buy a summer home at Neil's Harbor? I know a guy who's got one up for sale. It's a beaut, but you wouldn't want to live there in the winter. Not alone.

Atlantic Insight, December 1983

The Cottage Was Fine

We never worry about the house, only the cottage. Surely the sea wind will pick up a fir tree and swat the place flat. The carpenter ants will bring it groaning to its knees. Diabolical squirrels will turn the beds into garbage. Lightning will crack the roof wide open, and as the cabin dies in flames, no one will witness its last agony.

Or "they" will get inside. "They" are all its unknown human enemies, the petty thieves, the secret takers and window-breakers. They are all those who, for one bent reason or another, find joy in the systematic and imaginative destruction of something a stranger loves.

We don't worry about the city house because it has neighbors, good neighbors. The street is a tight huddle to keep out the worst marauders of crime and weather. But the cottage confronts the terrors of the open Atlantic. It is alone. You can't see it from road or beach. Its enemies may ravish it in the luxury of privacy. It is three hours away by car. Distance makes the heart grow fearful.

Only a few years ago owners of summer cabins in Nova Scotia often bragged that, at least down here, you could still leave your cottage safely without bothering to lock the door. You no longer hear that boast.

Dune buggies, motorcycles, jeeps and picnickers on foot find our gravel beach every hot summer Sunday and on Mondays we go along the shore to harvest the shards of brown glass, the slimy Kleenex, the bread wrappers, chunks of half-chewed food, the cans and crud. Some people just leave the stuff on the blackened rocks of their dead hotdog fires. Others, more genteel perhaps, prefer to tuck it into the trees so no one will see it till they're gone. Still others move a few feet into our woods to deposit their excrement and discard the unmistakable evidence of their love-making.

Are "they" moving closer and ever closer to our tender, beloved and helpless little cabin? And what might the hurricane have done to it? The storm has just ripped her way up the length of the province, with winds gusting up to 85 mph. The newspapers brandish photos of exploded house trailers and bowled-over summer cabins, and now, we approach our place with even more unspoken apprehension than usual.

Ah, sweet miracle! Neither vandal nor arsonist, burglar nor bum, rotten little kid nor midnight creep has harmed the old place in any way. And the storm has spared her, too. We see a porcupine, a deer. We revel again in the moods of the volatile bay and the seascape is as new as it was the first time we saw it, and in the days we're there, only one four-wheel-drive station wagon appears on the beach. It doesn't leave behind so much as a cigarette butt. Everything is better than we had dared to hope out loud, and all the way back down the 180 miles to Halifax, the survival and magic of the cabin continue to fill our heads. The city is damp, shady, strange.

We pull into our driveway. That's funny, there's a basement window broken. We unlock the front door, push it open. A tiny hurricane seems to have torn through the house. Something has messed the clothes in every drawer in every room, scattered the mail, plucked the ornamental wooden box off the piano and thrown it down on the living room floor. The box used to contain 85 dollars in quarters. They're gone. Someone has used the upstairs toilet, and failed to flush it.

The 4th Estate, August 1975

Athletes, Like Children, Should Be Seen and Not Heard

The loose-hanging, loose-jointed, fastball-firing Leroy Robert "Satchel" Paige was not only the best pitcher Dizzy Dean and Bob Feller ever saw, and not only a talker comparable to Muhammad Ali. He was also a mystery man. There were things about him no one knew. He may have been 76 when he died last June, or he may have been some other age. A goat, he said, ate his birth certificate. "I want to be the onliest man in the United States," he said slyly, "that nobody knows nothin' about."

Thank you, Satchel, and, wherever you are, God bless you.

Paige's strange ambition confirmed the glory of his uniqueness. The first of his Six Rules for a Happy Life was, "Avoid fried meats which angry up the blood," but his goal was to be amazing and, at the same time, to keep his private life private. How endearingly oldfangled! Today's pro athletes want to be the onliest men and women that everybody knows everythin' about. "Troubled" superstars, tortured by marital crises, homosexuality or drug addiction, regularly spill their untidy guts to reporters. Sports magazines suddenly

176

read like biographies of Hollywood has-beens or rejected scripts for the soaps. Superstars sometimes try to charge sportswriters for interviews, but since the athletes reap mountains of money whenever they're not fretting about their childhood traumas or current sex lives, it's the writers who should be doing the charging. By the hour, like any self-respecting psychiatrist.

"There is no one he [Steve Garvey] can release to," Dusty Baker, a Los Angeles Dodger outfielder, told William Nack of *Sports Illustrated*. Garvey, however, had no trouble releasing to Nack. Indeed, he unloaded on him. Recalling the day he cleaned out some drawers after he and Cyndy Garvey had agreed to a divorce, Garvey told *Sports Illustrated*'s several million readers, "Every drawer had memories. It was like a cassette of the last 10 years. It was like going back on rewind, then fast forward to the present, then back on rewind, then fast forward. Ten years of it.... The memories will never go, but you can't go back to what once was. Sure there were tears.... They were the toughest days of my life.... I failed. Of course I failed. I had never failed before. It's not failing for the first time, it's failing at what I've thought to be the single most important thing we can do in life. I do feel guilt...a lot of frustration and guilt.... I want that sense of guilt to go away.... You're going to talk about guilt, you're going to talk about agony, essentially."

Had enough? Does this sort of thing angry up your blood? Do you wish Garvey would shut up, and maybe obey Paige's second rule for a happy life? It goes like this, "If your stomach disputes you, lie down and pacify it with cool thoughts." The third of Paige's rules was, "Keep the juices flowing by jangling around gently as you move," which is what Pete Rose should do to cure his bad back. Rose, says Roger Director in *Inside Sports*, has a girlfriend named Carol—her navel is an "out-ie"—who gave him so many back massages her fingers got sore. He also has a sorrowful ex-wife named Karolyn, who as a gut-spiller rivals Garvey. She thinks Pete's real problem isn't his back but the fact that he can't accept the love that she and the kids still feel for him.

"Sometimes I think Pete is probably very lonely. And it's a shame."

She still loves him, and that's a shame too, because Pete, who is not known for having difficulty finding women to treat his back, told Director, "She don't know what the hell she's saying.... What do I need a wife for? As far as being lonely, baseball is my substitute." Director already knew that. Indeed, Director knew that Rose had bartered his soul to the devil for baseball immortality and that, "as the pay-out on his pact with devil baseball," Rose was now "a man who has brutalized the feelings of those who loved him and supported him as he went about his child's play." But by comparison with Garvey, the brutalizing Rose was at least succinct. Asked about his, ahem, active social life, he said, "If a guy doesn't like women, he's queer, so if you want to say, no I'm not queer, then I'm not queer."

By Rose's definition, I guess, Dave Kopay, a former running back in the National Football League, *is* queer. Kopay admires tennis star Billie Jean King, but with regard to the press conference in which she admitted her lesbian affair with Marilyn Barnett, he thought it seemed "a little silly to think they'd call a press conference to say, in effect, 'Hi, everybody! I'm queer.'" Kopay had been satisfied merely to write an entire book, with the help of Perry Deane Young (*The David Kopay Story*), about his life as a homosexual in pro football. It was a best seller, too. Now, *that's* coming out of the closet.

Martina Navratilova, the second most famous sometimes lesbian in tennis, might have been a tough interview for Robert Friedman. She was known to hide her emotions. A friend said she had the demeanor "of an ox"; but Friedman, on behalf of *Inside Sports*, got her to sing like a bird. They had dinner together, and by the time she dug into her mud pie, "her feelings of inadequacy were on the table." He felt "she still had not discovered the secret of happiness," and she couldn't satisfy her parents. "You know how parents are: You're still their little girl no matter how old you are, and you can never really please them." She found it particularly hard to please her stepfather with the fact her lover was a woman. Indeed, he'd told her he'd prefer her to take up alcoholism or sleeping with a different man every night.

Talking, and talking, and talking about the terrible effect on her of parental judgement, the oxlike Navratilova said, "I didn't talk about it to anybody—I still don't like to talk about it because it's personal—but definitely it influenced my tennis." Another time, she "stretched out on a sofa in her villa and related a dream she had had a few night earlier." It was a nightmare. Chris Evert Lloyd was making her run up and down huge hills to return shots.

Evert Lloyd felt Navratilova's game wouldn't straighten out "until she straightens out her life," but glamorous golfer Jan Stephenson played better and better the more her "private" life degenerated. "The thing that gets me is, the more trouble she has, the better she plays," rival JoAnne Carner complained in *Sports Illustrated*. Sportswriter Barry McDermott explained that Stephenson had "broken her right foot, been fined $3,000 and been ordered to undergo a psychiatric examination. Also, her assets have been frozen, and whether she currently has one, two or no husbands depends on what a court has to say." Her frantic personal life suggests she should follow Satchel Paige's fourth and fifth rules. The fourth: "Go very light on vices such as carrying on in society. The social ramble ain't restful." The fifth: "Avoid running at all times."

McDermott seems to be *Sports Illustrated*'s specialist on Jan Stephenson. He calls her "the wee ice maiden," but easily thaws her. He sees parallels between her and Marilyn Monroe: "And, like Monroe, Stephenson's life isn't all that terrific. 'It's all screwed up,' she says half seriously about every 15 minutes. Sex symbol? All you need to know is that Stephenson says she has never danced with a man." She spews her deepest yearnings at McDermott: "I would love very much to have a good personal relationship.... I want somebody who cares about me, someone who's all mine, who's just crazy about me whether I play badly or not, who thinks I'm wonderful.... And, it goes without saying, he'd have to be in good shape physically....Sometimes I feel like I should give up waiting for Prince Charming.... I guess faithfulness is more important to me than anything.... I just want one thing that will really be all mine, that nobody can touch." And so on. She should avoid Rose, go for Garvey.

Love, however, is not a preoccupation of Al Davis, fierce boss of the Oakland Raiders (now Los Angeles Raiders) football team. "I feel the role of love belongs to other people," he tells Gary Smith in the course of a 4,000-word revelation for *Inside Sports*. An admirer of Hitler's audacity, Davis is so tough that writer Hunter S. Thompson once said, "He makes Darth Vader look like a punk," but he does worry about death. "You can't dominate that son of a bitch," he complains.

"Don't look back," Paige advised in his sixth and final rule. "Something may be gaining on you." It finally caught Paige, and I miss him. With respect to his personal life and the things that haunted him, he kept his integrity intact by keeping his mouth shut. He had class.

Quest, December 1982

Hatelash and the French Fact

An announcement in French turns a Toronto hockey crowd into a rout of wolves. "*Bière*" on a beer label turns a bluenose redneck white with rage. A man from Warburg, Alberta, urges us to "take our guns and have it out with Quebec" and, having won, send all French Canadians "back to France." A Montreal journalist explores Toronto and finds a virulence of anti-French feeling there such as he's never known before. Another Montreal journalist journeys across the Prairies, describes the West's "open hatred" for all French Canadians. And Pierre Trudeau sweats.

I've got something to say about all this, but I'll leave Trudeau out of it. I'll leave Joe Clark out of it, too. Other matters I refuse to consider are the Official Languages Act, language law in Quebec, the Quiet Revolution, the October Crisis, air-traffic control, Pierre Vallières, René Lévesque, Keith Spicer, *deux nations, maitres chez nous*, the revenge of the cradle, conscription-if-necessary-but-not-necessarily-conscription, trilingualism in Switzerland, Wolfe's victory over Montcalm, Diefenbaker's French, and the relative greatness of Macdonald, Laurier, Howe and Beliveau.

I'll leave such issues to deeper thinkers, and talk about hate. Anyone whose work attracts mail knows that, sprinkled about the country, there are tortured people with aimless anger in their heads. The anger floats, like an obscene and unkempt hawk; and the meat upon which it swoops is any group of strangers known only by a label. Jews, blacks, Chinese, Italians, East Europeans, hippies, Torontonians, the rich, the poor, Americans, Catholics...you name them, somebody out there thinks he hates them. An Albertan wrote to tell me that every Nova Scotian miner who ever went West was a dirty, illiterate, drunken skunk who couldn't dig his way out of a sandbox, and wallowed among squaws (whom my correspondent didn't much like either).

Now this was almost funny, but I couldn't laugh. Even after getting crank mail for years, I remained reluctant to open letters from strangers. Who needed further proof that the bird was insatiable? Still, I was at least confident that he was merely the foamy-beaked emissary of isolated and friendless creeps who dribbled away the midnights of their lives in the mad glory of getting hate out of their heads and on to paper. Now, however, I am not so sure.

Maybe hate is contagious. Maybe thousands of English-speaking Canadians who were easygoing yesterday are full of hate today. Maybe the bird is breeding, and whole flocks are clucking and pecking the lice out of their greasy feathers before they get up to darken the sky in a mission of hatred against French Canadians. Something smells worse than it did last year, and it is us.

181

I address the following to everyone who decides he or she detests French Canadians: Do you know one? Have you talked for hours with a French-Canadian salesman, in the bar car of a train that's rumbling across his big nation? Have you sat in the kitchen of a Gaspé home; watched a moonlit hockey game on a brittle night in Beauceville; fallen in love with a French Canadian? No, I do not ask you to discover the soul of French Canada, or even to learn French. I ask you only to have the Canadian decency to refuse to hate people you do not know. Some hate hurts the haters more than the hated.

There's something else. Despite the "good riddance" theory about Quebec, I cannot imagine a more boring, greedy, screwed-up, squabble-prone, spiritually feeble and suicidally inclined excuse for a country than a Dominion of English-speaking Canada. Canada is an idea. Without Quebec, the idea is nothing. Canada is nothing. It took me 40 years to discover that this is the world's best country in which to be alive, and that this is true not just because the character of French Canada adds to its joy but also because it is the kind of society in which a French Canada can thrive. I *like* Quebec. I don't care if she doesn't like me back, and I want no part of a Canada so loutish it allows hatred to speed Quebec out of Confederation. If it came to that, I'd rather be a citizen of the independent Republic of Nova Scotia.

The Canadian, December 1976

Hatelash Revisited

In response to worries I expressed in "Hatelash and the French Fact," a man from Brantford, Ont., writes to tell me "Wolfe won the war against Montcalm fair and square, so *they* have no comeback"; an articulate veteran from Waubaushene, Ont., says of French Canada's war record that "it is easy to stand firm for your rights providing someone else is doing the dying"; a woman from Calgary is hopping mad over French on cereal boxes; a fellow from London, Ont., says the real problem with French Canadians is their religion; an anonymous authority from Kapuskasing, Ont., says, "Most of us do not care if Quebec separates or not."

The letter-writers who disliked my urging that we not hate French Canadians gave the impression that, if our belief in Confederation ever does collapse, it will be because we nurse grudges against Quebeckers for wartime sins most of them are too young to have committed, or because we make monsters out of molehills. "Streets" are fine; "les rues" are vile. Oh why, oh why must we endure the damnable insult of finding at our English-speaking breakfast tables, "Commencez votre journée avec des Shreddies"?

There is profound zaniness in this anger. It is as strange as the ingrained absurdity that, somehow, Quebec runs Canada, that Quebec has fantastic power over Ottawa and, from Burnaby Island to Bonavista Bay, is "ramming French down our throats." The letter-writers who cherish such crap are unlikely to believe me, or Languages Commissioner Keith Spicer, or anyone else who tells them the truth. One truth is that in the federal public service (that hive of evil Frenchmen), Francophones still don't get their fair share of jobs. In executive positions, for instance, English-speaking Canadians outnumber them five to one.

Okay, those letter-writers were the bad news. Now for the bewildering news. I was scared rather than mad in the hatelash column, but a fellow from Neepawa, Man., says I have "a real vocabulary of nasty words...if Bruce got any madder he could perhaps insult a snake." A man from Regina says my distaste for hatred and bigotry actually proves I'm full of hatred and bigotry. A Winnipegger somehow reached the same weird conclusion: "Quebec at heart was never part of Canada. Yet today she rules Canada, and our politicians are ready for an outright surrender. Therefore, go back to your Republic of Nova Scotia, Bruce. We will not miss your hate for Western Canada, which is so evident in your diatribe." No rational reader of what I'd written could possibly have interpreted it as an attack on Western Canada. It was an attack on hate among English-speaking Canadians, and what can I say to those who recognized themselves in it? I can say, "If the shoe fits, for God's sake take it off."

And now, at last, the good news. The love-mail smothered the hate-mail. The letters from men and women who loved Canada, wanted Quebec to remain part of it and feared the English-speaking hatelash far outnumbered those from what one correspondent called Canada's "uglies." Nor was there any regional pattern. The good guys wrote from Vancouver, Calgary, Winnipeg, Toronto, Ottawa, Montreal, from small towns on the edge of the Arctic, from the office of the Speaker of the Senate, from the faculty of medicine at the University of British Columbia, from a skyscraper suite on Dorchester Blvd. Most wrote in English, a few wrote in French, all of them wrote as though they truly gave a damn about the future of an idea called Canada.

A young Toronto postal clerk named Andrew Hurlbut, an appreciator of "the pure grace of dawn," sat down at 7:20 one morning and, in a neat hand, filled five lined pages with 1,600 words. They are as moving an expression of patriotism as I've read in years. "Being Canadian," he says, "is more than a passport entry; more than a birthright. It is a great and continuous responsibility that embraces the finest dreams of mankind." I like that. I think Hurlbut knows what Canada is for.

The Canadian, January 1977

184

The Town That Shaped Bob Stanfield

> Truro is a place of preeminent beauty, and when its
> blooming valley first burst on my view I thought of
> the words of St. John: "I saw a new Heaven and a
> new earth." I have conversed with travellers who
> have been in England, in the United States, and in
> Canada, who all declared that they had scarcely
> ever seen a more lovely spot than the Village of
> Truro.
>
> —The Memorials of the Reverend John Sprott,
> in 1847

Robert Lorne Stanfield was born here 67 years later—on
April 11, 1914, to be precise—and by then the Village of
Truro, no longer content to be merely a new Heaven and a
new earth, was calling itself The Hub of the Province, and
there were no fewer than 36 freight trains and 34 passenger
trains running in and out of town every single day, and if you
chose not to believe the local boosters on that particular
point, well, then you could go right on down to "one of the
costliest railroad stations of any town along the line of the
Intercolonial Railway" and count the trains for yourself.

The railroad station was, as they say, *some* big; and the
ICR had built it to last, out of the finest red sandstone. It had a
dining room, a carved wooden counter of exceptional quality,
an ample number of ice-cream chairs, plates of fruit and sugar
buns under handsome glass bells, potted plants of the very
best kind, gorgeous silver cash registers, a sufficiency of
spittoons, and since a man had only to go five miles into the
hills to kill all the moose he could haul home, the Truro
railroad station also had no fewer than 17 mooseheads on the
walls. It was a pretty good town in which to find oneself

suddenly alive, and named Stanfield.

Bob Stanfield's hometown made a statement about the people who lived there and the statement was that if men will only apply hard work, hard heads, horse sense and thrifty business practices they can arrange their corner of the world to suit themselves.

Truro's population amounted to about 7,000 souls in the years that Stanfield was growing from infancy to boyhood, but it had as many house telephones as most towns of 10,000. It had its own street-lighting plant and 600 lights under the eternally beautiful elms and maples that brought midsummer shade to the people and the horses on its streets, and 152 of these lights were exceptionally handsome three-globe clusters of the sort you might see in London, England, or Paris, France.

You would say that such facts could scarcely have interested the boy Bob Stanfield. Little boys do not ponder the satisfactory state of municipal affairs. They do not go to bed at night, reminding themselves that the Truro town council consists of one mayor, and two councillors from each of three wards. And yet...he *was* a Stanfield. He could not help but know that his father's opinions mattered a lot to whatever mayor and whatever six councillors happened to be in office at any one time. Boys absorb some knowledge without even trying.

Moreover, there's just the plain old educational fact of small-town life. The essential economic and social and political information in a Truro, N.S.—the number of trains, the number of street lights, the number of black neighborhoods, the fact that just about everyone spoke English and *only* English, the facts that the Presbyterians outnumbered the Anglicans two to one and that there were only 400 Roman Catholics in the whole town, the fact that the 340 boys and girls who boarded at the provincial normal school spent $70,000 right here in Truro every year—these things were known to virtually everyone. They might intrude on you even if they did not fascinate you. They were like stories about the scandals of the local rich. Known.

Such information becomes a part of your sense of place because the town is yours in a way in which no city ever belongs to anyone, and when you step out your front door and close it firmly behind you and walk along Prince Street and all the way down to the railroad station, you still have not even left your house, not entirely, because the whole town is a kind of extension of the house. In Truro, this was particularly true if your name happened to be Stanfield.

"Bob was not an unusual boy in any way," his third and youngest brother said half a century later. His name is Gordon D. Stanfield but everyone calls him Pete. His voice is flat, dry, both assertive and quavering. It is uncannily similar to Bob's radio voice, and he clearly did not want to grant an interview about their boyhood together. "He grew up normally.... He generally didn't drag his kid brother along.... [The interview] can't help my brother in any way politically...."

Not an unusual boy in any way. He grew up normally. They all tell you the same thing. They're middle-aged men now, guys with paunches and shiny heads of their own, and they've got jobs in car lots or tourist offices or soap companies and they, too, have been gone from Truro for a long time, and their own sons are already older than they were themselves in the time they knocked around with Bob Stanfield. They all say he was "likable." He was "more or less of a reserved type." Once you got to know him, and that *did* take a while, he was "an exceedingly fine fellow." He was not wildly popular but he was certainly "a nice fellow to be with." He was good at hockey, good at English rugby, good at swimming, pretty good at tennis, pretty good at paddling a canoe. He was a good trader of postage stamps, a good lover of Duke Ellington, and by the time he was 13 or 14, he was already a good guy to play cards with at a summer cottage. He preferred his friends to pay their poker debts. Bob Stanfield was "a fine, good, solid kid," and that's all.

Nobody recalls much more about him. One fellow does remember that he and Bob and some other guys used to sneak out at night and silently push a neighbor's car down the street. Then, they'd turn on the engine and go for clandestine joy rides, and those nights were the closest Bob ever came to a life of crime. They do not prove much, except that once, in a forgotten summer, people left their cars out all night with the keys in the ignition.

Another guy remembers that Bob Stanfield, even as a boy, was "an awful stickler for the truth. With Bob, everything had to be straight and right." On occasion he also had a hot temper, but among the Stanfields, there was nothing unusual in that. "You know," recalls a man who was once their neighbor, "you'd walk past their house at the dinner hour and, my God, you could hear them fighting all the way out on the street, and Bob's voice right in there with the rest of them.... I've seen him put a couple of real good lickins' on Pete, too."

Bob was the third of four sons (he has an older sister as well). The first two were destined to take over the family business and he apparently sensed at an early age that, if he were going to excel, he would have to do it in ways his brothers had not considered. He became the town's most distinguished bookworm in short pants. His family called him The Professor, and an old school teacher recalls that by the time Bob reached grade nine he already had so firm a grasp of political history that his teachers, half-kidding, would say, "There goes the next Prime Minister of Canada." (The old teacher is a Tory.) He was studious, quiet, but not shy. Composed. Every teacher should have one.

A housewife who was born in Truro, and now finds herself drifting down to her sixties in southern Ontario, recalls that she had "a terrific crush" on Bob and, not only that, so did "half the other girls in the school." He had dark hair and sensitive eyes. A Stanfield-watcher, of whom there are many in Truro, says Bob was "perhaps the most considerate of the lot." He was not the sort who puts pigtails in inkwells. He was athletic, brilliant, thoughtful. And rich. Every little girl should have one, too.

The Stanfields were rich but they were also careful. They

188

did not blow their money on trips to Europe. In the summers of his earliest boyhood, Bob's family would leave the mansion in Truro and go to live in a plain old farmhouse on a hill outside town. The place had an outhouse, and a wall-box phone with a crank. There was no running water, no electricity, and nothing much for small boys to do but dam the brook, trim the trees, pick wild berries, fetch the milk from the real farm farther down the hill, and pretend to help the farmer with his chores.

If the farmhouse was good enough for Bob's father, it was good enough for anyone. "There was no side to Frank Stanfield," recalls one old Tory. "There was never a Stanfield yet that was a snob. That was their secret in politics. They were all so damn *natural* the people had to vote for them."

The lieutenant-governor of Nova Scotia, the Honorable Frank Stanfield, died in his sleep in a black and early hour of Friday, September 25, 1931, and thereby startled not only his immediate loved ones (including his fourth child, Bob, 17), but also virtually everyone else who called the little province home. His death was not appropriate. "I'm just beginning to live, my lad," he'd told a newspaperman only a few days before he stopped living. He was only 59. He'd been King George V's official representative in Nova Scotia for less than a year. He died of a heart attack in the big bed at Government House, which was (and still is) right downtown in Halifax and, a funny thing, he'd been home in Truro only the day before, only a few hours before, and if you'd run into him then, if you'd seen him striding along under the great elms of Prince Street the way he always used to—with a bouquet of late-summer roses swinging in his right hand—well, the last thing that would ever have crossed your mind would have been the death of Frank Stanfield. He looked that well. That night, the Thursday night, he caught an evening train back to Halifax, a city which Truro people have had various good reasons to distrust for more than 200 years.

Frank Stanfield was tall and his shoulders were square. He had a rugged sort of physical grace. His cheekbones were high, and the long slope of his cheeks drew down the corners of his mouth in that faint and involuntary expression of hauteur that's so familiar in the face of Bob Stanfield. His face was heavier than Bob's is now, and at the time of his death, he had a rich crop of white hair. Newspaper eulogists described his features as "aquiline." They said, too, that "he never asked for advice; he gave it and, if he were in a position of authority, insisted that his opinion be followed."

Frank Stanfield was strong, that was why his death seemed so incorrect. Everyone said he was strong. Strong-minded. There are a lot of old men in Truro who remember him yet, 41 years later, and they're still saying he was strong. "Well, yes, Frank Stanfield could be hellish outspoken at times," recalls a man in his eighties. "Yes, he could be abrupt. He could swear. God save us, it didn't matter what, he'd come out with the damnedest things, and whatever he told you, you *did*!" Yes. Well then, sir, would you say that Robert Stanfield's father was a domineering man? "I would not say, sir, that he was an *unfairly* domineering man."

Charles Stanfield, 61, Bob's older brother, simply advises that "Dad always knew where he was going, and went that way." It was Frank, with his brother John, who turned their father's knitting mill into an immensely successful and world-famous underwear empire. That was shortly after the turn of the century. Today, Charles is vice-president of the empire (his nephew Thomas is president), and on a wall in his huge, brown, plainly furnished office on the second floor of the mill, there's a solemn group photograph. It was taken more than half a century ago when Charles was a little boy and Bob was scarcely more than a tot, and it shows The Men Behind Stanfield's Unshrinkable Underwear. They're in their Sunday best and they plainly know where they are going, and intend to go that way.

Preston Wilcox, a retired gentleman who went to work for the Stanfield trust company in Truro some time before Lindbergh flew the Atlantic, says that Frank Stanfield was "rather what you would call a stern man. He ran the show, there was no doubt about that. We all called him 'The

Governor.' I remember he'd put mottos up for his employees, and he'd sign them himself. One said, 'Don't guess. Think. And Know.' He was a real individualist I guess you'd call him. He was a fellow who just did things as he chose to."

The Governor was a mediocre orator, his sons were mediocre orators, and clearly, oratory is not everything in life. Nor even in politics. Frank Stanfield disliked making speeches about Frank Stanfield. He would not talk to the press about himself ("His more intimate fancies and adventures," a Halifax newspaper observed, "were kept to himself"), and in this respect, he was very much like his own father, Charles, who so loathed personal publicity that he refused even to be photographed. There are many respects in which Charles, if he were alive in 1972, might recognize his grandson Bob. And Frank Stanfield would *know* the stubbornly reticent attitudes inside the bony head of the middle-aged man he last saw as a teenaged boy during the deep Depression in the lost summer of '31. Every son, whether he likes it or not, is a chip off the old block.

Life around the Stanfield house during Bob's childhood was not so solemn and dark as descriptions of The Governor might suggest. Father definitely let everyone know that he knew best, but he was not entirely an oppressor. And although it was not the Stanfield style to throw expensive parties for adults, there were often a lot of neighborhood kids hanging around the place.

The house itself, which stood on the site of what is now Keddy's Motor Inn (the Stanfield's wrought iron fence still cuts across the front of the property), was one of the biggest wooden mansions in Truro, but it was not an extravagant display of the wealth that everyone in town knew the Stanfields possessed. It had a circular driveway out front, a fourth-storey turret, a bit of gingerbread embroidery, and a lot of dark wood inside. It also had manicured lawns, lush flower beds, one of the biggest private libraries in town, a stock of classical music on records, and a tennis court that doubled as a hockey rink in winter. The Stanfield house had

191

one other extraordinary advantage over other houses. Her name was Sarah Emma Thomas Stanfield. The Governor's wife.

Mrs. Stanfield was born in Truro of Welsh and Irish descent. She was not a famous beauty but her photographs indicate she was far from homely and, more important, that she was a woman of remarkable warmth. She knew how to put people at ease. She was highly aware politically, and as Senator Fred Blois of Truro says, such women may have "great influence on any man's political future. I think she had a great many of the attributes of Bob's present wife."

"What a lovely and gracious woman she was," says an ancient Tory. She was, says the former premier of Nova Scotia, G.I. Smith, a delightful, charming lady, a very, very nice delightful person. She was, says the Stanfield's retired chauffeur Aubrey Borden, a lovely woman, a wonderful person. You could sit right down at a table with her, and talk about your troubles, and Borden says, "I can't ever remember meeting another woman of her standard." She was, says her son Charles, "a little bit of a thing," but the music, the books, the reading programs for the children, the color and lightness of life at the house on Prince Street were all due to her gentle and powerful influence.

The Stanfields were loyal adherents and discreet bene-factors at St. John's Church, the first Anglican church built of stone in all of Nova Scotia, but Mrs. Stanfield had broader Christian interests as well. On assorted missions to help the poor, Senator Blois recalls, she'd visit places "I'd be afraid to go into." She gave money to Zion Baptist Church, the black congregation to which her chauffeur adhered; she gave money to good causes and hard-pressed individuals; she was up to her concerned ears in Red Cross and Salvation Army work; she backed various politicians with hard cash; and, along with her husband, had the knack of "going calling." The Stanfields, despite their awkwardness on a platform, were beautifully comfortable while chatting in someone's barnyard, and on many a golden Sunday afternoon, Mr. and Mrs. Stanfield would be miles away from town, up in the hills, paying their casual respects to families they had not seen for a while.

People in the Twenties seldom thought of women as politicians, but in the years in which Bob Stanfield was growing up gracefully in Truro, his mother may just have been the finest natural politician in Colchester County. She's been dead for nearly a decade, but even now, you can't find even a Grit who'll bad-mouth Sarah Emma Thomas Stanfield.

The Stanfields are all Tories, and therefore any good Grit will tell you that they're a bunch of cheapskates who sit on their wealth and never do a damn thing for the town that's helped line their pockets. Any good Tory, on the other hand, will tell you that the Stanfields are too modest to erect public edifices in honor of themselves but that every last one of them has performed hundreds of secret good deeds for impoverished widows, destitute old men, starving children. The truth is that the Tories are partly right, which is one reason why the voters invariably reject even exceptionally gifted Grit candidates in favor of Stanfield men.

The Stanfields are secretive about their good deeds. One does not advertise that one is an easy mark, and flaunting one's wealth is not merely bad politics it is something even worse. Bad business. The wife of a Stanfield worker died suddenly in the Twenties. "She's to have a first-class funeral," Frank Stanfield told his plant manager. "I'll pay for it but don't you tell the undertaker. You just say you're doing it yourself. If he knows it's me, he'll soak us." The widower would know, without being told, who had bought the funeral. That was enough. Charity need not be folly.

The Stanfields' most *effective* charity, politically, was a part of their business. It grew out of a highly paternal regard for the well-being of their own workers. They bought flowers for employees' funerals. They paid grocery bills, sick pay, rent, unofficial pensions. At the height of the Depression, Frank Stanfield Jr. achieved the relative miracle of avoiding mass layoffs. An earlier admirer of the Stanfield underwear factory referred to the 200 workers there as "a sea of happy faces." They were also a sea of Stanfield voters, and they all had spouses, mothers, uncles, in-laws and friends, and these people too would have their day in the polling booth. Moreover, through the family-owned Acadia Trust Company, the Stanfields managed a lot of people's mortgages. It is unlikely that any family anywhere has ever managed to mix business, politics and charity more neatly than the Stanfields have.

Bob Stanfield was not eager to become a professional politician, but unless he'd retreated to a holy temple in the highlands of Tibet, it is difficult to see how he could have avoided his destiny. From 1907 until now, for 65 consecutive years, there has not been a day that a Stanfield, or a Stanfield employee, or a Stanfield in-law or, anyway, *someone* directly under the Stanfield influence has not held an elective office. In Stanfield country, no member of the family has ever been defeated in an election.

Gordon D. Stanfield was the youngest of the five children. He's 56 now, an engineer, a successful businessman in his own right down in Dartmouth, N.S., and once, not too long ago, he was heard to remark good-naturedly that nobody named Stanfield could ever tell him what to think any more. The remark may be apocryphal but it illustrates a truth: a refusal to let people tell you what to think is as true to the Stanfield family character as reticence is. Was The Governor a strong-minded man? "Well, you see," Preston Wilcox replies, "they're *all* strong-minded men ... and Bob, he could make up his own mind all right, and you scratch him just where you hadn't ought to and, boy, the sparks will fly!"

Wilcox recalls that Bob, when pressed, could be "very thorny." Wilcox himself did some of the pressing because he worked for the Acadia Trust Company, and for a brief unhappy spell, so did Bob. Bob was 25 or 26 then. At Dalhousie University he'd majored in political science and economics and won the Governor General's gold medal for the highest academic standing in the class of '36. He'd also graduated from the Harvard Law School. He had, as Wilcox concedes,

194

the broadest outlook and the finest brains in the Stanfield family. He also detested life in the trust company that his family owned. It was pretty clear that, if he'd just hang on, he'd eventually wind up running the place but he disliked the work and he disliked the management, and one day, after a particularly nasty confrontation with the manager of the business, he walked out and did not come back. He was not sure where he was going but he knew he was his own man.

The sparks used to fly around the house a bit, too. Oh, yes, Charles remembers, sure, "We'd argue to beat hell, mostly about sports, about hockey and baseball teams. Dad always followed the NHL and big-league baseball." At the mill in the daytime, at the trust company in the evening and at home on Prince Street, the meat and potatoes of Frank Stanfield's incisive discourse were business and politics. If the dessert course was a hearty wrangle over, say, what the "lively ball" was doing to big-league pitching, one imagines that Mrs. Stanfield and her one daughter Kathryn (Kit) must occasionally have fled, screaming, to the sewing room.

Kit, incidentally, was the entire audience late on the night that Bob stalked around the living room with his shoes in his hands, declaiming about world affairs and banging his shoes on a table to drive home his points. Kit was 22, Bob was 16, and before he was through, the whole family was wide awake. Even at that age, Bob had read more history than any other Stanfield had, and in whatever political debates raged within the family bosom, he usually stood as a minority of one against orthodox Toryism. "That Bob," said his eldest brother Frank Jr., "he's nothing but a damn Grit."

He was not so much a Grit, however, as a rebel against the overwhelming forces of town and family that threatened his power to choose the direction of his own life. As far back as his days as a teenaged counselor at a YMCA summer camp, there among the lore of the Micmacs, the smell of the spruce and the camaraderie of the cookout, young Bob Stanfield was trying to work out in words his own set of political beliefs.

Senator Blois remembers. "There was a time—it was after he finished Harvard, I think—some of us just wondered what his politics were going to be. He didn't seem to have any set views. He'd get groups of young people together, all over Nova Scotia, just to meet and talk politics. He said he was going to study the policies of everyone, the Conservatives, the Liberals, the CCF." How very strange. The CCF? Study their policies? For other Stanfields, it was enough to know that CCF stood for Cancel Canada's Freedom.

Senator Blois—who has worked for the Tories in every election, federal and provincial, since 1911—is pleased to remember that Bob Stanfield did finally decide that "the Conservative Party was the only one he could support." Bob was well over 30 before he allowed the Conservative Party into his heart. He was living in Halifax by then. Years before, he had decided that whatever his future might be, it did not lie in the new Heaven and the new earth of Truro, Nova Scotia.

Maclean's, May 1972

The Last Bat

We found three dopey bats when we opened our cottage one spring afternoon, and they horrified us. What is it about bats that makes you want to scream and run out of your own house? Is it half a century of vampire movies? Is it that bats seem to be neither bird nor animal, but some fiendish mixture of the two? Is it that they hide by day, fly by night and insidiously squirm indoors through holes not much bigger than headache tablets? Bats are all flutter and flimsiness. They're just half-ounce mammals with wings, and if we could only be rational about them, we would appreciate their marvellous gobbling of flies and mosquitoes. But we can't. At least I can't.

"What'll we do?" I quavered.

"We've got to think of something," Penny said.

One bat was on a couch, the other two on the floor. They were mere lumps of fur with leathery points. They were not doing anything. In fact, they seemed to be dying. We had left two insect-killing strips in the cottage all winter, and maybe the bats had poisoned themselves by feasting on the poisoned bugs. Sick bats, however, are no less repulsive than healthy bats.

Country people would simply have smashed them with a broom, and thrown out the tiny corpses, but we're city people. We spent an hour removing shutters, unpacking food, putting pails under drainpipes to catch water and otherwise avoiding the inescapable challenge. The bats never moved. Then Penny boldly grabbed the broom and swept the bat nearest the door out onto the grass. I held the door open. One down, two to go. My turn.

I had to push the second bat 20 feet with the broom, and during the journey to the door, it began to revive. Its wings moved. As I swept it along, it curled itself into a tiny ball, as light as dust but strangely disgusting. More than 70 years ago, a vampire authority wrote that "sometimes, the vampire is thought to be the soul of a living man which leaves his body in sleep to go in the form of a fluff of down and suck the blood of other sleepers."

The third bat was the biggest and least lethargic. As Penny gave it a bum's rush with frantic broom strokes, its wings pounded the floor. Outside in the grass, it lay on its back, opened its tiny mouth, bared its tiny fangs, uttered tiny shrieks of rage, flopped around a bit, then lurched through a few feet of air to the woods. "I've never seen a look of such hatred," Penny said, "and there was something about its face that was almost human." Almost like Bela Lugosi?

Our next bat encounter made the cottage adventure seem tame. The cottage is on a bluff overlooking Chedabucto Bay in eastern Nova Scotia, and it is only a dozen years old. The farmhouse, which sits on the highway a little way inland, has been home to five generations of Bruces and God only knows how many bats. My great-great-grandfather Richard Bruce built the place in the mid-1840s. That would be around the time the young Queen Victoria fell in love with the Scottish Highlands, Marx and Engels wrote the *Communist Manifesto*, and Bram Stoker was born. Half a century later, in 1897, Stoker would write *Dracula*, the novel that turned the vampire legends of eastern Europe into a macabre and enduring branch of the entertainment industry.

The house and its rooms are small, built for short, 19th-century Bruces. "It started out as a plain square of a house—parlor, dining room (The Room), kitchen and bedroom downstairs and four bedrooms up, each with the upper part of one wall slanted by the pitch of the roof," my father once wrote. That was still the arrangement when my wife and I took over last summer. All we did was destroy the downstairs bedroom to double the size of the kitchen, and this enlarged area, still unfinished, served as our campaign headquarters during what we will always remember as Bat Saturday.

The bats were in the attic. We knew that. Two of my aunts, both of whom are older than a first edition of *Dracula*, had been harassed by bats in this same house only a couple of summers before, and I had hired a fumigator to come over from Antigonish. That, however, bought only a temporary peace. Now, as Penny and I snuggled under our quilt at midnight, we could hear things rustling, scratching, and scrabbling round just above our heads. Sweet dreams, dear.

I'd read enough to know that bats don't get in your hair or bite you on the neck and that although they can nip you nastily if you try to handle them (not one of my ambitions), you are more likely to win millions in a national lottery than to have a rabid bat come after you. The rest of my bat lore rested entirely on hearsay. One local theory was that the way to get rid of any bat zigzagging through your house was just to turn out all inside lights, open an outside door, turn on the outside light, keep your cool and wait. Eventually, the bat would follow the fresh-air current to the great black outdoors, leaving without any argument. I wasn't sure what purpose the outdoor light served but decided to incorporate the entire open-door policy into my strategy, which also called for mothball crystals. Bat-wise locals had told me your average brown bat hates mothballs. I bought the last two boxes of crystals at a Canadian Tire store, and on Bat Saturday, I mounted a bold offensive against the evil hordes.

Bats come out to play at dusk. As the sun sank in the west, I climbed a stepladder, pushed open the hatch to the attic and crawled into bat-held territory. Except for faint bars of evening light from the western vent, the place was in darkness. The day's trapped heat was stifling. Fourteen decades of dust clogged my nostrils. I could scarcely breathe, and I couldn't stand. From the ladder, Penny handed me a flashlight and three bowls of mothball crystals. I crept around among clots of ancient seaweed insulation, wondering if bats nested in desiccated eelgrass, and spaced out the bowls. Then I noticed that the western vent had no screen. The unscreened vent, to a bat, was like wide-open French doors to a cat burglar. I would seal the beasts in and force them out through another exit.

Penny fetched hammer, nails and a sliding, adjustable screen in a wooden frame. To direct the flashlight beam while I hammered the screen over the vent, she had to join me in the attic. It was claustrophobic's nightmare, and she is a touch claustrophobic. Country living, I told her, builds character. But as I hammered, bats began to stir and squeak, as though they were forming up in secret platoons or drawing straws to see who would lead the attack. Every time she frantically aimed the light towards the sounds, I frantically bashed my thumb. Maybe it was my screams and curses that inspired the bats to lay low till we were safely back at our command post in the kitchen.

Sweating like an overweight fighter who had just gone 15 rounds, I poured us each a slug of rum and water while Penny stationed herself so she could look down the skinny hall to the front door. We had left the upstairs hatch open to lure the enemy downstairs and outside. Fifteen minutes passed, and then the hall was suddenly filled with one bat.

"It's coming in here," Penny shrieked.

And so it was. It flew around about a foot from the floor and, in the dying light, seemed to have a wingspan of at least ten inches.

"Quick," I ordered. "Open the front door. Turn on the outside light."

It actually worked. The bat tore into the bug-ridden night like a bat out of...well, like a bat out of hell.

No sooner had it left than another arrived in the kitchen. But after cruising around us, it, too, flitted down the hall and shot outdoors. When this pattern was clear, I poured another drink, took it outside and lay on the grass.

"You just stay in the kitchen and discourage them from hanging around," I told Penny. "I'll stay out here and count them as they fly out the door."

"Thanks a lot."

Lying under the stars and counting bats was satisfying work. I kept score. "There's another one. That's six. There's seven. There's eight. Yahoo!" Once, three flew out together without even entering the kitchen. That was a high point of the evening, but occasionally I'd heard Penny's tremulous complaint that some bat was too stupid to leave and kept swooping around her head. "Don't worry," I shouted. "They've got radar. It'll never touch you."

When the score reached 13, the exodus ceased. None came out for half an hour. I went inside, closed the door, doused the light, reported to headquarters for a nightcap, turned on the kitchen lights. Number 14 popped into the room. I raced to open the front door, but this bat refused to follow the proper route. The fact that there were two of us in the kitchen must have unnerved it, or maybe it was just an exceptionally perverse bat. It stubbornly hustled around us, and then wormed its way through a hole in the wall near the floor, a hole that we will one day cover with baseboard. One of our bats was missing.

We forgot him. We retreated to another room to finish our drinks, congratulate ourselves on our victory during this amazing evening and consider the alarming possibility that I had not counted 14 different bats but perhaps only seven.

What if they had flown out the door, then insinuated themselves back inside through some secret passage we would never find, and come out a second time. We were chuckling about this ludicrous fear when Penny glanced at the six-inch hole in the ceiling where we had removed a light fixture.

"Oh migod!" she said. "What's *that*?"

An elfin, claw-like hand appeared, and then a pointed joint, like an elbow, and a face, and then a brown body was dangling from the hole as though the brute were about to do chin-ups. Instead, it flew madly about, brushing this, thumping that, maybe searching for departed cronies who had flown the coop. Once again, we switched on the outside light, opened the door. Out he went. The last bat.

We slept the sleep of the exorcised. Nothing stirred beyond the wood above our heads. Nor have we seen or heard a bat in the house in the months that have followed. We don't know where our evicted tenants have gone. We don't know what influence the mothball crystals exerted on the events of Bat Saturday, but they're still up there. One day, I may retrieve the bowls, but not yet. I'm in no hurry. Bats, like vampires, have been known to return.

Harrowsmith, September 1984

The Ottawa Children's Crusade

No great political event in Canadian history has ever been so thoroughly dominated by teenagers as the recent Liberal leadership convention. By "dominated" I do not mean that they controlled the outcome. I mean that their singing, their prancing, their squealing, their frequently militant parading and their plain physical superiority all combined to give the political rites whatever wild color they had, and to give the whole event the smell of some sort of jolly children's crusade. I also mean that their strength and exuberance irritated and even tortured some of the very voting delegates that the convention had been called to assemble. On occasion, the kids drove these older people right out of the big official parties, and up to the peace of their bedrooms, and a quiet bottle with *old* friends.

If you were mildly sadistic, nothing was funnier than watching middle-aged drinking men arrive at the convention centre on the morning after. They'd gingerly disembark from a cab, make their troubled way up the outdoor stairs, open one of the glass doors, and then—aargh, no, no, help, please stop!—the noise would slam into them. Forty beautiful, powerful, full-sweatered, clean, clean, *clean* big girls, with their teeth gleaming, their hair flying, their eyes happily shining, with their pennants, their signs, their hats, all in raw red and white... and all of them *screaming*, "HELLyer, HELLyer, HELLyer," and pounding sticks on the pavement, and a brassy band going blaaah at your head and, for God's sake no, a *drum*. It was bad if you were a Kierans man. In fact, it was bad if you were a Hellyer man. All that crazy jailbait, and nowhere to hide.

If you escaped Hellyer's girls, you could be sure that some other posse of innocent, fresh-faced, adolescent fiends would hunt you down... pretty little girls bellowing, "Hey, hey, what d'y say? All the way with Allan J.," accompanied perhaps by no less punishing a mid-morning instrument than the bagpipes, and thrusting Nova Scotian apples in your face...or the black and golden Turner troops, who appeared to be in better shape than an Olympic gym team...or some nymphet shoving mints, green for Greene, under your nose. Have you no mercy, child?

The enthusiasm of the teenagers also forced some of the candidates themselves into postures that struck me, anyway, as awkward and sad. One night, Paul Martin came through the lobby of the Skyline Hotel, trailing a brass band and hundreds of ecstatic kids. They were singing, "Martin's the man, hey... Martin's the man, say...Martin is the man for Ca-na-da," but Martin, the man, looked so tired I was afraid he'd fall down. He'd been leading these kids through impossibly crowded hotel lobbies for several hours, and now, as he came on through the Skyline mob, he was still trying to shuffle a little in time to the music, he was trying to stare beyond the hard lights, he was sweating, sagging, ceaselessly grinning. His face was frozen, and 65 years old. He grabbed my hand, pumped it, and said, "We're all right, we're all right now." Then he grabbed another hand, and then he was gone, and the big Martin signs veered past like colored sails and the kids, still as fresh as the crocuses of Ottawa, kept on singing, "Martin's the man, hey...Martin's the man, say...Martin is the man."

Martin is not one of my favorite politicians but as he went around, employing the political style he could no longer change, I thought his tired bravery shone through the adolescent racket. I even felt sorry for Hellyer, as the Hellyer girls swept onto the convention floor, kicking and yelping like a Broadway chorus line...with him in the middle, tall as DeGaulle, flashing a smile that could not help being silly, trying to kick along with them while the band played a tune that naughty boys know as "Bullshit makes the grass grow green." Politics is a cruel mistress.

The social activities of the teenagers were so vigorous that, on the last night before the voting, some of the candidates imposed an "Adults Only" restriction. They closed their parties to everyone except delegates and alternate delegates. ("That's not fair," said one little Trudeau-bopper. "It's just not fair after all the work we've done.") At one point, the Mac-Eachen camp felt obliged to declare they would tolerate no deals with other candidates, no delegate dropouts, and no drinking by minors. "There were no young kids at our parties," one of MacEachen's men said piously, "as there were at some other parties I could mention."

Many of the youngsters attended the convention because it was a monumental public bash—the Ottawa papers kept comparing it to Grey Cup weekend—but some had slightly more exalted motives. "Any principal who wouldn't allow a student to work at the convention is narrow-minded," one boy announced. "If this isn't an education, I don't know what is." John Turner's army wore golden jackets, and one of his more serious hangers-on complained, "All these guys want those jackets for is to work under their cars and go fishing." A middle-aged chap from the Northwest Territories who, incidentally, had never seen or heard the word "teenybopper," rather liked the vaguely Kennedyesque quality of the Turner team. "At least," he said, "some of these kids have haircuts." He added, partisanly, "I haven't seen any here as bad as those with Trudeau."

Trudeau's kids may have been hairy-headed—after all, most of them were girls—but many of them were also intensely loyal. If other youngsters were at the convention for the "education," or to get jackets, or simply to be an In person back in the old classroom, a great many of the Trudeau kids were there because they idolized their candidate. They wanted to see him up close, hear him, meet his eyes, earn one of his smiles, touch him. During the last desperate efforts to bring down Trudeau, the Hellyer girls cheerfully joined the Winters girls and—like the Hellyer jazz band, whose members now wore photographs of Winters—they all marched around the convention floor together. I doubt whether the Trudeau kids could have done that. If Trudeau had lost when Hellyer did, I think, the Trudeau kids would have all gone home and had a good cry.

The official Trudeau girls, the ones in the orange uniforms from a fashionable Toronto boutique, were so fiercely protective that they may well have been the only beautiful bodyguards in Canadian history. A reporter, who'd been assigned to stick with Trudeau night and day, suffered several sharp orange jabs to the ribs before he said, "You've got great elbows, you girls." One of them smiled back, ever so sweetly, and said, "Ah oui, but the feet." At the door to a party that Trudeau was attending, a brunette orange girl, with tears of frustration in her dark eyes, gave a furious dressing-down to a dumpy, reprehensible, orange boy. "I *know*," she said. "*Everybody* wants to be here. But we have to have people at the other hospitality suite. You can't just break rank like that."

Trudeau had a casual and thoroughly natural way of kidding around, not only with those in the official ranks, but also with the girls who simply showed up to watch him go by. Once, when he was charging through a corridor, followed by a clutch of panting reporters, he spotted an extraordinarily pretty girl whom he'd met in some other city. "What are you doing here?" he said. "A delegate, a guest, what? You can be a guest any time." He moved on, thought a second, and shouted over his shoulder, "And say hello to your mother."

Trudeau also had teenybopper power when he needed it most. That was on The Night of the Signs. Other candidates had come onto the convention floor behind big bands and marching, strutting, precisely controlled parades. Trudeau had advised his youthful strategists that he did not want his followers coming on like Nazi storm troopers. They planted hundreds of sign-carrying kids around the stands. ("We understand," Charles Templeton seriously announced on television, "that the Trudeau people are going to attempt a spontaneous demonstration.") When Trudeau's turn to speak arrived, an astonishing blizzard of signs suddenly rose up, and from the highlands of the arena, the roar for Trudeau rolled and swept down upon the delegates. "What a coup," the man beside me said to no one in particular. "What a coup!" And it was. The swaying photographs of Trudeau had a curious, sad, saintly quality, and the whole eruption seemed like some sort of massive tribute, in an ancient time, to a religious prophet. At that moment, I was sure that if the older people here were to reject Trudeau, they would be sending the Liberal party to certain defeat, and possibly oblivion.

The Star Weekly, May 1968

Man and Superfan: Jock Watchers of the World Unite!

If you've never been sure why you keep blowing money on tickets at ringside, centre field, blue line or third-base line, rest assured: sports sociologists will soon have you all figured out. For you are part of what they call "fandom," or "spectatorship," or "the phenomenon of secondary sports involvement," or, if they happen to be French Marxist sports sociologists, of "the servile masses," in which case your passion for big-time sports is a symptom of the fascist oppression under which you toil. (The Marxists claim evil capitalism horribly dupes not only fans but also athletes. The human body, you see, is meant not for the morbid self-abuse of Olympic competition but for lovemaking. Well, I said they were *French* Marxists, didn't I?)

With your cigars, your flask, a warm furry coat on your back and a warm furry woman at your side, you may *think* you're having a swell time as the Eskimos clobber yet another effete eastern team, but actually you're just a victim of "emotional fascistification." (Repeat after me: Emotional fascistification, emotional fascistification, emotional fascistification.)

206

The phrase is Jean-Marie Brohm's. He's a French intellectual who insists that "the purpose of these meaningless dramas is to fill the masses' minds with trivia to prevent them thinking about political struggle.... Sport is a means of regimentation and dehumanization...a mass political safety valve.... The ceremonies at major sports competitions are just like big military parades or prefascist rallies, with their military music, the flag rituals, rhythmic marches, national anthems and medal ceremonies."

Sport, in short, drugs the masses. Thanks to gun-toting cops and brassy half-time spectacles, it also infects them with both a sheepish respect for law and order and a dangerous taste for military pageantry. That, it seems, is why Hitler was such a zealous sports impresario. A British writer agrees with the French Marxists: Sports are "manifestations of the essence of bourgeois ideology infused into every nook and crevice of social existence under capitalism, and are to be fought as such...from the primary school playing field to Royal Ascot, from college baseball to the World Series."

Baloney, you say? You have never for a second felt like one of the servile masses? Ah, then, perhaps you have felt like a monkey. One John Dickinson, an associate professor in the department of kinesiology at Simon Fraser University in Burnaby, B.C., suggests your average sports fan is like a monkey in a cubicle. When the monkey presses a lever, "a window in the cubicle flips open and allows [him] to look out into the rest of the experimental area with all its ongoing activity for a short time. This is sufficient reinforcement for that response to be well conditioned. The analogy with spectating is, I think, very close indeed. The urban dweller of today is not exactly locked into his cubicle, but is certainly fed on a relatively unchanging diet of sensory stimulation.... The stimulation provided by the game, the crowds of people, the shouting, cheering, etc., is probably a fundamental aspect of the reinforcement of spectatorship."

The monkey who presses the lever to see some action is thus a brother-under-the-skin of the boxing fan who fights traffic and shells out the price of two bottles of Chivas Regal to sit in a hard place while watching two sweaty brutes beat each other bloody. Yes, that's it, fan and monkey share a fundamental aspect of the reinforcement of spectatorship. They're trying to escape boredom.

The intriguing thing is that despite Dickinson's jargon and the sour extremism of the Marxists, such chaps are not entirely wrong. Not about the opiate part anyway. Fans often behave suspiciously like drug addicts. Daniel Okrent, perhaps the ultimate U.S. baseball fan, managed to get to 13 ball parks on 13 consecutive days to see 13 games. He saw no team twice. He saw all 26 major-league clubs, and he said he was in baseball heaven. Surely no junkie has ever gone to such ingenious lengths to feed his habit. Jonathan Yardley of Baltimore, Maryland, a self-confessed "passionate, irrational, screaming-bonkers Orioles fan," told *Sports Illustrated* readers that, in the grip of his addiction, he couldn't sleep until he'd heard how his adored Orioles had done.

When they were out west, he would huddle by his radio, following the play-by-play till 2 or 3 a.m. If he fell asleep too soon (the flesh is weak), he'd guiltily wake at dawn and dial a number for recorded scores. He reckoned up-to-the-minute Orioles' averages with his pocket calculator, scrutinized sports pages in six daily newspapers to keep abreast of all tidbits about Orioles' injuries, Orioles' moods and tantrums, Orioles' ups, downs, ins and outs. Yardley talked about the Orioles all day, thought about the Orioles all night and unless you, too, were an Orioles fanatic, it's unlikely you would want him as your barber.

Yardley and Okrent are scarcely alone. They are merely extreme examples of what four physical education profs at the University of Alberta call "The deeply committed male sports fan." The profs are Garry Smith, Brent Patterson, Trevor Williams and John Hogg. In a recent paper they observe, "A new strain of sports fan has been spawned— namely the sports addict." Not only that, they organized interviews with no fewer than 52 male champions of spectatorship in Edmonton. You couldn't even qualify for the interviews unless you first confessed a heavy commitment to following sport and, second, "met the minimum standards in at least four of the following five categories: 1) read about sports in the newspapers every day; 2) read at least three different sports periodicals a month; 3) watched an average of eight hours of sports a week on television; 4) attended an average of more than one live sporting event a month where [you] had to pay admission; and 5) talked about sports every day."

Superstars may come and go, but not superfans. All 52 Edmonton jock-watchers "stated unequivocally that they expected to maintain their interest in sport indefinitely." Asked if they could imagine *anything* that might dampen their passion for sports, 77 percent said no, they couldn't. A handful said greedy players and the legal battles that afflict professional sport might just cool their interest. An even smaller handful thought a death in the family, disease or unemployment might possibly turn them off sports for a while. When their favorite team lost, virtually all were either "very upset" or "somewhat upset." Most felt blue for a few hours but some "reacted more emotionally by taking their frustration out on inanimate objects like walls and furniture, or by swearing a lot, or drinking more." Still others "got insomnia trying to analyze what went wrong."

These guys were *committed*. Most of them always planned their spare time around sports events, and the rest sometimes did. Some travelled hundreds of miles just to see a game. Some had video recorders so that if two games were on TV at once they could catch both. Others let football schedules dictate the timing of their summer holidays or took TV sets on camping trips so the glory of the Canadian wilderness might echo to the mellifluous tones of Yankee sportscasters. And the voice of the Cosell was heard in our land. One guy actually postponed his wedding so he wouldn't miss a football game. The researchers do not reveal whether he sang, "Get me to the stadium on time." Thirty-three suffered mild guilt feelings over the time they squandered on their glorious indulgence, and at least a dozen admitted it was "a source of friction with other family members." Wives crabbed at them for ignoring their children. Quarrels broke out over control of the TV set. But "even at the possible risk of alienating family members, their enthusiasm for sport was not diminished."

How had they become like this? Surprisingly, the significance of the media was slight. Most of those interviewed had caught the condition from their fathers, as though it were a hereditary disease, but several also mentioned friends and coaches. Moreover, a taste for playing was a crucial factor. While the learned enemies of spectatorship depict fans as slack-jawed, fat-arsed, beer-swilling louts and cretins, these Edmonton men weren't like that at all. Indeed, nine out of 10 played at one sport or another at least once a week. The lesson, apparently, is that it's easy to love watching an activity you've loved performing. To put it another way, it takes a little primary sport involvement to really get your rocks off on secondary sport involvement.

It was predictable that among Edmonton fans, the favorite team would be the Edmonton Eskimos. The Montreal Canadiens were second, the Edmonton Oilers third, the Montreal Expos fourth. The Canadiens, however, also placed second among "least favorite" teams. Some felt the Canadiens, like the New York Yankees, had been dominant too long and hogged the sports pages. "The Montreal Alouettes and the Boston Bruins were perceived as being dirty, chippy teams who would do anything to win," but contempt for the least favorite team of all, the Toronto Maple Leafs, "was almost entirely due to the antics of their management." Typical comments on the Leafs: "Harold Ballard is a buffoon, he has no class.... Following this team is like a soap opera, they treat players poorly.... They act like they're superior. When they lose, they always make excuses."

Another hater of the Bruins and Yankees was American sportswriter Eddie Andelman. In his book *Sports Fans of the World, Unite!*, he charged the Boston team had brutalized hockey until "it would require wild animals from the African plains to cope with the Bruins' bludgeoning brand of warfare." Andelman, incidentally, recommended hating teams: "It's fun, it's relaxing, and surely it magnifies one's enjoyment of the game.... Surely there is plenty of room in our hearts for hate, especially where organized sports today are concerned." Surely there is. Most of those interviewed in Edmonton "had disliked a particular team for at least five years, and they seemed to get almost as much enjoyment out of the misfortunes of their least favorite team as they did out of the success of their favorite team." And who can doubt that one night last October, millions of deeply committed male sports fans went to bed ecstatic not because the Dodgers had won the World Series but because the Yankees had *lost* it and, in losing, had looked like stumblebums?

Speaking of the Yankees, the Edmonton fans ranked Reggie Jackson among players they liked least. As some put it, he was "selfish." He had a "big ego" and a "poor attitude." On the roster of the unpopular, Jackson was right up there with U.S. high jumper Dwight Stones ("poor loser...selfish...arrogant...pops off a lot"); and, since the Edmonton interviews predated the swift limelighting of superbrat John McEnroe, with tennis star Ilie Nastasi ("show-off... infantile...prima donna...superbrat").

Unpopular hockey players included Vancouver Canucks' Tiger Williams and the most heartily disliked athlete of them all, Bobby Clarke of the Philadelphia Flyers. The fact that Clarke also squeaked onto the list of the Edmontonians' *heroes* seemed to confirm one fan's opinion that he was "a Jekyll and Hyde personality." Clarke, he continued, "would slash his mother in the face. The sad part is that he is a good player, he doesn't have to resort to being a stick artist." Others said Clarke was "dirty...chippy." His values were "warped." He "hid behind teammates."

All in all, the least-admired players were mouthy, egocentric, vicious shit disturbers, the sort of guys you wish had never showed up for touch football on a Sunday afternoon. Can you imagine a friendly pickup softball game with the likes of Jackson, Stones, Nastasi, Clarke and Williams? Especially if Nastasi, say, owned the bat and ball? The heroes of the Edmonton fans were a different sort entirely. They were not only good players but also Good Men. The fans revered them for their support of "mainstream values" and for such Boy Scout virtues as "dedication, leadership ability, sportsmanship, modesty and community involvement." They were "predominantly Canadian, Caucasian hockey players who personify traditional values" (or, from Jean-Marie Brohm's seat in the stands, "the values of the capitalist jungle"). Enough hints? Okay. The men who led the rest of the hero pack by a country kilometre were Wayne Gretzky, Guy Lafleur and Gordie Howe.

There was one stunning exception to all this: Muhammad Ali. He was the only boxer among the heroes, and one of only three blacks, the others being basketball stars Julius Erving and Kareem Abdul Jabbar. Ali was not high on the list but he was in there with the likes of Bjorn Borg and Bobby Orr, nudging Jack Nicklaus and Jean Belliveau. Yet he had not only defied such mainstream values as the Vietnam War but had also swaggered through his time as the quintessential mouthy, arrogant, egocentric superstar. His hands were fast, but his lip was faster. So how come he made the hero list in Edmonton? The answer may lie in the way the Alberta profs categorized the 13 heroes. Twelve were "reinforcing" types. One was a "seductive" type: Muhammad Ali.

I'll buy that. Monkeylike, I could never resist pulling the lever to see Ali fight or hear his outrageous patter. In his prime, he banished boredom. I mean, he enlivened the "relatively unchanging diet of sensory stimulation" that I endured as "an urban dweller." God, yes, seductive. Ali was so seductive he could mesmerize anyone—even, I suspect, a French Marxist.

Quest, March 1982

From Barbados to the Beauce, Life's Finest Spectator Sports Are Free

The best soccer game I ever saw was within earshot of the luke sea in Barbados. Tamarind trees surrounded the park and I could smell strange perfume. Plumes of casuarinas, 100 feet high, swayed in the ceaseless trade wind, and after a day of lolling in the breakers and accepting enough sun to sting, I had the illusion of fitness. The light from the sky was pink. Longfellow called this the "Children's Hour." It was "Between the dark and the daylight, / When the night is beginning to lower." Since I wasn't quite ready for another shot from my $2 bottle of amber rum, I sat in the grass like a local and watched all these black guys emulate Edson Arantes do Nascimento, or as he's better known, Pelé.

I seek such experiences when I travel because there's no better way to sniff a culture than to join the people who are watching their friends, lovers and relatives at play. If I were in Louisville on Kentucky Derby day, I'd reject Churchill Downs in favor of a little league ball game. I'd like to see a village badminton final in Indonesia, a second-rate rodeo in Texas, a battle of kites in an obscure corner of Japan, mountainous men of the Scottish Highlands tossing the caber in the shadow of their own hills, and at an outdoor pavilion in a small town in China, local hotshots competing at table tennis. I'd like to gate-crash a yacht club in Sydney, Australia, on the day ocean-going sloops finish a race from Tasmania.

Some of the Barbadian players were skinny boys, others paunchy men. Some wore jogging suits, others white shorts. Most had sneakers, but a few cradled, dribbled and boomed the old ball with their bare feet. Some were sluggish but tricky, others flew along like deer. One had shoulders like

213

onetime middleweight champ Dick Tiger and a hard, glistening, slender torso that surely inspired reverie among certain women tourists. He moved like an acrobatic ballet star and scored twice with his head. The players knew one another by their first names, and whenever one made a flashy move, the others liltingly shouted their approval. Nobody argued with anybody. Laughter was as significant as feats, and the pleasure flowed up and down the field until the sun plopped out of sight and the players and spectators drifted off with their wives and girls. Near the equator, the Children's Hour is too damn short.

The second-best soccer game I ever saw was outside the walled village of Obidos, Portugal. Obidos is a white, blossom-bedecked jumble of little old houses, shops, bars and churches. It is impossibly pretty. Even centuries ago, it was so enchanting that Portuguese kings would give the whole town to their wives as a wedding gift. It's 50 miles north of Lisbon, but some people with jobs in the capital nevertheless choose to live there. Crenellated walls, towers, parapets and spires are a magnificent backdrop for the soccer field. If you banned automobiles, you could shoot a movie about a medieval siege here, but it was a milder contest that consumed my Sunday afternoon in Obidos.

With some old men who wore caps, and naturally spoke in their own strange, sibilant tongue, I sat on a bluff that faced the stands—at most, they seated a couple of hundred villagers—and, beyond them, the fabulous skyline of the fortress. The clouds were the fat, towering, boiling kind that promise rain and harbor giants. Police in grey tunics lingered near the stands, but their manner was sunny and lethargic rather than coplike. The players, despite having uniforms, were as motley as the Barbadians. This was a game for those with bandy legs, pipestem calves, swaybacks and potbellies, for the hairy and the hairless, the shrimp and the hulk, the endomorph and the ectomorph, the quick and, at times, it appeared, the almost dead. This was a game for auto mechanics, shopkeepers, farmhands, schoolboys and waiters. The thing about getting within smelling distance of those who play for love rather than money is that you see them not as professionally perfected shapes on television but as vulnerable creatures who sweat, sigh, exult and grunt.

The game was clean, cheerful, hard fought. It was also messy, but no one cared, least of all me. Watching those fellows chasing a ball for two of their hours on earth, under the spectacular stone evidence of a millennium of local history, made me feel for a moment that I knew what it was to be Portuguese. I felt more in tune with both Portugal and myself than I had in any museum or hushed and cavernous church, or even in the Lisbon *fado* joints where women singers wrenched tears from the eyes of tourist and Portuguese alike. When you attend a two-bit game in a foreign country, you not only share a people's passion, you also cease to be an obvious tourist. You're rubbernecking, sure, but so are the locals. They're all watching the game too, and they do not notice you with your odd clothing, pricey Pentax and inability to communicate. Just for a while, you are *part* of the country.

At Mawnan Smith in May I found a cricket match. Mawnan Smith is near the coast of Cornwall in southwest England, and I was staying at the Meudon, a comfortable country hotel whose staff fed me as though they thought I should be fattened for slaughter. One Sunday afternoon I decided to pass up tea and scones with strawberry jam and gobs of clotted cream. Leaving the garden and its assertive rhododendrons, I ambled down a winding road. Tall hedges flanked me and rustled with secret life. A shower had rinsed the air. Sunlit steam hovered over the grass. The trees were heavy and friendly, and I wondered why songbirds were more fluent, throaty and mellifluous in rural England than anywhere else.

I rounded a bend, heard men shouting beyond my starboard hedge, negotiated a gate, and there I was—standing on damp sidelines with the girls in their summer dresses while chaps in white cavorted at cricket. It is a game I'll never understand, but I knew this scene was quintessentially English. When a warm cloudburst caused ladies to squeal and gentlemen to hoot, and all of them to scamper together for cover, I was, in the words of the immortal Dylan Thomas, as "happy as the grass was green." If you'd seen that English grass, you'd know I was extremely happy.

South of Quebec City, up the Chaudière River toward the Maine border, lies the Beauce country. Though John Crosbie is fluently bilingual compared to me, I once chose to spend a weekend there. The language barrier made it a time of apology, confusion and queer loneliness but, looking back, I would not trade the inter-village hockey game I saw on natural ice in Ste-Marie for a seat on the blue line during the seventh game of a Stanley Cup final between Toronto and Montreal.

The night was black, the air cold enough to kill. Along with 50-odd townspeople, I stood on the snow that was banked against the boards of the rink and watched local heroes whistling up the ice, knocking one another flying, gasping under bright bulbs and grim hills. Everyone was calling the players by name and yelling things in French. The teams weren't part of a highly organized league. The players, whose ages ranged from about 16 to 40, were not grooming themselves for the NHL. They played hockey simply because they loved to play hockey, and it was one hell of a game. The memory of enjoying it with people to whom I could not even talk has stayed with me for 15 years. I got a frostbitten ear that night, but it was worth it. For sports spectators far from home, the best things in life are still free.

Quest, November 1983

The "Acadian Nightingale" Starts to Soar

She's "the Acadian nightingale" but sometimes she eats like a wolf. Now, with her blonde curls, powerful eyes, scarlet dress, black buttons, scarlet and black earrings, and white and black necklaces of pearl, she is flashy, but tastefully flashy, precisely as flashy as a diva should be, and she's eating wet, red rib steak without remorse. Her silky coat, made of black mink, occupies its own chair at the round table. Animal lovers may object to fur coats but, she jokes, mink are nasty, destructive creatures who deserve no better fate than to keep her warm. Besides, Fernard Doucet gave her the coat. He's her husband, and she misses him. She's on the road eight months of the year. She's on the road right now.

At a plain café in stone Quebec, she engorges good lunch. She's within singing range of the old Laval campus where her father-in-law studied medicine, and she studied music. She's so close to the rented room where she and Fernand once met for pre-marital trysts that, if the street revellers would only shut up, she might reach it even with her soft floating *pianissimo*. After all, a critic wrote in Tokyo, her *pianissimi* would "go on spinning a thin silk thread of words and melodies, across space and across time."

She is Rosemarie Landry, a globe-trotting soprano, and here in Quebec City, during the excessive winter carnival, she feels she belongs. That's how she felt as a girl on long-gone Sunday evenings at her grandfather's house in Caraquet, N.B. Her grandfather played fiddle. So did her father. He had three brothers and two sisters and, what with the fiddles, guitars, a mandolin and piano, they amounted to "an Acadian chamber orchestra." Two of her six cousins played piano, and they all sang. At five, she was studying piano. At nine, she was competing in music festivals throughout northeastern New

217

Brunswick. "My mother used to say the two most important things in life were going to school and practising piano," she says. "I loved piano. It sure beat washing up the dishes." Moreover, although not all nuns were nice, "there were nice nuns at Caraquet," and they fanned her love of music.

The soup's gone, the steak shrinks, the cake with whipped cream and chocolate sauce is doomed. ("I am addicted to Belgian chocolate," she volunteers, rolling her eyes. "Ah, it is to die!") At 12.30 p.m., the Acadian nightingale needs her energy. "Energy" is one of her favorite words in English. For hours before a performance she eats nothing because she does not want the act of digestion to absorb even an ounce of her onstage energy.

"Discipline," to Landry, is an even more important word. She believes in discipline for herself the way Captain Bligh believed in discipline for the Royal Navy. Her back is straight, her gestures as quick as her broad smile. She is stubborn, studious, single-minded, abstinent. Yes, she is vivacious, and almost fluffily feminine. ("Is that the queen?" an awe-struck girl asks while a photographer grabs a shot of Landry outside the restaurant. It is a flattering question. The queen of the Quebec Winter Carnival, chosen last night, is a teenager. Landry's in her mid-30s.) To an anglo male, she is the strangest combination of iron determination and *joie de vivre*.

No Canadian could possibly have come by these qualities more naturally than Landry. From her painted fingernails, to the planes of her forehead, to the roots of her singing heart, she is Acadian; and the story of the Acadians is a story not just of determined survivors but also of joyful survivors, lyrical survivors. On both her father's and mother's sides, Landry is a descendant of Alexis Landry. Born in the Annapolis Valley in 1720 and ejected by the British in the Great Expulsion of 1755, he settled at Caraquet around 1760. British raiders drove him out in 1761, but he soon returned. Stubbornness runs in the family.

Historian W.F. Ganong called Alexis "the most prominent and no doubt the earliest" of the Acadian founders of

Caraquet. In 1784, just 200 years ago, the government granted land to 34 French-speaking families in Caraquet, and among them were Cormiers, Gallants, Boudreaus, Poiriers, Thibodeaus and, already, no less than six sets of Landrys. Rosemarie's parents, seven generations after Alexis, still live on his land grant. That's where she grew up, and that's where she goes when she comes home to see her family. The telephone listings for the Caraquet neighborhood include nearly 400 Landry households.

She was not an entirely good little Acadian girl. Her parents, Hedwidge and Adelbert Landry (lumber, pulpwood, construction) sent her to a convent school in Moncton, but she was so uncooperative the nuns kicked her out. "I hated it from the moment I went in," she says. "I am too much of an individualist." If she refused to attend mass it was because she wanted to go in her own good time, not when the nuns commanded. "I don't like people telling me what to do." (Folksinger Edith Butler was a schoolmate in Moncton, and novelist Antonine Maillet taught at the same school. Landry still sees not only them, from time to time, but also singer Angèle Arsenault and actress Viola Léger, and what is it about the Acadian culture that has lately spawned so many creative women?) Her parents now tried a similar school in Montreal but, once again, nuns expelled their "stubborn girl."

It was in Montreal, however, that she met the right nun at the right time, a voice teacher named Sister Rolande Ouimet: "Before I met her, people thought I was gifted, but I was nothing special. I did not discipline myself. She taught me how to work, how to make my work effective, and how to love the ideal of perfection." While studying voice, piano, music history and theory at the Université de Montréal, Landry endured a schedule so tight that Sister Rolande Ouimet insisted on giving her voice lessons at 8:30 a.m. "That's almost unheard-of," Landry says. "Your body's just not ready in the early morning. I know singers who won't open their mouths till two in the afternoon. . . .

"Sometimes I would just hate her. I met her when I was

219

19, and I became a workaholic. For four years, I didn't live except to train to be a singer. . . . But she believed in me. That woman gave me a love of discipline, and it has never left me. She was a very, very special woman, a wonderful woman." The nun's in Haiti now. They keep in touch.

After graduating from the Université de Montréal, Landry earned her master's degree in voice from Université Laval. Meanwhile, she had met Fernand Doucet, a fellow Acadian from Campbellton, up Chaleur Bay from Caraquet. They married in August, 1970. The reception was at her parents' house on the ancient Landry property, and naturally the family orchestra performed. The couple stayed at a friend's house for a three-day party. "The amount of liquor was absolutely astonishing," Landry recalls. "It was just an in-*cred*-ible party. We still talk about it."

They've lived in the heart of Toronto for 10 years, ever since Landry won a Canada Council scholarship to study opera there "so my voice could grow and expand." Doucet, a civilian employee of the Department of National Defence, teaches courses in career development to the military. He's a trim, engaging man with a dark, full, neat beard. It makes him look like a rising young naval officer in Edwardian England. Doucet's father's people are from the Chéticamp district of Cape Breton Island. "I love it there," Landry says. "A big part of his father's family is there, and when they meet him, they go back through four generations to decide, 'Now we know you'. . . ." Quebecois sometimes point out that New Brunswick French is charmingly archaic, but Landry says Chéticamp is "so removed, the French language didn't grow and change there. It's like the 17th century still. The accent and the use of verbs, it's so beautiful."

Landry's own accent appalled the late Pierre Bernac when she first took lessons from him in Paris. He was a master of the French art song, and she explains, "it requires a very specialized form of language, and purity of tone. He said I could talk with whatever accent I wanted, but I could not sing French art songs with an Acadian accent. We worked on nothing but my vowels for months on end." Along with

Gérard Souzay, "one of the great French singers," from whom Landry has also taken lessons, she is now among the dwindling handful of superb interpreters of French art song. Her recitals, however, are not quite like those of any other classical soprano. For in response to cries of *encore* in concert halls round the world, she returns to the stage to toss off an Acadian folk song. Soon she'll be performing with the Singapore Symphony, and it's not every day that steamy Singapore gets a dollop of culture from cool Caraquet.

But here in Quebec City, downriver from the Plains of Abraham, she talks not about Singapore but about what it takes to be a singer. Dessert disappears down the little red lane and aromatic coffee arrives in a creamy cup, but she refuses cognac. Nor did she take even a teaspoon of wine with her steak. She likes cognac and wine, but "they dry the throat, and also make me talk too much," and that's bad for "the voice." Ah, "the voice." Sometimes she simply means the human voice, "the most beautiful and delicate of all instruments"; but more often "the voice" is her voice, the Rosemarie Landry voice, the voice that requires pampering, coaching, the attention of specialists, ceaseless motherly concern. It is as though the voice were the last, fragile child of a reigning monarch. "I *must* keep the voice healthy," she says. And, "I make sure the voice gets regular check-ups."

The voice. A Montreal critic praised its "sensual elegance"; a Toronto critic lauded its "soaring purity"; another Toronto critic referred to Landry's "beautifully limpid line and deft skill"; and a writer in the *Kitchener-Waterloo Record* said the voice was the "ideal medium" for the songs of Richard Strauss. It was "warm, effortless and vibrant, but never heavy or aggressive." Overseas, *Music & Musicians* responded to her London début with praise for her "highly polished platform manner...exuberant singing, and finely spun tones"; *Le Monde*, Paris, described her "superb interpretation" in an opera première in Lyons; and a critic in Tokyo confessed that, after hearing a Landry recital, "I was filled with happiness on my way home." Even this tribute was restrained beside that of the Icelandic music lover who, after her recital in a place called Austurbaejarbio, wrote that her renditions of songs by Gounod, Debussy, Strauss and Poulenc proved her soul was "as deep and beautiful as theirs." Landry remembers Iceland. "I sang in a movie theatre," she laughs, "between two thrillers. We had a packed house."

The voice has taken her to Italy, Czechoslovakia, Ireland, Hong Kong, North Dakota, Colorado, Arkansas, New Jersey; to the glitter, black ties and bejewelled crowds, all smelling of money, at Toronto's Roy Thomson Hall; to good old boys and girls down home at Caraquet during the annual Festival Acadien; to vice-regal splendor at Rideau Hall, where her singing for the out-going governor general, Edward Schreyer, was nationally televised; to a concert hall in the Quebec City neighborhood of Ste-Foy where she will open tomorrow night in the title role of a French version of *The Merry Widow* (*La Veuve Joyeuse*). For the first time in her life, she'll dance onstage. At tonight's dress rehearsal, she'll waltz with her romantic lead, tenor Daniel Cassier, but she'll scarcely sing at all. The voice, you know. One must always look after the voice.

"If I am very careful not to abuse the voice," she says, "I should be performing till I am perhaps 55. Sometimes one has to quit earlier, but I studied at university for 10 years, and I created a very good foundation of technique. If I can sing 20 more years, I'll have time to really build a career. To build a career, that is a life investment." And it means ruthless scheduling and restraint.

"I don't smoke, of course," she says. "I rarely drink anything alcoholic, and in the weeks of rehearsing or performing, I never touch it at all. Sometimes, I talk as little as I can. I may be talking too much now. I work extremely hard, from morning to night, and I am fortunate to have excellent health. It's so good I rarely even suffer jet lag." She dislikes team sports, can barely swim, and detests jogging. Yet she endures an exercise workout program that eats up two hours of every second day. Why? "I decided I wasn't going to grow up as an old flabby woman." Also, and more important, "for my singing. It helps my stamina. It was excruciating at first, even when I did it slowly. I was ready to die. But now I feel so much better. It improves my performing. I feel better and can do more. In rehearsal, I sometimes have to stand for hours, and now my legs are more fitter to hold me."

She flirted with tennis as a route to fitness, actually liked it, then quit. She knew she'd never have time to get good at it, and couldn't stand being mediocre. "I cannot do anything by halves," she explains. She could not be a good singer and, at the same time, a good mother, so she denied herself children. Singers with children feel guilty while away from them, and guilty while away from their work, "and I couldn't live like that." The fact that Maureen Forrester could amazes her. Landry has often performed with the celebrated contralto— and mother of five—and marvels that "some years, she's been away eleven months. It's bringing up children by telephone. She is just an incredibly strong, healthy woman. I have never known anyone to have such energy."

Landry is not so fond of everybody in her business. Sopranos, she suggests, don't get along all that well. Percussionists sometimes hang around together, or violinists, or woodwind players, but you're unlikely to find sopranos who meet regularly for lunch. Indeed, opera stars often loathe their rivals. On PBS TV, Grace Bumbry and Leontyne Price sing a sisterly duet of unearthly beauty, but unless you're privy to the trade gossip that a Rosemarie Landry hears, you'd never know that these two great, black divas "absolutely detest each other." But what about Landry? Is she temperamental? Does she occasionally find she's not exactly hitting it off with a rival?

That, she suggests, is a naughty line of inquiry. All she'll allow is that she's glad she's not one of the two performers in *The Merry Widow* who can't bear each other; that temperaments must inevitably clash in her business; that professional singers "are individualists. We have strong egos. You need a strong ego to protect yourself." Moreover, not liking someone is finally irrelevant. The complete pro knows that, no matter what's bothering her—a fight with a manager, a sleepless night, a wounding review—she must always strive "to be better than the last time." Sometimes, "you have to sing a duet with a man who has a terrible, garlicky breath, or who is otherwise totally disgusting." It doesn't matter. You do the best you can with the voice.

"I know many people with just beautiful voices," Landry says, "but they cannot face the pressure of being onstage and revealing your soul like that." The human voice is not a manufactured instrument like a clarinet, violin, or piano. It is a God-given expression of yourself. It is *you*. That's why nasty reviews cut so deeply. The two nastiest that Landry's endured appeared in Ottawa and Montreal, a fact that won't surprise critics who believe Canadian artists suffer most at the hands of Canadian critics. She kept telling herself, reasonably enough, that no one could please everyone, "but I could not face the fact that people did not like my voice, did not love *me*. It just destroyed me. It's really silly."

Lunch consumed, she strolls up St. Jean Street, then down to the historic neighborhood where she first lived with Fernand Doucet. "I have a very supportive husband," she says. "I trust him very, very much." She hopes that some day they'll be able to afford to have him join her in all her travels as her personal manager. "That I would love." She picks up her rented car at the Chateau Frontenac, and drives to the house in St. Augustin where she's been staying with Pierre Pouliot, a prominent Quebec City lawyer, and his wife, Hélène. They've been friends of Doucet's for two decades, of Landry's for 16 years; and now, in their living room, she unlimbers the voice. She stops. "I knew it," she says. "I talked too much at lunch. I spoke too much today."

But she continues for 45 minutes, clowning for a photographer, singing to the Pouliots' canary ("my competition"), flashing her eyes and teeth, offering snatches of *The Merry Widow* and snatches of old Acadia, and only occasionally letting the voice soar till it threatens to lift the roof. She is enjoying to the hilt every second of the late, darkening afternoon, but at 4:30 sharp it's time to report to the concert hall for a dress rehearsal that'll last till midnight. She is punctual to a fault. As she leaves, Hélène Pouliot gives her a

224

snack in an orange, plastic lunchbox, decorated with a familiar mutt. "My God," someone will soon marvel in the dressing room, "a diva with a Snoopy lunchpail."

Tomorrow night, Saturday night, *The Merry Widow*
will open to a full house, and the tension is building. Rosemarie Landry need not worry. When the curtain falls at midnight
and it's her turn to bow alone, the crowd will jump to its feet,
the clapping will turn rhythmic, screams of *bravo* will mingle
with approving whistles, and up in the balcony a man who's
come all the way from Toronto will be doing his bit to keep
the applause rolling, a man named Fernand Doucet. He'll be
more than welcome at the backstage party, you may be sure.

Atlantic Insight, April 1984

Movin' East

When I was six and my father 34, I called him a fool. I liked
the word, and I wanted to see what would happen. He was a
stocky, round-shouldered man, and quick when aroused. He
rose from his chesterfield, spun me around, spanked my bum,
and said, "I may be a fool but you're sure as hell not the one to
say so." The incident was not serious. I think he was trying
not to laugh. He never struck me again, and I don't believe he
ever laid a hand on any of my three brothers. I decided a long
time later he was like a superpower with the ultimate
weapon; he was afraid of the damage he'd do if he ever got
physically violent with us. For he was capable of terrible
rages.

His face turned red when he was angry, and his eyes
bulged dangerously behind his thick glasses. You didn't move

till he was through with you. Fury makes many men inarticulate but my father's tongue-lashings were masterpieces of precise language. He documented his grievance against you as though he'd been nursing it a long time and could no longer contain himself. My mother sometimes wanted to say, "But why didn't you tell me sooner you felt this way?" These tirades were memorable but, thank God, rare. Anyway, he let her administer the few spankings my brothers and I endured. She used the back of her hairbrush.

He also let her tend the coal-burning furnace at our house in central Toronto, put up the storm windows, build bookshelves, paint walls, and do minor electrical repairs. He rarely mowed the lawn or shovelled snow. He left the vegetable garden entirely in my mother's hands. After all, they had healthy sons, and we did help around the house, though not as much as we should have. I once tried to hit a golfball over the house with a softball bat, but the ball shot straight through a dining-room window. My mother sent me down Yonge Street for a sheet of glass, brads and putty, and taught me how to install the new pane. I fixed a lot of windows after that.

My father didn't object to her giving us weekly allowances—"What can you do these days on two dollars a week?" I once sneered, a risible complaint that I did not live down for a long time—but he barred her from paying us extra for jobs such as raking leaves. He was a farmer's son from Nova Scotia. Children did not charge their parents for helping to look after their own home.

His uselessness as a handyman seemed natural enough. For he was the breadwinner, and he was also the artist. It's his poetry and fiction that preserve his memory but it was to Canadian Press, the national news-gathering agency, that he sold his days and sweat. He worked hard, long hours for CP, hard, long years, and rose to become its General Superintendent. Six-day weeks at CP were routine for him, and often he reported to the office on Sundays, as well. Among many other things there, he was the ruler and watchdog over grammar, spelling and copy style throughout CP's empire.

Others who cared about correct prose in daily journalism recognized him as an authority, and while preparing style guides for their own newspapers, consulted him. John LeBlanc spent decades as a CP reporter, mostly in Ottawa, and shortly after CP recalled him to its head office in the mid-Sixties, the man seated behind him in a Toronto streetcar murmured in his ear, "LeBlanc, you never did know the difference between 'that' and 'which.'" The man was my father. They hadn't seen each other in years.

At home, too, his passion for correct English usage hovered on the pleasant side of pedantry. He was the first person I ever heard fume over what has now become the ubiquitous misuse of "hopefully." When arguments arose over the meaning of a word or correct usage, he'd impatiently get up and march to the *Oxford English Dictionary* or *Fowler's English Usage*. He actually read *Fowler* for pleasure.

He carried fat, black, soft-leaded pencils in an inside breast pocket of his suitcoat. The words "Canadian Press," in silver letters, were stamped into each pencil, and he used a pocket-knife to keep the tips as sharp as pins. I remember the silky lining of his suitcoats, and their stench. His staff worked in their shirtsleeves but he always wore his suitcoat at CP, even on the most sweltering days that summer inflicted on Toronto. The smell of his jacket in our front-hall closet warned that he was tired, and after supper he'd lie down on his chesterfield and sleep.

Then he'd get up, fetch the pencils, lie down on his back again, hold a pad of soft copy paper on his stomach—and start to write. Once, while he was doing that, I asked him about a small, white, oval-shaped mark on his cheek. He said it was the scar from a knife-wound he'd suffered during a bar-room brawl in Trinidad. I proudly believed him till I made the mistake of checking the story with my mother. "He had a mole removed," she drily advised. Another time, my brothers and I were flat on our stomachs reading the daily comics and bickering and chatting. My mother called us out to the kitchen to say, "I wish you'd be more quiet. I *think* your father's writing a novel." He'd been writing it in exactly that fashion for at least seven years. It was *The Channel Shore*, which appeared in 1954 and lost the Governor General's Award only after a three-way tie vote among the judges.

The pencils were only the most tangible link between CP and his creative writing. Though his news work provided few images for his poetry—and maybe the poetry was an escape from the other—he believed good news writing and good poetry had things in common: precision, economy, order, the search for the perfect word. Moreover, his work on the chesterfield turned him into a successful poet and novelist, and this helped him downtown. It gained him respect, not only at CP but on newspapers across the country. He actually did what so many news people merely yearn to do. He became a creative writer.

He was revered, however, not only for his talents but also for his humanity as a boss. His only superior at CP, Gillis Purcell, was an organizational genius of ferocious energy. He was also a martinet. In press clubs across Canada, men who endured his time at CP still yarn about the abuse he heaped upon his underlings, and how he kept them trembling hour after hour, year after year. They tell their stories proudly, like men who've survived floggings in the French Foreign Legion, and with a lot of laughs. You get the impression the experiences are funnier in the telling than they were in the living. If you're a son of Charlie Bruce, you also get the impression that while Purcell was The Tough Guy at CP, Bruce was The Nice Guy. We are talking here about 17 years in the administrative history of the most important news-gathering agency in the country.

When I became a reporter myself, I'd hear from older newspapermen that if it weren't for my father they'd have long since quit CP. They described his fairness, warmth and the basic decency he surely owed to his Nova Scotian up-bringing. After drink had conquered courtesy, someone invariably told me that no matter how smart I thought I might be I'd never be the man my father was. This didn't bother me. I was pleased to know I was the son of a news demigod, and fascinated to hear about qualities of his character he hadn't always revealed at home. They were talking about a good Charlie Bruce, but I knew it wasn't the only Charlie Bruce.

There's an old expression about a man's being "a street angel, and a house devil." That's too harsh a judgment to apply to my father, but at the same time these men revered him for his ability to *understand* them, and I remembered all the times he'd failed to understand me. They were times that hurt us both.

When I was 11, and my father 40, he sent me by train from Toronto to Montreal, where I caught the Ocean Limited to the Maritimes. I got off at Truro, boarded a train bound for Cape Breton, and some time after midnight found myself alone on the platform at Monastery, shivering under the stars in the strange, crisp air of backwoods Nova Scotia. A car awaited me, and I climbed in beside my father's sister, Bess. I had never met her before. She was only 54, but I thought of her as an old lady. (She is 93 now.) Moreover, she was a schoolteacher. Summer was supposed to offer freedom from teachers but Bess, I knew, would be my boss for all of July and all of August.

With the beams from the headlights drifting on the gloomy spruce, the car trundled its way over 20 miles of sharply curving dirt roads to Port Shoreham on the north shore of Chedabucto Bay. To me, the drive was an eternity, but I stiffly refused to snuggle against Bess and fall asleep. I resented this whole adventure, and already yearned for the voluminous hardwoods, deep ravines, corner movie houses, sullen heat, and fresh-water fragrance of summertime Toronto.

I had no idea that the seaside farm I would see for the first time in the sunshine of the coming day—and the countryside that had been home to my Bruce forebears since the 1790s—would grip my soul for life. How could I know that 40-odd years down the road I would at last succumb to this grip, and report to that same ancient homestead for a sojourn that I now expect will continue till my last breath. Like Bess, whose teaching job was in Alberta, I was *home* for the summer after that long train ride in 1946. Unlike Bess, I didn't know it.

Flu felled me. When my California cousins arrived, I was a puking, quivering mess. I hated Port Shoreham, and wept for my lost Toronto. To a child, however, two summer months are half of forever, plenty of time for things to get a foothold on the mind, things like a chorus of birds at dawn; the gurgle of a tidal gut in mid-morning; the smell of hay and fir in the afternoon; cowbells at dusk; the distant sound of surf-sucked gravel late at night; and all day long, the laughter of the bluenose kids on the farm next door. Just before Labor Day, on the train back to Toronto, I wept again. I wept for my lost Port Shoreham.

When I was 12 and my father 41, he decided to do what fathers were supposed to do: take the boy out to a ball game. The Toronto Maple Leafs were an International League team of big-leaguers on their way to oblivion, hotshots on their way up, and journeymen who'd reached their natural level and weren't on their way anywhere. Maple Leaf Stadium, long since demolished, was a grey, grubby, echoing, pigeon-haunted affair. It looked vaguely like the Roman Colosseum, and was a fine place to chew hotdogs and watch, say, Luke "Hot Potato" Hamlin zing his hot potatoes past batters from Syracuse, Newark or Montreal. If the game got boring, you could watch the ships entering Toronto Harbor through the Western Gap, which lay beyond the outfield fences. I liked sitting there and daydreaming while the summer breeze delivered the smell of water from Lake Ontario, set the ballpark pennants fluttering, swept over the players, and caressed my face. I liked sitting there beside my father, the war correspondent and poet.

Before my birth in Toronto in 1934, he'd played amateur ball in Halifax, and he still cherished his glove. It was already so out of style it looked to me as though Abner Doubleday himself might have used it. My father understood baseball. He filled out his scorecard at the game in Maple Leaf Stadium, using a CP pencil. The Leafs loaded the bases, with one

230

man out. Up stepped a Leaf batter. He popped an easy infield fly toward the shortstop, but the umpire ruled him out even before the shortstop had snagged the ball. The umpire had applied a standard baseball rule to prevent an infielder's deliberately fumbling the ball to set up a phony doubleplay. If you know much about baseball, you know what "the infield-fly rule" means; but I didn't know much about baseball.

"Do you know why the batter's out?" my father asked.

"Oh sure." I wanted him to think well of me.

"Well, what happened out there?"

The moment I started to stammer an explanation, he nailed me.

"You don't know, do you? Have the guts to admit it. Don't you *ever* pretend you know something you don't. You hear me?"

Now this was flawless advice for students, businessmen, lawyers, and especially journalists, and I never forgot it. But my father offered it with such intense irritability that I prayed for rain to stop the game so we wouldn't have to sit together all afternoon. I knew we wouldn't be talking. After that day, he'd get two tickets—CP always had free ones for pro hockey, football, and baseball—and give them to me. I'd take some kid of my own age.

The hockey tickets caused a minor family row. I was a fanatical little fan of the hockey Leafs all through their glory years in the late-Forties. For mid-week games at Maple Leaf Gardens, though not for Saturday nights, CP's free tickets actually went begging; and, therefore, on countless Wednesday nights during the regular season, I saw my darling Leafs pound the dastardly Red Wings, Bruins, Rangers and Black Hawks, and also the detestable Canadiens.

But my brother Alan, two years older than I, finally insisted it was his turn to show the Leafs to a friend. We disliked each other—we don't now, and haven't for a long time—and he was not a hockey fan. To assert his claim, he had chosen a Stanley Cup play-off game against Montreal, and I believed his real motive was to see the tears that now rose in my eyes. He was not even a fair-weather friend of the

Leafs. He knew nothing of the divine excellence of Turk Broda or Syl Apps. He just wanted to hurt me by revelling in the fashionability of attending a Stanley Cup final, and with some jerk he knew. Without the truly loyal in the Gardens, without me, the Leafs might lose.

I couldn't scream these suspicions without looking ridiculous, but I'd been devouring U.S. sports magazines for months, and something I'd read enabled me to blurt a desperate argument: "But that's like the World Series. The poor people go to all the games all season but when the World Series comes the rich people hog all the tickets." Wouldn't it be undemocratic to let Alan go instead of me?

"I don't know what in the world you're talking about," my mother said. "You've seen dozens of games, Alan hasn't seen any. It's his turn. It's only fair."

"Now wait a minute," my father snapped. We were elbow-to-elbow at the narrow kitchen table where we ate every meal except Sunday dinner, which my mother served in the dining room. He was looking at her, not me. "Harry's got a point. He's not expressing it very well, but he's got a point."

He announced no decision. The next night, however, he brought home two tickets to the big game for Alan, and two for me, in a different part of the Gardens. One pair was the usual set from CP, and the other, I've always believed, was a couple he'd gone to the Gardens to buy out of his own pocket. I still remember Howie Meeker as he flew over the blueline in the first period of sudden-death overtime, collected a pass from a fellow Leaf, and tucked a deft backhand behind the flailing Montreal goalie, Bill Durnan. I also remember that no matter how excruciating some of my confrontations with my father were, he was forever looking after me in ways he kept to himself.

When I was 17 and my father 45, I ruined what should have been one of the happiest events of his life. That's what he told me anyway. He'd won the Governor General's Award for poetry in 1952 for his collection *The Mulgrave Road*, and Mount Allison University in Sackville, N.B., had promptly

232

awarded him a D. Litt. He hated pretentiousness, and refused to let people call him "Dr. Bruce"; but because the honor came from Mt. A it meant more to him than Oscars meant to actors, or knighthoods had once meant to Canadian politicians. He'd graduated from Mount Allison in 1927 after four of the finest years of his life, and now, a quarter-century later, that beloved, cosy college was calling him back to prove its pride in his talent. I went along for the train ride, but due to a crime I'd committed in Toronto the night before we left, the ride was agony all the way.

He was already disgusted with my high-school report. By spring it was clear I was so lazy I'd flunk half the nine courses I'd need for my Senior Matriculation. Alan, by comparison with me, had been an ace student in Grade 13, but his performance during his first year at the University of Toronto was disappointing. We were a feckless pair. We still weren't getting along all that well, but sometimes my father would come home from a murderous day at CP and find us together on the front porch, puffing cheap "wine-soaked" cigars. We were lolling in the living room one night while the family Marconi brought us the lewd growl of Eartha Kitt. My father came in the front door with his briefcase and before he'd even removed his fedora, he snorted, "Turn that goddamn thing off." I can't remember who got to the switch first.

Early in '52 he decided that come September, whether we liked it or not, he'd pack the two of us off to good, old Mt. A. With my Grade 12 from Ontario I could enter as a freshman, and might some day graduate. I'm sure my father thought Mt. A might even improve my frivolous character. By May of that year my high-school marks were so abominable that skipping a week's classes couldn't possibly make matters worse, and he asked me to be with him in Sackville while he made a speech and got his D. Litt. That way I could sniff around the place where I'd soon begin to serve time.

We were to leave Union Station early on a May morning, but I chose the night before to say farewell to a girl. (Three years later, I would marry her.) I was 17. She was 16, and fragrant. The streetlights lit up the tender, green spray of the new leaves. The soft smell of the lake wafted through the city, and we fooled around in a ravine.

I got home at 1:30 a.m., hoping to find the house in darkness. But the downstairs lights were on. There he was, sitting in his favorite stuffed chair, his hands squeezing the arms. The face was red, the eyes bulged behind the thick glasses. The words were hard. What did I mean coming home at such an ungodly hour on this of all nights? I was the epitome of selfishness. I had ruined forever what he'd hoped would be one of the happiest events of his life. Now I could shut up, and get the hell up to bed.

The fury of his overkill silenced us both for days. The train rattled along the north shore of Lake Ontario, past the Thousand Islands, and on to Montreal, and all along the route, spring sweetly exploded on farmland and forest, and we never spoke a word. We sat there side by side, father and son, like tense zombies.

We boarded another train at Montreal. It trundled through the Eastern Townships, past the sliding St. Lawrence, over to the Matapedia River, which spring had turned foamy, raucous and Alpine, and on into New Brunswick; and still, 30 hours out of Toronto, we had not spoken, or let our eyes meet, not even in the dining car. But we sat together, and I *was* with him on these trains. He had not cashed in my ticket. Did he hope that this mute, painful journey, which had now given me severe constipation, would somehow teach us something true and favorable about each other? Even yet?

The train was hurtling southward through bleak forest a few hours north of Sackville when he pushed past my knees to join a man who'd also attended Mt. A in the Twenties. They sat in the booth behind me, and sometimes I could hear them. The man was Sackville-bound to see his own son graduate. Such a worthy son he was, too, class president, and valedictorian, just as my father had been in '27. The two fathers murmured about ancient campus hijinx, and about the worthy son, and then my father raised his voice a trifle, and I've always thought he did it so I'd be sure to hear him:

"You know, Jack, I envy you. I don't know why, but I've

never been able to get *close* to any of my boys. I wish I could."

Our base turned out to be a small room in the Fort Cumberland Hotel, Amherst, N.S., where for a further three nights we exchanged barely a word. Amherst is ten miles from Sackville. In a rented car, we zoomed in silence across the spooky and hay-fragrant Tantramar marshlands. My father had known and respected Sir Charles G.D. Roberts, who'd been dead for six years, and Roberts had described these same marshes in verse:

> Miles on miles they extend, level, and grassy, and dim,
> Clear from the long red sweep of flats to the sky in the distance,
> Save for the outlying heights, green-rampired Cumberland Point;
> Miles on miles outrolled, and the river-channels divide them,—
> Miles on miles of green, barred by the hurtling gusts.

The prime minister, Louis St. Laurent, was also receiving an honorary degree, and what looked like all of Sackville turned out to hear "Uncle Louie" speak. The crowd overflowed Charles Fawcett Memorial Hall—a wooden, Romanesque affair, named after a dead stove-manufacturer—but the university thoughtfully set box-shaped loudspeakers on the lawn. So on a balmy May afternoon, I lay on the tender spring grass of a strange town, listened to St. Laurent's clichés about Canada's glorious future, and admired three girls from Sackville High who'd soon be my classmates; and then when it came time for the president of Mount Allison to intone Latin over my father's bowed head, I went inside and stood at the back of the hall.

At the alumni dinner that night, the university served up "Rhubarb and Ginger Cocktail, Roast Turkey with Dressing and Cranberry Sauce, Frosted Peas, Fingered Carrots, Whipped Potatoes, Ice Cream Puffs with Strawberry Sauce, Salted Nuts, Coffee," and my father. He brought tears to a lot

235

of eyes with an emotional address about what Mount Allison had meant to him. I had never before heard him speak in public, and his skill as an orator amazed me. Before an audience, this sometimes dour literary man became an eloquent ham with a powerful voice. Pretending to grope for the right words, he asked:

> How can you express in words—in any form of communication, really—a thing that isn't a matter of thought at all?
>
> How can you define in thought, or measure in memory, what has become as much a part of you as breathing and sleep?
>
> No one knows better than the man who has worked with them, what inadequate materials words are. You work them over with the tools of thought and judgment and self-criticism....And find that what you have produced...well, it may be a polished thing, a piece of expert craftsmanship... but it hasn't caught what you were after. Perhaps it never does.

There were times, then, when he was no more capable of finding the right words than he was of getting close to his boys.

"How you feeling?" he asked the next day, an hour before we climbed aboard The Ocean Limited for the long ride home.

"Okay, I guess, but I haven't gone to the bathroom for four days."

"That sometimes happens when you travel."

He went to a drugstore, bought a package of Ex-Lax, shoved it into my hand, and said, "Here, eat that. That'll fix you up."

It did, too. We were not garrulous on the return journey, but neither were we enemies.

When I was 18, and my father 46, I went to Mount Allison to get a three-year dose of the Maritimes. I wore his 30-year-old

Mt. A sweater, a woolly, garnet-and-gold bum-hugger with a thick collar I could pull up to cover my ears. For hitch-hiking, that Joe-college sweater was a godsend, and I did a fair bit of exuberant kicking around in such places as Truro, Moncton, Amherst, Halifax, and along Nova Scotia's South Shore. By now, I'm sure my college years would look good to me even if I'd spent them at the University of Manitoba. The point is, I did not, and the fine times of my youth are inseparable from the smell of the pines and the Atlantic wind at Point Pleasant Park in Halifax, the beer I drank in Truro, the ferry on Northumberland Strait, the people I knew in Sackville.

When I was 19 and my father 47, he arranged for us to spend a few days together at Port Shoreham. It was as though he wanted to strengthen whatever addiction I'd felt for the place as a boy. A few months later, however, what he surely wanted to do was throttle me. For I had managed to get myself expelled from the men's residence at his beloved Mt. A. My crime was co-sponsoring a drinking party at which university property, a bedsheet to be precise, mysteriously vanished.

I tried to con my father into believing my expulsion was neither important nor fair. I wrote him a jaunty letter. Since my brother Alan had chosen to live off-campus, I began like this: "Well, you now have not one but two sons who are not living in residence...." I went on to explain that the party really hadn't been my fault at all, and that the body that had banished me, the Men's Council, was a kangaroo court of stupid jocks who regularly got drunk themselves but disliked intellectuals such as me. In view of all this, I told my father, he should not worry about my having in any way tarnished "the Bruce name" at Mount Allison.

My letter was disastrous strategy. Its flippancy enraged my father. His blistering reply was hand-written in ink. He usually typed his letters on a big, square Underwood—I still have that typewriter, and it reminds me of an antique car—but in the heat of his rage he must have just grabbed the nearest sheet of paper and started to scribble. He was so mad his pen nib punched holes in his letter. I recall nothing of what

237

he said, except, "You must stop betraying those who love you," and I remember that only because it remains the one time in his entire life that he used "love" in a letter to me. He was so furious with me in the winter of 1954 that he forgot the word embarrassed him.

But when I was 20 and my father 48, I actually got my BA, complete with Honors in English, and this time it was I who got the parchment in Fawcett Hall. My father came down from Toronto, and at the right moment the president invited him to the stage to place the hood over my shoulders. Back in Toronto, he suggested I try to get a job as a reporter, not on one of the mighty Hog Town dailies but on a medium-sized paper in Ottawa. I'd learn about different beats there, he said, and at the same time absorb a sense of the whole country's political life, so why not try the *Ottawa Journal*.

The managing editor of the *Ottawa Journal* was a small, tough, pale man of Irish descent. "Well, Bruce," he said, "we normally start junior reporters at $38.50 a week, but you're a college man so we're going to give you $41.75. How does that sound?" It sounded wonderful. I decided to get married and settle down in Ottawa. After all, I was 20, and the first time I'd applied for a job I'd landed it. I was a newspaperman. But I could barely type, and I was too cocky and dumb to know that I could not possibly have failed to catch on at the *Journal*. My father had made sure of that. He had good friends there.

When I was 24 and my father 52, he suggested I show the homestead to my Toronto-born wife. She and I drove all the way down there in our sky-blue Renault Dauphine, and stayed for a week with Bess, who'd come home from Alberta for good, with her mother Sarah. My wife and I built massive bonfires on the beach, and had a fine, old time. When I was 26 and my father 54, he hired a lawyer to establish beyond all doubt that the Bruce family had title to that same beach.

His motive was "the future possibility of some member of the family setting up summer living quarters there." I knew nothing of this correspondence, but by 1969 my wife and I did indeed yearn for a chunk of the Nova Scotia coast. We were not thinking of the homestead. Sarah and Bess lived there. Two of Bess's sisters descended on the place from the States each summer. My own three brothers, and some American cousins seemed to have as much right to it as we did. Pursuing the homestead would be complicated. Owning it would mean custodial responsibilities we weren't sure we wanted.

When I was 35 and my father 63, I returned to the Toronto house where he had lived since even before he'd first packed me off to Port Shoreham. I wanted his advice on land in Nova Scotia. He sat in his favorite chair, and smoked his pipe. The chair faced east. I was considering the Northumberland Strait because the water there is fairly warm.

"Oh sure, it's fine for swimming over there," he said, "if you like muck, eelgrass and seaweed."

What about the South Shore?

"It's pretty all right, but pricey, just a dormitory for Halifax, really. For rugged beauty, I like the Eastern Shore."

Should we buy on the Eastern Shore then?

"Well, you'd get a good deal along there, specially if you don't mind fog three days out of four. Of course, at Port Shoreham, the weather's more like you get in Cape Breton. Lots of sunshine."

He took a drag on his pipe, and gazed at the eastern sky. His health was poor, and it was too late for him ever to go home for more than a visit.

"You know," he said, "you should consider the homestead. We could work something out with Bess, and it wouldn't cost you much."

He talked about a 10-acre knot of forest that Port Shoreham had long known as "Bruces' Island." It was actually a peninsula. No one had ever built anything on this gnarled hump of fir, spruce, moss and wire birch, but it included the family's entire salt-water frontage, almost a thousand feet of it. He said he'd always thought the highest point of Bruces' Island would make a terrific site for a cabin. From up there, at the edge of a steep bluff, you could see gulls sail among tree-tops at your own eye level, or you could look down on the backs of birds cruising the surface of the water, or you could look across the whole, great sliding bay at the purple and cobalt hills of the far side, or you could look eastward and you'd be so high you'd see over Ragged Head and right out to the long, empty horizon of the open Atlantic.

He was finding all the right words.

When I was 36, and my father 64, he did indeed "work something out with Bess." She agreed to give me Bruces' Island. That was not the only reason why my wife and I abandoned Ontario in the spring of '71, and brought our three Toronto-born children to Halifax; but that gift of ocean-front wilderness, that fragrant earth, was a magnetic link to my summer of '46, and to Bruces who'd disappeared in the mists of time. We built the cabin on the spot my father cherished, and sure enough gulls still sail among tree-tops at our own eye level.

He never got to see our cabin.

When I was 37 and my father 65, he sent a hand-written note: "Been having a spot of trouble with personal health—general weakness and some dizziness—so temporarily I'm going out only when accompanied by Mum. No damned energy. My medico is watching things closely so I'm hoping to have it cleared up before too long. Basically poor circulation, I think. Anyway, I'm taking things easily. Best, Dad." Ten days later, he was dead. A dozen years later, my wife and I bought the entire Bruce homestead from Bess.

Some day, a Torontonian will visit us there, and he'll say, "Migod, this makes Orillia look like Manhattan. How come a city slicker like you has ended up in a backwater like this?" From my favorite chair, I will gaze at the eastern sky, and I will say, "I'm not quite sure, but I don't think I had much choice."

Port Shoreham, N.S., June 1985

240